Sport Policy and Governance

Sport Policy and Governance
Local Perspectives

Dr. Neil King

ELSEVIER

Amsterdam • Boston • Heidelberg • London • New York • Oxford
Paris • San Diego • San Francisco • Singapore • Sydney • Tokyo
Butterworth-Heinemann is an imprint of Elsevier

Butterworth-Heinemann is an imprint of Elsevier
Linacre House, Jordan Hill, Oxford OX2 8DP, UK
30 Corporate Drive, Suite 400, Burlington, MA 01803, USA

First edition 2009

British Library Cataloguing in Publication Data
A catalogue record for this book is available from the British Library.

Library of Congress Cataloging-in-Publication Data

King, Neil A.
Sport policy and governance : local perspectives/Neil King. -- 1st ed. p. cm.
Includes bibliographical references and index.
ISBN 978-0-7506-8547-4
1. Sports and state--England--Liverpool. I. Title.
GV706.35.K56 2009
796.09427'53--dc22

2008054449

ISBN: 978 0 7506 8547 4

For information on all Butterworth–Heinemann publications
visit our website at books.elsevier.com

Typeset by Macmillan Publishing Solutions
www.macmillansolutions.com

Printed and bound in Great Britain

09 10 11 12   10 9 8 7 6 5 4 3 2 1

Working together to grow
libraries in developing countries

www.elsevier.com | www.bookaid.org | www.sabre.org

ELSEVIER   BOOK AID
International   Sabre Foundation

To Sarah, Isaac and Rory.

Contents

List of Illustrations

Figures

Tables

Acknowledgements

First and foremost, I would like to thank the many people who contributed to the development of the book through interviews and providing access to documentation, particularly officers and former officers of Sport and Recreation Services within Liverpool City Council; senior personnel within the voluntary sport sector; representatives of local schools; members of the Liverpool Sports Forum and commercial and professional sports organisations. Second, I would like to thank officers in other local authority departments including Education, Health Promotion, Youth Services and Planning and those local councillors who were prepared to discuss sport policy and practices across the city. Finally, personnel representing the Merseyside Sports Partnership, North-West Sports Board and Sport England North-West are also acknowledged as are senior officers in neighbouring local authorities in Merseyside.

I would also like to thank the many professional colleagues who have at various times supported my research, most notably Professor Barrie Houlihan at Loughborough University.

Selected Abbreviations

ABA	Amateur Boxing Association
ACF	Advocacy Coalition Framework
ARC	Association of Running Clubs
ASA	Amateur Swimming Association
BAALPE	British Association of Advisors and Lecturers in Physical Education
BGA	British Gymnastics Association
CCPR	Central Council for Physical Recreation
DCLG	Department of Communities and Local Government
DCMS	Department of Culture, Media and Sport
DfEE	Department for Education and Employment
DfES	Department for Education and Skills
DH	Department of Health
DNH	Department of National Heritage
DoE	Department for the Environment
ECB	England and Wales Cricket Board
ESC	English Sports Council
GOR	Government Office for the Regions
HAZ	Health Action Zone
HEA	Health Education Authority
LCC	Liverpool City Council
LCSR	London Council for Sport and Recreation
LEA	Local Education Authority
LSF	Liverpool Sports Forum
LSSF	Liverpool School Sports Federation
MSF	Multiple Streams Framework
MSP	Merseyside Sport Partnership
NGB	National Governing Body (for sport)
NOF	New Opportunities Fund
NPFA	National Playing Fields Association
NRF	Neighbourhood Renewal Fund
NWSB	North-West Sports Board

ODPM	Office of the Deputy Prime Minister
PCT	Primary Care Trust
PDM	Partnership Development Manager (for school sport/physical education)
PEAUK	Physical Education Association of the UK
SAZ	Sport Action Zone
SDO	Sports Development Officer
SENW	Sport England North-West
SPAA	Sport and Physical Activity Alliance
SSC	Specialist Sports College
SSCo	School Sport Coordinator
SSP	School Sport Partnership
UKA	UK Athletics
WNF	Working Neighbourhood Fund
YST	Youth Sports Trust

CHAPTER 1

Introduction

CHAPTER CONTENTS

WHO IS THIS BOOK FOR?

First, this book is intended for use by students undertaking sport-related degree programmes and academics developing and delivering sport courses. Students of public policy and politics may also find the text of interest. *Second*, the book may be of utility to practitioners and policymakers, particularly those working with a sport and physical activity remit, in local authorities, schools and the voluntary sector. Those personnel based in the health, education, planning or community regeneration sectors, with a physical activity or sport-based remit, or who work in partnership with sport sector personnel may also find aspects of this study useful, perhaps as a reflective tool in making policy or delivering programmes. *Third*, as the core research involves a series of case studies in the city of Liverpool, students of sport policy in urban contexts, or of Liverpool specifically, may find the text of interest. *Fourth*, policy theorists may wish to employ the case studies in developing existing frameworks for explaining policy processes.

RATIONALE

Since the mid-1990s, sport as a policy concern has gained greater salience within central government priorities, both in terms of elite sport development (DNH, 1995; Green, 2004a,b; Green and Houlihan, 2005a) and through instrumental uses of sport in meeting social policy goals, particularly in respect of urban regeneration, education and health (Collins and Kay, 2003; DCMS, 1999, 2000, 2002; Gratton and Henry, 2001; Houlihan and White, 2002). Subsequently, the last decade in particular has witnessed a restructuring of the sport policy area, its governance and resourcing, both in the public sector and in the voluntary sector for sport. This book assesses this restructuring and evaluates the consequences for sport interests, with a particular focus on the local level of policymaking and implementation.

The study is arguably timely in raising questions about the changing parameters of influence in the sport policy area at the local level, given the 'modernisation' of both local government and the voluntary sport sector. Moreover, although there have been a number of recent publications on sport policy and development (Bergsgard et al., 2007; Green and Houlihan, 2005a; Houlihan and White, 2002; Hylton and Bramham, 2008) and in respect of the role of sport in social policy (Coalter, 2007; Collins and Kay, 2003), almost all focus on the policy process at the national and/or international levels. To date, there has been an absence of published research that explores the local level. This text therefore seeks to expand knowledge of sport policy and practice within local authority areas.

The relative absence of policy research at the local level is perhaps surprising, given that local authorities allocate far greater financial resources to sport per annum than the central government department responsible for sport and the Lottery Sports Fund (LSpF) combined (Lord Carter of Coles, 2005). Further, the text highlights the significant role of local authorities in elite sport provision and development, as this component of their activity is often unrecognised in published research, given that most studies of sport at the local authority level foreground policy and practices to increase participation. Finally, in respect of sport in social policy, there is very little published work that explores relationships between local authority policy for sport and policy in adjacent sectors, including education, health, land-use planning and community regeneration. This text explores these dimensions as partnership-working across policy areas has become a significant feature of sport development and provision. Additionally, sport policy at the local authority level is arguably under-theorised, and therefore the book seeks to explain local sport policy with reference to appropriate theoretical frameworks.

AIM AND OBJECTIVES

The aim of this book is to explore the politics of sport policy processes at the level of the local authority area. In order to achieve this aim, key sport policy actors with a stake in sport policy are identified and their policy aspirations, priorities, beliefs/values, resources and dependencies are assessed in order to evaluate the relationships between them. Further, the book seeks to identify and evaluate the strategies and instruments utilised by sport policy actors in pursuing their interests. This analysis is set both within the changing local and national organisational and funding contexts in which sport policy actors formulate and implement policy and within broader political, economic and socio-cultural contexts that shape policy. Moreover, the author provides a historical context to the study through tracing and analysing the evolution of local and national sport policy processes, as policy decisions and actions tend to emerge from prior policy processes. The final theme and thread of the book concerns an evaluation of the utility of major meso-level explanations of policy in order to understand contemporary sport policy processes, particularly at the local level.

FOCUS

It should be noted that this book concerns recreation and physical activity and is not solely about 'sport', although policy relating to sport is the primary focus. Also, as the content includes an analysis of the changing relationships between sport and non-sport policy actors, it is, to an extent, a book about public policy as opposed to sport-specific policy, although Chapter 6 highlights the storylines of specific sports. Although the focus is primarily public policy at the local authority level, and therefore it concerns central and local governments, the study does not exclude voluntary sector sport policy, and to a lesser extent commercial and professional sport, where interests have influenced decisions made in the public sector.

Further, it is not a book solely about Liverpool, although sport policy and practice in this city forms the core of the empirical work underpinning this book. It is argued that there is significant scope for generalisation across local authority areas and between cities with a similar socio-cultural, political and economic history. Further, this study does not treat 'Liverpool' solely as the municipal area, although this is the core focus, given that political and geographical boundaries do not constrain the reach of sport as a socio-cultural phenomena. Moreover, the text is not comprehensive in researching all aspects of sport in the city or all the sports played in Liverpool. Instead, the case studies of specific sports serve to highlight aspects of policy processes that may assist in theory construction.

Finally, the book does not centre on professional football, horse racing via the Grand National event, major golf events or the recreational use of the River Mersey, whilst recognising the importance of these components of the sporting identity of the city and region. With the local authority being at the hub of the research underpinning this book, the focus instead is on those sports prioritised and to an extent, resourced by the city council. Nonetheless, two sports that are located outside of these priorities are included for comparative purposes. Due to limitations of space, other sports of note in the city, such as baseball (incorporating rounders and softball), basketball (the Everton Tigers are a semi-professional club), badminton, bowls, a range of disability sports, golf, hockey, both rugby codes, sailing and water polo, to name only a selection, are not included in this edition of the book.

STRUCTURE

The book is divided into five parts. Part 1 is concerned with the study of sport policy. Sport Policy: Theory and Analysis (Chapter 2) details a series of theoretical approaches that are utilised for understanding public policy processes. The author then selects an approach for researching sport policy at the level of the local authority area. Part 2 describes and analyses sport policy at the national level in order to provide a context to policymaking at the local level, particularly in respect of the local authority. The Evolution of National Sport Policy (Chapter 3) highlights the development of sport policy in England since the 1970s in order to identify the changing parameters of the sport policy area and to highlight the key influences shaping policy.

The chapter draws upon the work of key sport policy analysts, most notably Bergsgard et al. (2007), Coalter, Long and Duffield (1988), Coghlan and Webb (1990), Collins and Kay (2003), Gratton and Henry (2001), Green and Houlihan (2005a), Henry (1993, 2001), Houlihan (1997) and

Houlihan and White (2002). The account of sport policy is divided into timeframes based primarily on analyses by Henry and Bramham (1993), Green (2004a), Houlihan (1997) and Houlihan and White (2002).The chapter highlights political rationales and ideologies underpinning government involvement in sport; the changing organisation and administration of sport; relationships between the key organisations within the policy area and the funding context in which policy is made and implemented.

Part 3 of the book concerns sport policy in Liverpool. The Policy Context in Liverpool (Chapter 4) centres on the socio-economic and political contexts in which sport policy processes emerge and change (e.g. Bianchini et al., 1993; Couch, 2003; Murden, 2006). The infrastructure for public sector sport is mapped, highlighting the funding and organisational context and relationships between Liverpool City Council Sport and Recreation Services (LCC Sport) and internal and external bodies. Following on from this analysis, The Evolution of Sport Policy in Liverpool (Chapter 5) is an account of the changing role, remit, priorities and actions of LCC Sport (LCC, 1997, 2003a, 2008a).

Part 4 of the book is a series of local case studies set within policy change at the national level. Sports Development (Chapter 6) examines three of the six local authority 'priority sports': namely, boxing, gymnastics and swimming, particularly in respect of interests around performance and events. The case studies on athletics, grass-roots football and tennis are not included in this edition of the book. For each sport, a storyline is identified that facilitates an analysis of policy priorities, content, instruments and determinants. This analysis of local sport-specific policy and practice is located in a policy context where central government and governing bodies for sport influence local policy processes. However, as the chapter highlights, it is the local authority that has been the key driver in local sport development for a number of sports. The chapter also provides a policy-related analysis of two sports that are located outside of local authority priorities, namely, cricket and road running, in order to evaluate the extent to which being outside of core Liverpool City Council (LCC) priorities makes a difference to the development of a sport.

School Sport Policy (Chapter 7) examines the relative influence of interests in policy and practice around school sport through tracing the evolution of policy processes at national and local levels. The chapter reviews national policy change during the Conservative administrations during 1979–1997 and, in particular, under New Labour during 1997–2008 (e.g. Ball, 1993; Green and Houlihan, 2005b; Houlihan, 1992, 1997, 2000a; Kirk, 2003; Penney, 2004; Penney and Evans, 1999). The chapter then draws on empirical research in Liverpool.

Sport, Physical Activity and Health Policy (Chapter 8) explores the evolving relationship between sport and health interests in Liverpool within the changing national policy context. The chapter reviews policy change in the health sector in England (e.g. Adams et al. 2002; Ham, 2000, 2004; Klein, 2003; Oliver and Exworthy, 2003) and relates these changes to policy where health and sport interests overlap (Robson, 2001; Robson and McKenna, 2008). The chapter constructs an account of the emerging relationship between the sport and health policy areas from a review of central and local government policy statements and strategy documents due to the paucity of published literature that concerns the policy spill-over between these two policy areas (e.g. Acheson, 1998; DCMS, 2002; DH, 2005a,b; LCC, 2000a, 2005; Liverpool First for Health, 2002).

Sport, Land-Use Planning and Playing Fields Policy (Chapter 9) examines policy impacting on the protection and usage of playing fields and other green spaces, including pitches for sport. The analysis of policy in Liverpool is set within the changing contours of national policy and the wider socio-economic context where many interests compete for scarce land resources including both a range of sport and recreational interests and a range of non-sport interests. Given the relative paucity of published academic research specific to this aspect of sport policy, this chapter relies primarily on empirical work. Sport and Community Regeneration (Chapter 10) investigates the role of sport and physical activity in social policy objectives around social exclusion (Coalter, 2007; Collins and Kay, 2003; DCMS, 1999) through the practices of the former Liverpool Sport Action Zone (SAZ) and more recently, the Sport and Physical Activity Alliances (SPAAs). This chapter describes and analyses a series of local area case studies that serve to highlight issues and challenges in policy implementation.

Part 5 of the book attempts to analyse and explain sport policy at the local level based on the empirical research that forms Parts 3 and 4 of this book. Analysing Sport Policy in Liverpool (Chapter 11) provides a summary of the key themes of the investigation. Theorising Sport Policy at the Local Level (Chapter 12) assesses the relative utility of the theoretical approach utilised in this book. It is contended that the findings of the study cannot be fully captured by any single policy framework, theory or model, but the theoretical approach selected does nonetheless offer a degree of descriptive, analytical and explanatory utility. Recent studies of sport policy have drawn on these theoretical frameworks (e.g. Green and Houlihan, 2005a; Houlihan, 1997, 2005; Houlihan and White, 2002) and insights from these studies inform this discussion and conclusions. Finally, future research directions are briefly considered where the book acts as a 'point of departure' for similar studies.

OVERVIEW OF THE RESEARCH STRATEGY

In agreement with Rorty (1980), social scientists should not attempt to discover facts but should advance critical interpretations of processes, for example policy processes. This is the case as our understanding is both context-dependent and mediated through language. In undertaking research to underpin this book, the goal was to pursue a provisional rather than a determinate explanation, and the study is therefore exploratory, recognising the value of rival webs of interpretation (Bevir and Rhodes, 1998: 99). A qualitative approach to research was adopted, recognising that qualitative methods have contributed to the study of political behaviour by 'seeking to understand political actors as conscious social beings who shape the world of politics as well as being shaped by it' (Devine, 1995: 137). Specifically, qualitative methods draw particular attention to contextual issues in which to locate interviewees' perspectives, for example, in a bid to capture meaning, process and context (Bryman, 1988: 62).

The study undertaken is inductive in the sense of being open-ended, empirically informed and 'grounded' inquiry, as opposed to deductive research that tests pre-set assumptions. The author is in agreement with Greckhamer and Koro-Ljungberg (2005: 738) who state that 'staying "truly" open for data, allowing data to have voices and meanings of their own, becomes difficult if researchers are using careful and systematic procedures to discover meaning because in this case researchers are controlling the data and not vice versa.' However, this study does recognise that the research is, in practice, theory-laden and therefore deduction is a feature of the analytic strategy. The aim of the approach taken was to develop generalisations on the basis of careful observation of empirical phenomena, both in order to provide opportunities for subsequent testing of these generalisations against other cases (Hawkesworth, 1992) and in order to develop theory. Hence, the study's analytic strategy was iterative or recursive; that is, the data collection and analysis proceeded concurrently.

The book is based on case study research that is essentially 'a narrative-based account of a limited number of select instances, which belong to a social or behavioural phenomena as it occurs in its natural setting' in order to highlight the perspectives of those subjects 'within' the case (Marinetto, 1999: 63). The objective is to describe and explain a case that has yet to be studied in any detail, to capture its uniqueness and to provide an appropriate context for linking theory with practice (Yin, 1994). The approach taken does not, however, attempt to include an analysis of *all* possible factors shaping policy processes, as the 'boundary' of a case study is difficult in practice to specify. According to Peters (1998: 141), 'good case researchers accept complexity and multiple causation as a crucial characteristic of their research, rather than a bother to be eliminated.'

In this study, a triangulation of research strategies is used to further validity (Denzin, 1970). Forms of triangulation used included data triangulation, involving the collection of data from different people, in different places at different times; theory triangulation using different theoretical frameworks and methodological triangulation using interviews, document analysis and observation. An overview of the methods employed in researching this book follows.

Research methods

In agreement with Becker (1970b: 5), researchers must 'try to make the bases of [their] judgements as explicit as possible so that others may arrive at their own conclusions'. Hopefully, the case studies in this book, coupled with a description and explanation of the research strategy utilised, will provide such an opportunity. In terms of methods, Devine (1995: 141) states that 'the crucial question is whether the choice of method is appropriate for the theoretical and empirical questions that the researcher seeks to address.' The three components of the research strategy utilised in exploring local sport policy are briefly detailed as follows. First, document analysis was undertaken of LCC Sport and recreation strategies (LCC, 1997, 2003a, 2008a); internal departmental papers; minutes of meetings of the City Council, Executive Board and Select (or Scrutiny) Committees 1997–2008 and minutes of the Liverpool Sports Forum (LSF) 2002–2008. Documentation pre-1997 was scarce with the author relying on public library records and interviewee recall.

Document analysis can be considered an 'essential technique' for studies of public policy. Moreover, on a pragmatic level, much of what takes place in a policy process is recorded in written form and is accessible. In this study, a qualitative analysis of documentation (Altheide, 1996: 15) was used, through the application of thematic coding (Flick, 1998), in order 'to understand how different discourses structure the activities of actors and how they 'are *produced*, how they *function*, and how they are *changed*' (Howarth, 1995: 115, cited in Green and Houlihan, 2005b: 8; also see Bacchi, 2000; Ball, 1993). Of note is that the study undertaken analyses a series of policy-related documents over time as the 'contemporary features of policy life have been influenced by longitudinal developments and processes' (Marinetto, 1999: 73).

Moreover, in policy-related research, documents are considered to be 'sedimentations of social and political practices' (May, 1997: 157). Texts can be seen to be attempting to impose authority on the social world in setting parameters so as to prioritise certain interests or exclude others. Further, Bulkeley (2000: 745) observes, 'the ways in which understandings of problems are forged through the policy process and the crucial role of discursive constructions of particular issues [is instrumental] in enabling and constraining policy change.' Therefore, any analysis of documents should focus not only on factual detail relating to organisation, relationships and resource allocation, for example, but on the beliefs, values and preferences of policy actors. In sum, documents are not 'neutral artefacts' that report social reality, but are a medium through which political power can be demonstrated and legitimised. May (1997: 164) concluded that documents 'do not simply reflect, but also construct social reality and versions of events'.

However, it is argued that an analysis of the language of texts cannot fully address the aims and objectives of this book, and therefore document analysis is combined with an analysis of the 'material context' in which decision-makers utilise their influence. This 'material context', whilst recognising the significance of economic structures and processes, highlights the 'primacy of politics', acknowledging that documents have political origins. Further, Scott (1990) considers the *quality* of documentary sources in terms of authenticity, credibility, representativeness and meaning. The key consideration when addressing these concerns is to establish the social and political context in which the document has been produced (May, 1997: 170). As document analysis clearly involves a process of active choice, idealisation, selection and closure by the researcher, the method was triangulated with interviews and observation.

The second research method used in researching this book was interviews with personnel in the sport policy area. Fifty-five semi-structured interviews were conducted with senior personnel within LCC and representatives from other organisations in the sport policy area, including national, regional, county and local representatives in the public and voluntary sectors, between late 2004 and mid-2006, with a number of follow-up interviews conducted in mid-2008. Semi-structured interviews are used by researchers in order to acquire an agent-informed account of policy processes and allow distinctions to be made between the 'rhetoric' of policy-related documentation and an interpretation of 'reality' from the perspective of policy actors. Specifically, this method facilitates access to actor's beliefs, values and norms, embodied in policy preferences and priorities, and provides insights into the factors/influences perceived as constraining or facilitating action (the structural context in which policy actors operate). Using this method, evidence of indirect forms of power can be inferred, given that 'all social activity takes place within the context provided by a set of pre-existing social structures' (Lewis, 2002: 19).

Semi-structured interviews consist of informal probing into issues via open-ended questioning in order to facilitate opportunities for interviewees to express their interpretation of events with minimal constraint. Semi-structured interviews are in effect 'guided conversations' (Loftland and Loftland, 1984: 59). Thus, the 'assumptive worlds' (Young, 1977) of policy actors can be explored, in order to highlight the significance of agency in an account of sport policy processes. Further, the use of this method allows insights into the strategies employed by policy actors in the pursuit of their interests and, moreover, in the mediation of other's interests. Although there are potential 'weaknesses' in employing this method (Devine, 1995: 141), particularly when interviewing senior personnel (Richards, 1996) or in 'expert interviews' (Flick, 1998: 91–92), Devine (1995) addresses these 'weaknesses' by locating interview data in the 'material context' in which policy actors make decisions, as in the case of document analysis. For this study of sport policy, an 'interview guide' was composed of questions around the themes identified in *Table 1.1*.

Third, given the limitations of interviews, components of ethnographic research were introduced into the research strategy. This approach included both participant observation as a member of a local sports forum and

Table 1.1 Interview themes

Theme	Example
Organisational and administrative arrangements.	The location of 'sport' in local authority policy processes.
Funding context.	Timescales and conditions influencing policy-related decisions.
Relationships between interests.	Partnerships and tensions between policy actors.
Patterns of interests.	The identification of 'clusters' of interests.
Exogenous factors mediating the sport policy area.	Central government priorities, economic context, influences from other policy sectors.
The historical context.	'Focusing events', prior policy/embedded interests.
Capacity for policy delivery.	Strengths and weaknesses of the local infrastructure.
The strategic actions of decision-makers.	Actor responses to the changing policy context.
The consequences of policy, intended or unintended.	Policy learning/policy success or failure.

non-participant observation at local authority public meetings and events. Both methods facilitated access to interviewees. Gratton and Jones (2004: 159) argue that 'Observation is ... the most neglected research technique in sport, yet it has a number of advantages.' Observation, it is argued, complements other methods in case study research, particularly as interviews and documents are based on self-reporting. In respect of the research underpinning this book, observation had utility for uncovering subtle features of policy processes; for example, meanings, values and beliefs of personnel that may not be revealed in documents or interviews (Hammersley and Atkinson, 1983).

Further, accessing events when they happen, and in their 'natural setting', bypasses the potential difficulties of interviewee recall. It can be noted too that although observation is relatively neglected as a research tool in contemporary studies of policy processes, respected studies such as those conducted by Heclo and Wildavsky (1981) were based, in part, on the author's observing and recording policy processes in action. In respect of using observation in research, Becker (1970a: 37) highlights solutions to the problems of subjectivity, interference and proof in observation. The weaknesses of observation can be offset by triangulating methods, and in combination with interviews and document analysis, a plausible account of the policy processes can emerge over time. Although the method is more appropriate for descriptive rather than explanatory research, the use of this method did generate questions for the research that in turn assisted in analysis and explanation of policy.

As important as the selection and use of methods in qualitative research is the interpretation of data, as interpretation shapes the conclusions regardless of how the data was collected. In this study, thematic coding (Flick, 1998) was considered the most appropriate technique for data analysis. Although normally used in comparative case studies, the technique can be used for single case studies where elements of comparison exist, such as in the research underpinning this book. In this approach, sampling is oriented to individuals and groups whose perspectives are likely to be instructive in addressing the research questions. The collection of data is therefore conducted using a method that will guarantee future comparability, usually achieved through semi-structured interviews.

In terms of procedure, thematic coding was applied in 'steps'. The first step is to develop a short description of the case study, document or interview. This is continuously rechecked and modified during further interpretation of the data. The data is 'coded' into conceptual categories, in this case, 'themes'. As Miles and Huberman (1994: 56) note, 'Codes are tags or labels for assigning units of meaning to the descriptive or inferential information compiled during the study.' This process was applied to not only documents, but interview transcripts. Coding is taken as a starting point for addressing four types of questions: conditions (background information such as, What has led to the situation?); interaction among actors (Who acted? What happened?); strategies and tactics (Which ways of handling situations? Avoidance or adaptation?) and consequences (What did change? What was the outcome?). For an overview of coding techniques, see Gratton and Jones (2004: 220–221).

Finally, all research strategies have their limitations. As Mackie and Marsh (1995: 180) observe, 'It is impossible to produce a flawless research design; the trick is to acknowledge, and cope with, as many of the problems as possible.' Further, Devine (1995: 152) observes that 'No single method can resolve the complex issues involved in the study of politics.' Therefore, the author sought to reduce the level of complexity of the empirical work by emphasising only a limited range of relevant causal or explanatory factors. In sum, it is contended that it is possible to evaluate a 'research problem' without necessarily establishing *proof*, as there are degrees of positive confirmation. This *degree* of confirmation is shaped by constraints such as access to data, the author's own limitations in understanding the findings and problems of interpretation resulting from the limits of the theoretical apparatus used in the study.

In sum, it is argued that the research methodology and methods employed in this book offer the potential to provide a satisfactory account of sport policy at the local level. Marsh et al. (1999) identified specific criteria for researchers engaged in policy-related studies, and it is this framework that the author draws on in considering an appropriate research strategy and in selecting a theoretical approach for understanding sport policy at the local level. Chapter 2 details this approach.

AN INTRODUCTION TO SPORT IN LIVERPOOL

Liverpool has a diverse history of sports that dates back to the early nineteenth century, with athletics, boxing, cricket, gymnastics, rugby union, rowing, sailing, swimming and tennis, to name only a selection of sports, all thriving before the advent of association football towards the end of the century. In fact, Liverpool hosted its own Olympic Festivals as early as 1862 (Physick, 2007). The history and evolution of sport and recreation in the city, across the public, voluntary and commercial sectors, has produced a unique local cultural heritage that mediates contemporary sport and recreation policy. However, in terms of public perceptions, Liverpool in the era of professional and commercialised sport is perhaps most recognised for the success of its two professional football clubs and the annual Grand National horse-racing event, albeit the event is not in the Liverpool local authority area. However, sport as a socio-cultural phenomenon does not end with the municipal boundaries of the city. Liverpool Urban Area (as defined by the Office of National Statistics) or 'Greater Liverpool' would include parts of Sefton and Knowsley and many would include urbanised north-east Wirral as 'Liverpool'.

Since the early 1970s, LCC has invested in sport and recreation, including parks, community leisure facilities, event organisation and sports development programmes for specific sports, and it is the policy and practices of LCC Sport that is central to the text (see Chapters 4–6 in particular). Apart from the local authority, a raft of public sector bodies are involved in delivering sport and physical activity for social policy purposes such as health (see Chapter 8) and community regeneration (see Chapter 10). Further, schools are at the hub of sport-related policy and practice (see Chapter 7), where playing fields policy within wider land-use planning concerns (see Chapter 9) has had a bearing on sports provision.

Arguably, local-authority-formulated sport policy cannot be fully understood in isolation from developments in the voluntary and commercial sectors. A process of mutual adjustment can be observed between and across the three sectors over time (see Henry, 2001: Chapter 6). In the voluntary sector, as of 2008, there are approximately 860 sports clubs in the Liverpool local authority area including junior sections, with the vast majority being football. In grass-roots football alone, there are 15 leagues across the city consisting of numerous clubs. The city also features 15 boxing clubs, 12 tennis clubs, 7 cricket clubs, 4 rugby union clubs, 4 swimming clubs (within the local authority area), 3 badminton clubs, 2 sailing clubs, an outdoor education centre and 3 universities incorporating a wide range of sports clubs with extensive participation in competition structures, and this list is not comprehensive. A great deal of voluntary sport activity also takes place in schools (see Chapter 7).

From the 1990s, Liverpool has witnessed an expansion of commercial sector leisure and sport provision with organisations including David Lloyd, Total Fitness and Greens all expanding their operations. The City Council has sought to attract commercial sponsorship for hosting events to market the city and attract tourism. The extent to which the local authority is a direct provider of sports events has changed over the last 20 years with an expansion of the commercial sector with one such example being road running (see Chapter 6). Liverpool is also noted for its success in some sports such as amateur boxing, gymnastics and swimming; long-standing organisations such as Liverpool Cricket Club, Sefton Rugby Union Club, Liverpool Red Triangle Karate Club and many boxing clubs such as Rotunda and Golden Gloves at the Belvedere Community Activity Centre (BCAC); and more recently for disability sport with the Greenbank Sports Academy being the first fully inclusive sports facility.

In summary, a mixed economy of provision for sport and recreation exists in Liverpool. Despite public perceptions of Liverpool as a 'football city' – and football is the dominant sport –, the range and diversity of voluntary sector sport locally should also be noted in contributing to the social and cultural fabric of a 'city of sport'. However, prior to an analysis of aspects of the local sport policy area, within national policy parameters, Chapter 2 considers theoretical approaches to explaining sport policy and practice in Liverpool.

PART 1

Studying Sport Policy

Sport Policy: Theory and Analysis

CHAPTER CONTENTS

This chapter will explore theoretical approaches in policy-related research that can inform an analysis of sport policy. The chapter identifies the specific approach utilised by the author in describing, analysing and explaining sport policy at the local level. In brief, the approach taken centres on a meso-level analysis of sport policy processes located, at the macro-level, within a neo-pluralist theory of the state. Given the nature of the empirical work underpinning this book, this approach is complemented with insights from the body of literature around local government and governance.

CHARACTERISTICS OF THE SPORT POLICY AREA

Before applying policy theory to sport policy analysis, it is necessary to identify the key characteristics of the sport policy area in order to provide a basis for the analysis. The sport policy area is characterised by recency, increasing government intervention, embedded beliefs, a dispersed administrative context and experiences of significant exogenous influences (Houlihan, 2000b). First, in terms of recency, Houlihan (2005: 163) observes that whereas 'few governments in the 1960s gave any explicit budgetary or ministerial recognition to sport, by the mid-1990s sport was an established feature in the machinery of government of most economically developed countries'. Second, related to the rise in political salience of sport is the increasing level of government intervention in sport policy (Houlihan, 1991, 1997), most notably in the period since 1995 (Green, 2004a). Third, the sport policy area is characterised by many competing ideologies and beliefs, both outside of the state and within it. Government policy preferences for sport embody values which reflect political 'positions' on the left/right political continuum and can be related to specific political ideologies (Henry, 1993, 2001). Also, sport policy preferences embody a range of causal claims, for example 'widening participation extends elite success' and 'sport/exercise alleviates social problems'. Fourth, the sport policy area is highly differentiated in terms of its organisation and administration, with a plethora of bodies representing many sports and different government departments and agencies with a remit for different aspects of the policy area (Houlihan and White, 2002; Roche, 1993). Fifth, the sport policy is to an extent shaped by interests and policy change in adjacent policy areas such as Education, for example, in repect of school sport. In sum, these characteristics shape the strategic action of policymakers and practitioners.

TOWARDS A FRAMEWORK FOR UNDERSTANDING SPORT POLICY

Houlihan (2000b: 1) argues, 'while the current state of theory building has provided a number of insights into the sport policy process, too many concepts, theories and frameworks have been either inappropriate or have required significant adaptation to fit the peculiarities of the policy field as it developed in the UK'. For example, major theorisations tend to assume that the policy process consists of a distinct set of policy actors working within a definable 'policy sector', whereas for sport, the boundaries of a 'policy area' are less distinct.

Further, policy theorists tend to view policy actors as possessing clear objectives, organisational capacity and specific resources. In this context, theories conceptualise the policy process in terms of power, pro-action, self-confident advocacy and effective strategising. Houlihan (2000b) suggests such theory building to be the product of research that focuses on policy sectors characterised by recognisable and relatively stable institutional arrangements and embedded interests including those of government and specialised groups. Policy areas where stable arenas for debate are sparse, for example, and where organisational capacity is fragmented and resources are scarce, are not widely researched or theorised, including non-statutory services in local authorities such as sport and recreation.

Moreover, in the study of sport policy, the very concept of policy-*making* may be misleading. Dery (1999) clarifies the distinction between policy-making and policy-*taking*, which may have utility for the analysis of sport policy. Dery states that policy-making 'implicitly presumes control over key variables that shape policy in a given area', whereas policy-taking 'denotes the pursuit of a given set of policy objectives, which is primarily or entirely shaped by the pursuit of other objectives ... the resulting policy ... [is] ... the by-product of policies that are made and implemented to pursue objectives other than those of the policy in question' (Dery, 1999: 165–166).

Houlihan (2005: 176) surmises that an adequate framework for analysis should allow an exploration of the structure/agency relationship, where 'structure' includes a focus on the administrative infrastructure of the state; the pattern of non-state interests that represent sport; the structure of beliefs, ideas, norms and values; and the interaction of interests and ideas. Given that sport services are delivered through government departments and agencies including, most notably, the Department of Culture, Media and Sport (DCMS), Sport England and local authority leisure/sport services, as well as county and regional bodies, it is important to recognise institutional history, context, resources and culture in any analysis of sport policy, including administrative and funding dimensions, that in part shapes the behaviour of policy actors.

In line with Houlihan (2005: 167–168), this study recognises criteria against which theoretical frameworks can be evaluated. First, the framework must offer the capacity to explain both policy stability and change (Sabatier, 1999). The framework should facilitate a historical analysis of policy change in a period of 5–10 years minimum, as a shorter time span would provide only a 'snapshot' of policy and may serve to confuse 'minor fluctuations' in policy direction with 'sustained change'. Further, over a time period such as a decade, 'significant explanatory factors' are more likely to be identified than over a year, for example. A proposed framework would have the capacity to explain policy stability and change if located within a historical context.

Second, analytical frameworks must have the potential to illuminate a range of aspects of the policy process, so that policy 'as a whole' can be evaluated, particularly given the broad-based and exploratory nature of the research. Howlett and Ramesh (2003: 48) state, 'What is needed in policy analysis ... is an analytical framework that permits consideration of the entire range of factors affecting public policy'. They further state, 'theoretical efforts ... should remain firmly rooted in the middle or meso level. That is, policy theory cannot and should not claim to be more than a part of the development of general theories of social and political phenomena ... careful empirical studies and careful generalisation can provide a useful middle-range theory and understanding of public policy-making' (ibid: 48).

Third, any proposed theoretical framework must have applicability and utility across policy areas, as the sport policy area experiences 'policy spill-over' from other areas such as education, land-use planning and health. Houlihan (2005: 168) argues, 'The application of analytic frameworks in policy areas beyond sport should result in greater sensitivity to the distinctive features of the sport policy area'. He further states, 'Comparison of policy areas allows greater insight into the significance of systemic factors such as bureaucratic processes, organizational culture, and political party ideology'. Fourth, a meso-level policy framework for analysing sport policy should be located, at the macro-level, within a theory of the state and therefore a 'theory of power'.

Considering these guidelines, the following sections outline the potential contribution of pluralism as a theory of the state and the related body of literature around policy networks and approaches such as the 'multiple streams' framework (MSF) and the advocacy coalition framework (ACF). It is argued that insights from neo-pluralist studies of local government and governance in urban contexts complement theoretical development for explaining sport policy at the local authority level. However, a general introduction to policy studies is arguably required to 'set the scene' for the selection of a framework to illuminate sport policy processes in local contexts.

POLICY STUDIES: AN INTRODUCTION

Policy research attempts to understand how the state and political actors interact to produce public actions. It is in part a study of 'how, why and to what effect governments pursue particular courses of action and inaction' (Heidenheimer et al., 1990: 3). Parsons (1995) identifies six approaches to policy analysis within a political context, namely *stagist* (Hogwood and Gunn, 1984), *neo-Marxist* (Offe, 1985), *institutionalism* (Hall, 1986), *policy discourse approaches* (Fischer and Forester, 1993) and the two approaches adopted in this text. These are the *pluralist-elitist* (Dahl, 1971; Bachrach and Baratz, 1962; Gavanta, 1980; Lindbolm, 1977; Lukes, 1974) for the macro-level analysis and the *subsystem approaches* (Baumgatner and Jones, 1993; Heclo, 1978; Rhodes, 1988, 1996; Richardson and Jordan, 1979; Sabatier, 1998; Smith, 1993) for the meso-level analysis. Nonetheless, it is recognised that 'policy analysis is an applied sub-field whose content cannot be determined by disciplinary boundaries but by whatever appears appropriate to the circumstances of the time and the nature of the problem' (Wildavsky, 1979: 15). In practice, policy studies have become increasingly fragmented as researchers attempt to describe, analyse and explain complex policy processes.

Policy itself has been defined in a number of ways, including 'a course of action or inaction rather than specific decisions or actions' (Heclo, 1974: 85), 'a web of decisions and actions that allocate values' (Easton, 1953: 130), 'a set of interrelated decisions concerning the selection of goals and the means of achieving them within a specified situation' (Jenkins, 1978: 15) or simply 'anything a government chooses to do or not to do' (Dye, 1972: 2). Of particular relevance to the research underpinning this book is the argument by Hill (1997: 41) that 'policy is the product of the exercise of political influence, determining what the state does and setting limits to what it does'. Reference to political influence 'alerts us to the assumptions of pluralist politics where power and resource control are not monopolised by holders of formal offices' (Houlihan, 1997: 4). Further, policy is a process as opposed to a single decision or decisions isolated in time and context (Ham and Hill, 1993). Therefore, policies cannot be viewed in isolation but can be viewed as a sequence or cluster of decisions.

In terms of specific areas of research, some authors have sought to identify 'policy regimes' where particular policy types and policy priorities are associated with political systems whereas others seek to identify 'policy determinants' or influences shaping policy (Hancock, 1983), with, for example, a focus on either macro-level socio-economic factors or micro-level behavioural factors in a search for causal variables underpinning policy. Others have focused on 'policy content', where Lowi (1972) stated, 'policy may determine politics' rather than the opposite. Salaman (1981) suggested research focus on policy tools or instruments used by government to steer policy. However, most academic studies tend to pay attention to the entire policy process, taking account of policy regimes, determinants, content and instruments in any analysis, as in this study of local-level sport policy. Studies of 'policy outcomes' are not a specific aspect of this chapter, as this text is a study 'of' policy rather than a study 'for' policy. In other words, describing and analysing policy processes and exploring the utility of policy theory in order to explain policy processes are at the core of the text, as opposed to an applied research focus concerned with policy effectiveness or impact, for example.

Policy stages

The 'stages approach' to policy acts as a heuristic device in understanding policy processes. This approach disaggregates and simplifies the 'real world' in order to 'impose some conceptual order on the policy process in order to comprehend it' (John, 1998: 22). Laswell (1956) divided the policy process into stages to describe how policies were made and how they *should* be made (see Howlett and Ramesh, 2003, for details of the stages). Subsequent versions of a 'policy cycle' followed (Anderson, 1984; Brewer, 1974; Hogwood and Gunn, 1984). A specific 'stage' of the cycle can be highlighted in research, such as issue definition (Crenson, 1971; Easton, 1965; Outshoorn, 1991), agenda setting (Kingdon, 1995), policy implementation (Pressman and Wildavsky, 1973) or evaluation (Guba and Lincoln, 1981). Critically, the 'stages model' draws attention to the interaction between the policy process and the context within which it takes place (Houlihan, 2005: 168).

The key disadvantage of the 'stages' approach is that it suggests policy actors make decisions and attempt to solve policy problems in a linear and rational manner (Jenkins-Smith and Sabatier, 1993b), whereas in practice, a policy may be made in response to the embedded interests or beliefs of policy-makers, for example, or as a response to a problem or crisis. Further, the stages 'model' fails to capture the complexity and 'messiness of policy-making' (John, 1998: 25). Moreover, this approach does not identify what it is that drives policy and therefore lacks explanatory value, particularly as it is not associated with any 'theory of power' (De Leon, 1999b; Sabatier, 1999). Houlihan (2005: 169) adds, 'The stages model is more effective in capturing particular moments in the policy process than in identifying patterns of influence and outcomes over a sustained period'. Given the limitations of the stages approach to policy, researchers have taken as their unit of analysis the policy 'sector', 'field', 'domain', 'subsystem' or 'area'.

In this text, the term 'policy area' is used, given the characteristics of sport policy processes (Houlihan, 2000b). A 'policy area' is conceived of as an arena in which policy is made and implemented whose membership typically includes at least one government department and a cluster of organisations with a policy concern. The concept 'policy sector', as described by Benson (1982: 147–148), implies a greater degree of organisation and cohesion than may be the case for sport policy in England, at least outside of elite sport (Green and Houlihan, 2005a). The interaction of policy actors in a 'policy area' is at the heart of the neo-pluralist analysis, to which this chapter now turns.

NEO-PLURALISM

Pluralist theory and analysis is concerned with the relationship between government (or more broadly, 'the state') and civil society. Pluralism has been defined as 'the study of the formation and intermediation of political interest groups as a precondition of competitive liberal democracy' (McLennan, 1995: 34). A key characteristic of pluralism is an emphasis on promoting institutional difference and diversity, given scepticism towards 'the state'; therefore, it is broadly supportive of a 'strong' civil society to place checks and balances on state power. Pluralists conceptualise society as a plurality of interest groups as opposed to a set of self-interested individuals. Thus, the pluralist case rests on the argument that competition and participation among organised *groups*, not among individuals, is pivotal to understanding policy.

The group approach is historically wedded to the incrementalist model of decision-making (Lindbolm, 1960, 1977, 1986). Far from being a 'rational' process, decision-making in the policy process is characterised as a 'partisan mutual adjustment' between policy actors, where policy-makers make 'selective limited comparisons' between policy choices. Policy therefore results from an incremental process characterised by bargaining between interest groups, where 'multiple pressures' exist (Richardson and Jordan, 1979: 22–24). Further, Lindbolm notes that incrementalism is compatible with the idea that powerful interests constrain policy change, and therefore he views groups as unequal participants in the policy process. Arguably, a focus on groups is a substantive starting point from which to investigate influence in sport policy processes.

In order to provide a satisfactory account of the influence of interests shaping sport policy, pluralist understandings of 'power' have particular benefit. In early pluralist studies, power was defined as 'the capacity of one actor to do something affecting another actor, which changes the probable pattern of specified future events' (Polsby, 1963: 5). This was underpinned by a methodology that focuses on *observable* behaviour and outcomes. Traditional pluralist methodology therefore quantified power in terms of the capacity of groups to coerce government in taking actions it would not have otherwise taken. Polsby (quoted in Lukes, 1974: 12) states, 'The researcher should study actual behaviour, either from first hand or by reconstructing behaviour from documents, informants, newspapers and other appropriate sources'. Although this approach is of value in the first stages of researching sport policy, it has its limitations. Bachrach and Baratz (1962) suggest that, in practice, power can be exercised by excluding issues and interests from the policy agenda and this should also be a feature of research. In other words, interests can exercise more power if they have the capacity to control the political agenda.

Lukes' 'third dimension of power' involves the use of power to shape policy actor's preferences so that neither overt nor covert conflicts exist (Ham and Hill, 1993: 70). Therefore a 'manipulated consensus' may exist and can be maintained by powerful interests. Ham and Hill (1993: 23) conclude that 'the most effective and insidious use of power is to prevent … conflict from arising in the first place'. Analysing the structural position of interests is necessary in policy analysis. Marsh (1995: 283) concludes that there are four questions that any theory of power needs to address: 'Who exercises power?', 'How do they exercise power?', 'Why do some people have privileged access to power?' and 'In whose interest do they rule?' Arguably, early pluralist studies addressed the first two questions. Revisionist pluralism has therefore acknowledged that the influence of groups does not derive solely from their resources but also from institutional and historical contexts. Smith (1995: 216) observes, 'To grasp the influence of groups it is important to assess the historical development of a policy area, to examine how groups became involved, what pressure groups were excluded and what policy-making institutions developed'.

In terms of analysing relationships between groups or clusters of interests, Bentley (1967: 269) notes, 'It is only as we isolate these group activities, determine their representative values, and get the whole process stated in terms of them, that we approach … a satisfactory knowledge of government'. In terms of quantifying the extent of the influence of interests, Smith (1990: 302–304) identifies six variables that can be utilised in research: the social position of a group or interest, the extent of its organisation, the skills and qualifications of its leaders, group size, the level of resources and the degree of its mobilisation.

Other critiques of pluralism have also been assimilated into the theory over time. For example, the focus on groups outside of 'the state' at the expense of the policy actors and groups within the state, where, in practice, most policy is initiated (Alford, 1975b; Nordlinger, 1981), has led to a contemporary research focus on groups both within and outside of government. Further, Smith (1990: 320) recognises that 'elected and appointed officials have organisational and career interests of their own, and therefore devise policies that advance these interests'. Thus, the state and state actors have interests that can be realised through the instrumental use of groups in policy development and implementation. Moreover, Smith (1993: 228) contends that rather than pressure groups 'capturing' government, 'state actors have incorporated groups in order to achieve their own goals'. In other words, 'Are groups responding to an agenda and policy opportunities created by government, or do groups themselves bring about changes in government policy which in turn give them new opportunities to exert influence?' (Grant, 1995: 125).

In fact, the institutionalisation of interest groups (and their interests), coupled with the marginalisation or exclusion of others, is one dimension of pluralist research (e.g. Jordan and Richardson, 1983, 1987). Early pluralist literature, for example Truman (1951), observed that 'institutionalised relationships between an agency and its attendant interest groups could develop, leading to the marginalisation of some interests'. Moreover, government can take account of the interests of 'unorganised and potential groups' (Truman, 1951: 448), only to ensure that some interests do *not* become organised and acquire influence. The empirical research of the local sport policy area should therefore explore the relationship between the local authority and interests both 'inside' and 'outside' of its sphere of influence.

A further revision in explaining the role of pressure groups in the UK context (Grant, 1989) emerged from changes in British politics and policy-making. The 1970s could be typified as the decade of 'bureaucratic accommodation' (Jordan and Richardson, 1987), where a consensus existed between government and interest groups including business interests and trade unions in respect of economic and social goals. Government worked with interest groups in regard to specific areas of policy such as education or health, where a 'negotiated order' could be identified. These structural arrangements existed as governments need groups for at least three reasons, namely as a source of policy ideas and expertise, to implement policy and to secure legitimacy for policy preferences.

However, in the 1980s, under the Thatcher administrations, a 'confrontational style' of politics emerged where policy was both reactionary and impositional (Richardson, 1982). From the perspective of the New Right, 'bureaucratic accommodation' between interest groups and the state was viewed as essentially malign, concentrating power in closed communities of 'vested interests' that in effect constitute 'an elite cartel in which participants collude to preserve the existing parameters of the policy-making process' (Grant, 1995: 37). As Olsen (1982) had concluded, as democracies mature so special interests become embedded and therefore state–group relations change incrementally, if at all. In fact, competition between interest groups may inevitably lead to some interests securing interdependent relationships with government agencies, resembling a corporatist form of governance (summarised in Evans, 1995: 244–245; also see Parsons, 1995: 257–262).

In corporatist arrangements of power, policy is perceived of as the outcome of a bargaining process concerning strategic issues, conducted between *elite* interests within the state and external to it. Again, neo-pluralists accept a significant role for elites in shaping policy, but emphasise that elites themselves are 'internally divided'. Moreover, Ham and Hill (1993: 33) argue that 'the existence of elites is not incompatible with pluralist democracy because competition between elites protects democratic government'. Given these structural arrangements, interests groups are less concerned to solve policy problems and more concerned with creating stable relationships of self-interest, thus avoiding conflict, policy change and policy learning. Brittan (1987: 262–263) concluded that 'democracy has degenerated into an unprincipled auction to satisfy rival organised groups who can never in the long run be appeased because their demands are mutually incompatible'.

Another example of change to pluralist theory is in the acknowledgement that forces 'outside' of the state including commercial interests can and do shape government behaviour (Lindbolm, 1977; Olsen, 1965; Smith, 1995). Further, Lindbolm (1977) suggests that as business benefits from structural power, it can avoid having to operate specifically through traditional lobbying channels. He conceptualises an 'imprisoned zone' of policy-making, in which the interests of business have the greatest political representation. Moreover, countervailing powers are not viewed as sufficient to check business interests. Neo-pluralists recognise the privileged position of business interests relative to the state and accept that business interests potentially 'skew' the democratic process, although theorists insist that 'history making' decisions are still within the control of democratic influences. Hence, a 'deformed polyarchy' thesis emerges in neo-pluralist thought (Dunleavy and O'Leary, 1987). In sum, neo-pluralist theory assumes that there are multiple influences on policy processes but the political agenda is potentially skewed towards corporate power and state power (Dunleavy and O'Leary, 1987; Held, 1996; Smith, 1995).

When tracing the development of neo-pluralism, Marsh (1995: 270–271) suggests the changes, within pluralism, to elite theory and Marxism have resulted in 'a convergence towards an elitist position'. The 'convergence' of theories of the state is reflected in the elite pluralist position (McFarland, 1987). Importantly, for the study of sport policy, Marsh (1995) details six specific aspects of convergence: first, the existence of structured privilege; second, a limited number of structural bases of privilege (economic and political resources, knowledge, gender, control of agenda and member-ship of policy networks); third, a role for agency in shaping political institutions and outcomes; fourth, an increased focus on the state; fifth, a focus on the contingency of policy outcomes; and sixth, a focus on ascribing primacy to politics.

Nonetheless, there are some important differences of emphasis. For example, pluralists accept structural privilege, but view conflict between interest groups as remaining at the 'core' of politics. Interpretation based on broad social categories (e.g. class or gender) are rejected in explaining political *outcomes*. Simply put, pluralist interpretations differ from Marxist and elitist accounts in terms of the degree of emphasis placed upon agency, contingency and intentionalism. In brief, in the transformation from 'classical pluralism' to neo-pluralism, pluralists have sought to retain an agency-led explanation of society, while accommodating and assimilating elements of structuralist thought into theory and methodology. These insights assist in interpreting the findings of a study of sport policy and practice.

Therefore, for the purposes of empirical investigation, the author accepts that 'political outcomes are … the product of conflict between interests … for the allocation of scarce resources in a context characterised by structural inequality' (Marsh, 1995: 273). The form of the state and civil society is therefore viewed as the outcome of past struggles. Hence, in conducting research in the sport policy area, the focus is twofold: on conflict between interests *and* on the structured context (historically formed) in which interests compete. Finally, in relation to sport policy, Houlihan (1997) argues that neo-pluralist analyses are one of the most persuasive frameworks for understanding power and that neo-pluralism provides an intuitively plausible account of the policy-making process, at least within Western industrial democracies.

THEORIES OF URBAN POLITICS, GOVERNANCE AND LOCAL GOVERNMENT

As the focus of this book is on policy at the level of a local government area, the body of literature around local government and governance (Stoker, 1991; Stoker, 2000; Wilson and Game, 2006) offers a point of entry for understanding sport policy and practice. Moreover, the research underpinning this text predominantly centres on Liverpool City Council sport and recreation services (LCC Sport) who have, to a large extent, shaped sport policy and practices (see Chapters 4, 5 and 6 in particular). The empirical focus on a city invites theories of urban politics into the study (see for example, Judge, Stoker and Wolman, 1995) where regime theory (Stone, 1989, 1993), for example, may have utility for locating sport policy in a broader set of policy processes, particularly as this approach has a close theoretical association with neo-pluralism and the policy networks literature drawn upon by the author.

Briefly, regime theory highlights business control over investment decisions and resource allocations made in the public sector, where a 'regime' is defined as a 'relatively stable group *with access to institutional resources* that enable it to have a sustained role in making governing decisions' (Stone, 1989: 4; original emphasis). The approach also foregrounds bargaining and brokering as important in understanding policy processes, as in pluralist theory. Regime theory focuses on partnership-working and highlights how cooperation between interests can result in effective policy-making and implementation (although competition between interests also shapes policy). The theory also offers utility in understanding policy change in an urban setting through addressing issues of power, where interests 'blend their capacities to achieve common purposes' (Stone, 1989: 55), hence a focus on the interdependence of governmental and non-governmental interests. Insights from regime theory may be of particular utility in understanding sport policy in the context of a city undergoing economic and social regeneration where 'sport' plays a role in city-wide strategy. Moreover, the theory has been widely used in research on single-city case studies. In these respects, the theory can be seen as complementary to the neo-pluralist meso-level analysis of the sport policy area utilising approaches such as policy networks and the ACF addressed in the following sections of this chapter.

Perhaps, the most important fact, however, is that regime theory offers a framework for analysing power relations. The theory identifies four types of power: *systemic power*, where interests gain influence through their location or position within socio-economic structures; command or *social control*, which involves the active mobilisation of resources to achieve compliance with policy goals and is therefore an issue of capacity; *coalition power*, where actors engage in bargaining in search of consensus, particularly where coalitional arrangements tend to be unstable; and *pre-emptive power*, where leadership is critical in complex policy areas to building and sustaining governing capacity. The coalitions that can retain influence over time are therefore those with systemic power, embedded within institutions and policy processes, who can mobilise resources relatively easily and are also able to manipulate their strategic advantage through bargaining and leadership in complex policy environments.

The body of literature around local government and governance also offers a point of entry for developing a theoretical framework for understanding sport policy at the local level. The key dimensions of the literature that may be of value in the study of sport policy in Liverpool include central–local government relations, local government financing and spending control, the internal politics of local government and relations between local interest groups and local authorities, each dimension being a component of a historical and evolutionary account of local government policy processes. These dimensions are briefly outlined as follows.

Dunleavy (1980: 105) observed that 'councils are located and locate themselves in what may be termed the "national local government system". This may be taken to describe the complex web of inter- and supra-authority relations which can exert a strong influence on the policies pursued in particular localities'. As Stoker (1991: xiv) notes, 'Local government has during the 1980s found itself buffeted and challenged by a range of forces including public expenditure constraints, economic restructuring, increased politicisation and changed public perspectives'. Liverpool, in particular, was at the centre of political and economic tensions between central and local governments (see Chapter 4).

Specific policy instruments used by central government to steer local government policy processes include the use of legislation, particularly in regard to education (see Chapter 8) and land-use planning (see Chapter 9). One example of central government setting the parameters of local authority activity, related to sport and leisure, can be found in the literature around competitive compulsory tendering (CCT) and its replacement, *Best Value* (Henry, 1993, 2001), and more recently, the comprehensive performance assessment (CPA) framework. However, the impact of central government policy on local authorities was not always as extensive as intended, with significant resistance encountered at the local and regional levels (Rhodes, 1981, 1988, 1996). In practice, an 'implementation gap' may undercut national policy aspiration. As Stoker (1991: 153) concludes, 'What emerges is a picture of increased control but over a narrow range of matters ... along with control has come unintended consequences, ambiguity and uncertainty. Resistance from local authorities has also been stiffened and politicised'. One solution for central government has been to create a parallel tier of government agencies with their own resources that simply by-pass local government policy processes. The Merseyside Development Corporation (MDC) was a case in point (see Chapter 4).

At the heart of central–local government relations are disputes concerning local spending. The *Local Government, Planning and Land Act 1980* is notable for introducing a new system for allocating central government financial support to local authorities, given that the Conservative government was committed to reducing spending on services not under direct central control. This legislation effectively meant that central government could decide what constituted local spending needs given greater central government control over local capital expenditure (Newton and Curran, 1985). The establishment of the Audit Commission and the setting of targets and penalties were further attempts to 'control' local government spending, particularly Labour-controlled local authorities. The 'capping' of local authority spending had a significant impact in Liverpool, particularly where an 'ideological gulf' existed between local and central government (again see Chapter 4).

In respect of the internal politics of local authorities, throughout the 1970s and 1980s, it was generally accepted that an elite of senior officers and members (councillors) in effect controlled policy (Saunders, 1979). However, Stoker (1991) argues that multiple sources of influence within local government have replaced elite control, identifying areas such as the ruling political party group (cf. Rose, 1984), individual departments and councillors as ward representatives and in addition to the 'elite' of senior officers and councillors at the executive board level. Policy is therefore mediated by officer–member relations and inter-departmental and intra-departmental relationships, for example. The *Local Government and Housing Act 1989* is viewed as important in this respect, as it made changes to decision-making structures to increase 'checks and balances' on party political influence (Stoker, 1991: 111). It can be anticipated that the internal politics of Liverpool City Council has had an influence on sport policy.

The relationship between local authorities and local interest groups is also of relevance to this text. Stoker (1991) identifies four types of interest groups: *producer groups*, including business and professional bodies in the sport sector; *community groups*, such as play groups; *'cause' groups*, such as those representing playing fields conservation; and *not-for-profit groups*, such as voluntary sector sport clubs. Clearly, some group types span more than one category. In this book, the relationship between the local authority and voluntary sector sports bodies, as it impacts on sport policy, is one focus of the case study analysis.

In terms of theorising this relationship, the pluralist/elitist 'debate' has dominated research. The elitist view assumes local authorities are enclosed organisations 'unresponsive, oligarchic and inward-looking' (Dunleavy, 1980: 150) where power is concentrated at senior officer/member level and producer group interests achieve privileged access to policy processes. However, neo-pluralist accounts of local government, although recognising the significant influence of 'elites', highlight the increasing strength of local interest groups, an increasing diversity and complexity of local interest group politics and the growing structural influence of some interests. Given that there is therefore an 'ambiguity' of power in localities, the actual distribution of power remains an empirical question to be explored in sport policy research.

In sum, studies of local government and governance sensitise sport policy researchers to the local institutional, financial and political context in which policy is formulated and implemented. These studies also foreground the significance of relationships between policy actors in shaping priorities and practices. However, a complementary body of literature arguably offers the potential for a more detailed analysis of the influences that shape policy at the level of the local authority area. The literature around policy networks and associated meso-level theoretical frameworks arguably has utility in this respect and is outlined as follows.

MESO-LEVEL APPROACHES TO UNDERSTANDING POLICY

Policy networks

Benson (1982: 148) defined *policy networks* in terms of 'a complex of organizations connected to each other by resource dependencies and distinguished from other ... complexes by breaks in the structure of resource dependencies'. The term 'network' is therefore used by social scientists in focusing on the inter-connected relations of policy actors which, for proponents, is the key to understanding how policy is made and how it changes. Rhodes (1981, 1988) identifies different structures of dependences that vary along five key dimensions, namely the 'constellation of interests', 'membership' (e.g. balance of public and private sector actors), 'vertical interdependence' (e.g. central and sub-central actors), 'horizontal interdependence' (i.e. the extent of network insulation from other networks) and 'the distribution of resources'. As a starting point to the analysis of sport policy, identifying networks or 'webs of influence', in reference to these dimensions, is of value.

Richardson (1982) developed the idea of *policy communities* in a comparative analysis of policy styles, defined as either anticipatory or reactionary (i.e. a tendency to anticipate or react to policy problems and events) and as either consensus seeking or impositional. Rhodes (1988: 78) states that policy communities are characterised by a 'stability of relationships, continuity of a highly restrictive membership, vertical independence based on shared service delivery responsibilities and insulation from other networks and invariably from the general public ... They are highly integrated'. This may be the result of shared values and beliefs and therefore shared policy preferences and priorities (Rhodes, 1988; Richardson and Jordan, 1979). Houlihan (1997: 16) adds that probably *the* defining characteristic of policy communities is 'the emergence of a core set of values that will inform the way in which problems are identified and defined, and also the way in which solutions are selected'.

However, value consensus alone may not be a powerful enough spur to policy cooperation, as competition for scarce resources will produce a conflict between policy actors even where there exists broad agreement on policy priorities. Hence, any analysis of sport policy should include a focus on patterns of resource dependencies alongside the values held by policy actors. As Smith (1993) claims, networks are the manifestation of prior policies, ideologies and processes, and therefore 'to explain the origins, shape and outcomes of a network it is necessary to examine why some interests are privileged in a given network or, if no interests are privileged, why the network is open' (Marsh and Stoker, 1995: 293).

Issue networks can be defined, by comparison with policy communities, as 'looser' in terms of integration and as a set of interests and therefore less exclusive and stable. Rhodes (1988: 78) states, 'The distinctive features of this kind of network are its large number of participants and their limited degree of interdependence. Stability and continuity are at a premium, and the structure tends to be atomistic. Commonly, there is no single focal point at the centre with which other actors need to bargain for resources'. Issue networks are likely to exhibit characteristics of conflict as groups with differing perspectives and agendas struggle for recognition and resources.

Of note is that whereas a policy community can have a sustainable impact on policy process, an issue network does not have the capacity to achieve this. Thus, policy continuity can result from the influence of a policy community although a community can also produce inertia and inhibit policy change and learning. In issue networks, groups in positions of relative weakness acquire legitimacy and resources through conformity with how issues are defined by more powerful interests. Rhodes (cited in Thompson et al., 1991: 204) observed, 'The prime example in British government [of an issue network] seems to be the field of leisure and recreation'. Smith (1993) views that *issue networks* develop where low political priority is given to the policy area in question or where a new issue has not been institutionalised, which characterises the sport policy area to some degree. In the last decade, apart from an emerging policy community around elite sport (Green and Houlihan, 2005a), the sport policy area can still be characterised as a series of issue networks.

Smith (1993) highlights the significance of the state and state actors, such as local authorities, who, it is argued, increase their autonomy and influence through being 'integrated' into policy networks. Smith (1993) suggests that although policy networks can be 'sites of resistance' through their relative control over policy implementation, government can make a considerable difference to the influence of a particular group or coalition. Rhodes (cited in Thompson et al., 1991) states that central government can 'specify unilaterally, substantive policies, control access to the networks, set the agenda of issues, specify the rules of the game surrounding consultation, determine the timing and scope of consultation, even call a network into being'. Further, central government can 'create a nexus of interests so that co-operation flows from a sense of mutual advantage' (Richardson and Jordan, 1979: 105). However, government also retains the option of coercion if the 'manufacture' of consent proves ineffectual. This is achieved through the active use of the resources it controls to shape policy networks in its own interests and image. Smith (1993) adds that *policy communities* will emerge in specific contexts, for example, where the state is dependent on networks for implementation of policies that are valued by government or where government seeks to avoid a policy failure or where interest groups hold significant resources.

Authors such as Kickert et al. (1997) highlight government 'steering' strategies to gain consent for policy priorities, including the use of legal instruments (orders and prohibitions), economic instruments (financial incentives) and communicative instruments (the selective use of information) or the government can stimulate cooperation, bargaining and compromise and attempt to create transparency and trust (including identifying and promoting the mutual advantages of cooperation) or the government can attempt to provide a 'vision' or common purpose, thus creating a strategic consensus within a given context. This may require restructuring the inter-organisational dynamics of a policy area, including creating policy networks with a government department or agency at its hub. Being at the 'hub' and possessing the greatest resources, government bodies may be able to shape the context, perceptions and actions of non-government actors in the policy process.

In any analysis of state–network relationships, it should also be noted that policy networks may not have supplanted party political channels of communication and influence. As Rhodes (cited in Thompson et al., 1991: 209) observes, 'The effects of party are pervasive. It spans levels of government and communicates a range of interests. Most important, it spans the policy network'. In any analysis of local authority sport policy, it is accepted that political parties, committee structures and actions, and individual councillors can influence policy depending on the issue. However, the influence of political parties is an area of controversy in comparative politics (cf. Castles, 1982;

De Leon, 1999a). To what extent local political control makes a difference in shaping sport policy is one component of the case study analysis to follow (see Chapter 4).

In a revised policy networks framework (Marsh and Smith, 2000), the authors argue that there are three interactive or dialectical relationships that explain the role networks play in the development and implementation of policy. These are (i) the structure of the network and the agents operating within them, (ii) the network and the context within which it operates and (iii) the network and the policy outcome. *Figure 2.1* highlights these dialectical relationships. The authors conclude that networks are structures that constrain and facilitate policy actors and the culture of the network also acts as a constraint and/or opportunity for members of the network. Further, Marsh and Smith (2000) stress that networks involve the institutionalisation of beliefs and values in addition to rules and routines, given the previous conflicts that have shaped networks. Hence, power relations are entrenched to some extent. Moreover, policy outcomes impact on the character of policy networks and vice versa. These conclusions again highlight the shift in pluralist thought towards a neo-pluralist position, where,

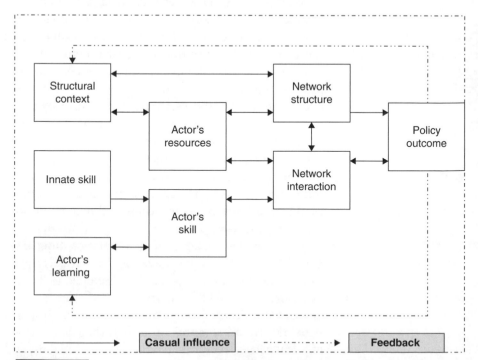

FIGURE 2.1 *Policy networks and policy outcomes: a dialectical approach. (Source: Marsh and Smith, 2000: 10.)*

in particular, the networks framework recognises the value of institutionalist perspectives in understanding policy.

Also of importance to the aims of this book is Marsh and Smith's (2000) discussion of the method by which networks change. Some authors stress endogenous factors (e.g. resource dependencies) and others exogenous factors (e.g. ideological or political context, or policy spill-over from other sectors). Marsh and Rhodes (1992) contended that networks change through a dialectical relationship between endogenous and exogenous factors, especially where the boundaries of policy networks are difficult to identify, as in the case of the sport policy area.

In sum, Marsh and Smith emphasise that, first, the formation of a network is affected by a combination of external factors and decisions by agents; second, policy outcomes are the product of interactions between agents and structure; third, the change in a network involves an interaction between network and context; and fourth, outcomes affect networks. Evans (2001: 544), in reviewing Marsh and Smith's dialectical framework, highlights the key factors that impact on a policy network, identifying history, culture and beliefs; ideologies; macro-economic variables; institutions; interest groups; other networks and 'agents' (individual policy actors) as the significant influences. Marsh and Smith, however, argue that it is *political authority* that is the most significant external factor in determining network change.

In relating the policy networks approach to a theory of power, Marsh and Smith (2000) draw on Benson (1979, 1982). The revised theoretical framework contends that the network is a site of conflict between competing interests and conceptions of purpose (beliefs, ideas and values). In essence, the authors maintain that there exists an interdependent relationship between ideas, interests and power in policy actions. In sum, the dialectical network analysis focuses on the process through which network arrangements are generated and sustained through the interests, ideas and power of policy actors.

Atkinson and Coleman (1992: 176) conclude that network approaches 'serve as a kind of conceptual crossroads for ongoing theoretical and empirical research'. Houlihan (1997: 15) states that policy networks fulfil an important function in providing 'a step towards a more theoretically informed explanation of policy processes. Moreover, the approach provides a set of concepts and tools that facilitates the comparison of detailed case studies'. This approach is therefore useful for exploring sport policy at the local authority level, as macro-level theories pay little attention to mediating processes, while micro-level theories tend to ignore the impact of broader structural factors on micro-level decision-making (Evans, 2001).

Arguably, the revisions of the policy networks approach by Marsh and Smith (2000) offer much for an analysis of sport policy, and their insights provide a 'point of departure' for a study of sport policy. More specifically, for the study of sport policy, the literature around policy networks serves to foreground processes of negotiation and bargaining, coalition building, resource dependencies and the mobilisation of influence within a complex policy environment (Jordan and Richardson, 1987; Marsh and Rhodes, 1992; Richardson and Jordan, 1979).

Finally, researchers utilising this meso-level approach reject the idea of the policy network being a rational form of organisation, but view the network as an 'arbitrary system unevenly imposed upon events and insecure in its hold of the policy environment' (Evans, 2001: 546). This insight directs the study of sport policy towards utilising insights from the MSF.

The multiple streams framework

The MSF (Cohen, March and Olsen, 1972; Kingdon, 1984, 1995; March and Olsen, 1976, 1984; Zahariadis, 1995, 1999, 2003; Zahariadis and Allen, 1995) focuses on agenda setting and choice between policy alternatives under conditions of ambiguity. Zahariadis (1999: 6) notes, 'Complexity, fluidity and fuzziness are particularly appropriate characterisations of policy-making'. Therefore, decision-making situations are characterised in terms of 'organised anarchy', where argument, persuasion and reasoning are central in policy formation (Fischer and Forester, 1993). Further, this approach assumes that the adoption of specific choices is, in part, dependent on *when* policies are made. A growing number of policy analysts consider timing to be important in understanding policy processes where the structure of political time is a critical variable of policy choice. The theoretical approach also elevates the significance of ideas in policy-making and analyses how ideas emerge, are adopted or are rejected, particularly at the agenda-setting stage of a 'policy cycle'.

The MSF identifies three processes or 'streams', namely 'politics', 'policy problems' and 'policy solutions', which interact to produce policy change. The *problem stream* comprises those issues which government has identified as requiring action (Houlihan, 2005: 171). Such issues may result from 'focusing events' (a perceived or actual crisis, for example), indicators of the changing scale of a problem and/or feedback on the performance of existing policy or strategy. 'Problems' in the sport policy area may include 'a lack of national success in sport' or a 'decline in participation in sport'. Further, a problem may emerge from policy change in adjacent policy areas, hence the concept of policy spill-over (Dery, 1999). For example, focusing events in adjacent policy sectors, such as health – where a 'problem' is the 'growing obesity in young people' – can result in sport policy actors becoming assimilated into social policy objectives (see Chapter 10).

The *policy stream* comprises ideas that rise and fall from favour over time, supported by specific interests and, on occasion, advocated by 'policy entreprencurs'. Ideas gain a foothold on government agendas if they fulfil specific criteria, such as whether the idea is compatible with dominant beliefs or values held by key policy actors or whether it is based on the feasibility of applying the idea to practice. The *political stream* comprises government, political parties and interest groups, as well as the 'national mood' or public opinion. The synergy of the three policy streams enhances significantly the chances that policy-makers will address an issue.

According to Kingdon, the three streams normally operate independently, except in the event of a 'window of opportunity', where 'policy entrepreneurs' act to couple the interdependent streams. Kingdon (1995: 165) defines policy windows, which generally have a short duration, as 'opportunities for advocates of proposals to push their pet solutions, or to push attention to their spccial problems'. Kingdon (1995) further maintains that some 'policy windows' are predictable (e.g. spending rounds) and others unpredictable. 'Windows' close when policy-makers believe they have addressed the issue/problem adequately, or actors have failed to generate action, or there is no perceived alternative available, or the crisis or 'focusing event' has passed. Kingdon also observes that policy windows may open and close as thc 'national mood' changes. However, policy selection criteria in the MSF are usually founded on 'value acceptability' and/or strategic feasibility, whcrc lcss favoured or 'unfeasible' policy options are likely to be rejected.

Although Kingdon's work focused specifically on agenda setting and alternative specification, Zahariadis (2003) extends the approach to explain other aspects of the policy process. First, the author extends the explanation of the role of policy entrepreneur via the concept of 'manipulation' (Zahariadis, 2003: 18–22), defined as 'systematic distortion, misrepresentation, or selective presentation of information by skilled policy entrepreneurs who exploit opportunities in a world of unclear goals'. These policy actors engage in 'context shaping', defined as specifying boundaries around what is of value (Stone, 1988). In essence, 'manipulation' aims primarily to provide meaning, clarification and identity, in a context of ambiguity. Specific 'manipulation' may involve the use of 'salami tactics', where policy entrepreneurs acquire agreement for, and commitment to, a policy, in stages, realising that a proposed policy would not find favour if presented in full 'from the outset' (see Zahariadis, 2003: 93).

However, this 'manipulation' may be limited in practice where structural factors, such as institutional rules or wider socio-economic forces in effect, constrain action. Second, in response to the critique of the MSF that it is ahistorical (Weir, 1992), Zahariadis (2003) revises the framework to include a focus on how the trajectory of ideas is influenced by the structure of policy networks in the *policy stream*. More specifically, the dimensions of integration (size, mode, capacity and access) are seen to affect the evolution of ideas. The author concludes that 'ideas are constantly accepted, rejected, or amended by various participants in the policy stream in their quest to forge coalitions and enhance the likelihood that their solution will eventually be adopted' (Zahariadis, 2003: 65).

Third, Zahariadis (2003: 86) argues that 'ideology is a necessary but not sufficient determinant of choice [where] ... This deficiency is ameliorated by opportunism'. As highlighting either ideology *or* opportunism in understanding policy processes can limit analysis, the MSF seeks to 'uncover' rather than assume rationality in the policy process. Kingdon (1995) too, in revising the MSF, states that political ideology is central to policy formation, as it provides meaning to action and a 'guide' to identifying which issues are seen as important. Therefore, 'ideology' is viewed as invoking 'idea-guided behaviour' in policy actors (Reich, 1990). Further, Zahariadis (1999: 80) maintains that 'the ideology of the governing party (or coalition) shapes the kind of issues that will rise to the agenda and demarcates the solutions available for adoption'. Therefore, the role and influence of *policy elites* is important in shaping policy. Again, these revisions indicate a shift towards a neo-pluralist account of power in policy analysis at the meso-level.

At face value, the MSF appears to offer insights into sport policy processes that can prove fruitful in any analysis, given the characteristics of the sport policy area (Houlihan, 2000b). However, as the MSF foregrounds the importance of argument and ideas in policy-making and downplays institutional power and systemic bias, it may not be able to *fully* explain sport policy. Further, the analytical framework may understate the significant influence of the state on policy, where it is contended that power in the sport policy area is concentrated (within the government) despite the existence of organisational pluralism. Clearly, the evidence of plurality (a multitude of organisations in the sport sector) does not support the normative preferences of pluralism (e.g. the widespread distribution of power).

Finally, the framework has undergone little empirical testing because it has no explicit hypotheses and therefore falsification is problematic, apart from its limited use by Chalip (1995, 1996). The author will therefore draw upon the insights offered by the MSF, but its direct application may be limited. In particular, Houlihan (2005) suggested the MSF offers a partial understanding of policy stability, although the relationship of ideas to interests is under-theorised and it is overly focused on agenda setting as opposed to the 'whole' policy process despite the revisions made by Zahariadis (2003). In sum, the strengths of the MSF are that it can easily integrate with concepts in other analytical frameworks such as policy networks; it has some utility for explaining policy change, given its focus on 'circumstance'; the concept of 'spill-over' of policy from other policy areas has value; and the framework facilitates analysis over time. Further, for understanding sport policy processes, the concept of 'policy entrepreneur' has utility in a context of a policy area characterised by weak systemic embeddedness (Houlihan and White, 2002).

Houlihan (2005) claims a potential utility of the MSF in sport policy research, given the degree of change and opportunism in complex policy areas such as 'sport' where a high level of organisational fragmentation exists. Further, in 'crowded policy spaces', there is greater scope for individual policy brokering or entrepreneurship, especially where interests have yet to become embedded in the political and administrative infrastructure, as in the case of 'sport', and by contrast with the embeddedness of interests with adjacent policy areas, such as education, land-use planning and health. Houlihan and Green (2006) note the significance of one such policy entrepreneur for school sport policy (see Chapter 6).

The advocacy coalition framework

The ACF complements and extends the premises of the policy networks and multiple streams theoretical frameworks, within a neo-pluralist theory of the state and conception of power. It arguably meets the criteria of a 'theory' (King, Keohane and Verba, 1994; Lave and March, 1975), as most of the critical terms used are clearly defined, with propositions clearly stated and internally consistent. It has two causal drivers (the core beliefs of actors and exogenous 'perturbations'), has many falsifiable hypotheses and is broad in application.

The development of the ACF can be seen as a 'progressive research program' (Lakatos, 1978) that has stimulated much published policy research; including recent research on elite sport policy (Green and Houlihan, 2005a). The ACF has been modified since the initial version (Sabatier, 1988) that attempted to synthesise the stronger features of the 'top–down' and 'bottom–up' approaches to policy implementation and to act as an alternative to and improvement upon the heuristic 'stages approach' to understanding the policy process.

As opposed to rational choice approaches to policy analysis (Ostrom, 1999), the ACF does not assume that actors are driven primarily by economic/political self-interest, but assumes that actors' goals are usually complex. Sabatier (1999: 130) states, 'an individual's ability to perceive the world and to process that information is affected by cognitive biases and constraints'. Policy actors are viewed as instrumentally rational in the sense of seeking to use resources to achieve goals, but self-interest need not be the causal driver. Instead, 'actors are driven by a set of policy-oriented goals comprising value priorities and conceptions of whose welfare should be of greatest concern' (Sabatier, 1999: 130). Hence, the focus of the ACF is on beliefs in policy processes, where pre-existing beliefs constitute a lens through which actors perceive policy, and further, it is policy core beliefs that provide the principal glue in coalitions of interests (Zafonte and Sabatier, 1998).

In the ACF, the unit of analysis is the policy *subsystem* (or area) in which advocacy coalitions compete for recognition and resources. Sabatier (1999: 119) states, 'A subsystem consists of those actors from a variety of public and private organisations who are actively concerned with a policy problem or issue ... and who regularly seek to influence public policy in that domain'. A policy subsystem includes not only interest groups, administrative agencies and legislative committees, but also journalists, researchers, policy analysts and individuals at all levels of government who are active in a policy area. Moreover, those involved in implementing policy are included in the subsystem, as the boundaries between policy formulation and implementation are blurred in practice. Moreover, those who operationalise policy have some influence on which ideas and interests are represented in practice. Further, Sabatier makes a distinction between a *nascent* subsystem (one in the process of forming) and a *mature* subsystem (one that has existed for approximately 10 years or more). He further defines a mature policy subsystem as where the participants regard themselves as a semiautonomous community who seek to influence policy and where an 'organisational residue' or an administrative structure including government agencies and interest groups exists.

Sabatier (1991) and Sabatier and Jenkins-Smith (1993) also explore the importance of policy subsystems in policy formulation and implementation. They emphasise the relationships within policy subsystems as the key to understanding how decision-making works. The ACF has much in common, therefore, with the *policy networks* approach. In the ACF, 'policy brokers' act to mediate between competing coalitions. This concept has parallels with 'policy entrepreneur' in the MSF. Further, in the ACF, knowledge plays a pivotal role and therefore parallels can be drawn with the concepts of epistemic communities (Haas, 1992) and discourse coalitions (Bulkeley, 2000).

Policy subsystems normally comprise between two and four *advocacy coalitions* (a concept similar to *policy community*) that compete for influence. The ACF assumes that actors can be aggregated into a number of advocacy coalitions composed of various government and private/voluntary sector organisations. Further, Houlihan (2000b: 8) suggests that 'coalitions' within a policy subsystem 'provides a potentially useful modification to the concept of the policy community with its assumptions of substantial value consensus'. Each coalition shares a set of normative and causal beliefs and engages in 'a non-trivial degree of co-ordinated activity over time' (such as policy-making). Sabatier (1999) argues that at any one time, each coalition adopts one or more strategies that involve the use of guidance instruments (defined as budgets, personnel, information and/or changes in rules) in an attempt to realise policy objectives.

In terms of beliefs, Sabatier (1999) organises the belief systems of each coalition into a hierarchical tripartite structure. This consists of, first, *deep core beliefs*, which are basic ontological and normative beliefs; second, *policy core beliefs*, a coalition's basic normative commitments and causal perceptions, including, for example, the choice of policy instruments; and third, *secondary aspects* of a coalition's belief system, for example, policy preferences regarding desirable resource allocations. It is argued that deep core beliefs are very resistant to change, whereas policy core beliefs are less fixed as they may change over time with the gradual accumulation of evidence to challenge the status quo. Following this line of argument, it can be expected that 'secondary aspects' of beliefs are the most susceptible to change. Public policies and programmes therefore include value priorities, perceptions of causal relationships and assumptions regarding the efficacy of policy instruments. As Sabatier (1999: 120) observes, the utility of the ACF lies in the fact that its 'ability to map beliefs and policies on the same "canvas" provides a vehicle for assessing the influence of actors over time'. In using the ACF, it therefore becomes necessary to investigate the beliefs of those seeking to influence policy processes.

Apart from beliefs, Sabatier (1999) conceives of two sets of exogenous variables that impact on the constraints and opportunities of subsystem actors. These are relatively stable 'parameters' including socio-cultural values, natural resources of the political system and basic constitutional structure, and relatively dynamic 'external (system) events' including changes in socio-economic conditions or public opinion. Although normative 'core beliefs' change slowly over time, changes in the policy core are 'usually the results of perturbations in non-cognitive factors external to the subsystem' (Sabatier, 1993: 19–20). These influences include changes in governing coalitions or impacts from adjacent policy areas. In terms of how and why policy changes, Parsons (1995: 196) states, 'Change in the policy subsystem is a result of the interplay of "relatively stable parameters" and external events, which frame the constraints and resources of the actors in the subsystem and the interactions within the policy subsystem itself'. The ACF is represented diagrammatically in *Figure 2.2*.

The ACF assumes that understanding policy change requires a time perspective of at least a decade in order to complete at least one 'formulation–implementation–reformulation' *policy cycle* (Hogwood and Gunn, 1984).

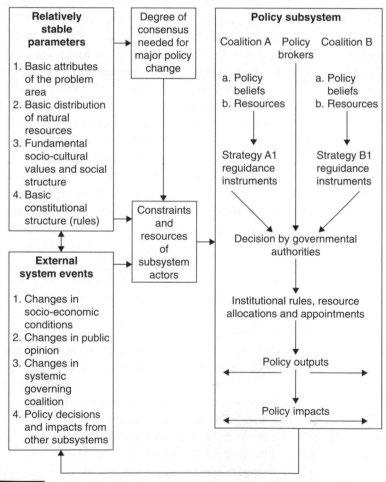

FIGURE 2.2 *The advocacy coalition framework. (Source: Adapted from Sabatier and Jenkins-Smith, 1999: 149.)*

The resultant changes subsequently feed back into the beliefs and resources of coalitions, a process of 'policy-oriented learning'. From Sabatier's perspective, policy-oriented learning may underpin a relatively long-term policy change (Sabatier, 1998: 104). *Policy learning* is generally considered to be either a concept restricted to the elite subsystem actors, where non-elites have 'neither the expertise, nor the time, nor the inclination to be active participants in the policy subsystem' (Sabatier and Jenkins-Smith, 1993: 223) or a broader concept to include the relationship of public opinion to public policy (e.g. Kingdon, 1995; Lindbolm, 1986). Importantly, the ACF does not assume policy-making systems are consensual or dominated by *stable* elites. However, Parsons (1995) questions whether successful coalitions are those that learn 'better' than others or those that hold greater resources and power. Parsons argues that coalitions may change as they advance core interests; hence, no rational learning process is required. Thus, the ACF may not be robust enough for understanding any 'mobilisation of bias' in policy-making.

Another critique of the ACF includes that of Bulkeley (2000: 733), who claims that the 'ACF does not address the ways in which actors "create" the social and political world in which they operate, in as much as it fails to grasp the interaction between actors within policy coalitions by conceptualising discourse as a means through which learning is communicated' (cited in Green and Houlihan, 2004). Green and Houlihan (2004) also note that the ACF lacks 'a fully articulated theory of power' which weakens the ACF's analytical capacity. In particular, these authors note that the ACF would benefit from giving greater weight to the organisational arrangements of the state and the relationship between the state and organisations in civil society. In this respect, the ACF can be complemented with insights from institutionalism (cf. March and Olsen, 1989; Thelen and Steinmo, 1992). For example, Thelen and Steinmo (1992: 2) observe how institutions 'shape how political actors define their interests and ... structure their relations of power to other groups'. Further, Howlett and Ramesh (2003: 27) note the 'relative autonomy of political institutions from the society in which they exist ... and the unique patterns of historical development and the constraints they impose of future choices'.

Institutionalism is relevant to the study of sport policy where authors have focused on the organisational infrastructure for sport as significant in shaping policy (Henry, 2001; Houlihan and White, 2002; Pickup, 1996; Roche, 2003). Further, the significance of the 'culture' of institutions has been researched by a number of authors focusing on, for example, disability (Thomas, 2003) or ethnicity (Carrington and McDonald, 2003). However, as Houlihan (2005: 170) observes, institutionalism cannot be viewed as an analytical framework, but as more of an 'analytic orientation or sensitizing concept'.

Houlihan (2005) assesses the value of the ACF in explaining sport policy and draws the following conclusions. First, the ACF offers valuable insights into policy stability, where 'stability is explained in terms of dominant coalitions and the persistence of deep core and policy core beliefs' (Houlihan, 2005: 173). However, the explanation of policy change is viewed as 'less convincing', given that the ACF relies on a combination of exogenous events, instrumental rationality and policy learning, as the basis for change. Moreover, membership of advocacy coalitions is 'only vaguely specified', and the implication that coalition membership is 'open' and accessible requires more empirical support than is currently available' (Houlihan, 2005: 173). Nonetheless, despite its limitations, as stated, sport policy analysts have recently used the ACF in policy research. For example, the ACF has been used in explaining (1) elite sport development policy (Green and Houlihan, 2005a), finding some evidence for the existence of advocacy coalitions in the UK and broad applicability of the framework; (2) the UK sport development policy (Houlihan and White, 2002); and (3) sport regulatory policy in the European Union (Parrish, 2003).

These studies support the idea that the ACF has utility as a 'point of entry' into understanding sport policy, particularly given its broad-based approach to the whole policy process in contrast with frameworks that highlight specific aspects or 'stages' of processes. Parsons (1995: 203) concludes that, despite some reservations, the ACF is 'a notable contribution to synthesizing a range of approaches into a coherent and robust theory which links the early phases of the policy cycle – problem definition and agenda-setting with decision-making and implementation'.

UNDERSTANDING SPORT POLICY AT THE LOCAL LEVEL: A THEORETICAL APPROACH

Houlihan (2005: 176) concludes that 'the most fruitful strategy for framework construction is to take the ACF as the starting point, due to its ambitions to be comprehensive, the extent of application in the field of policy analysis and its particular concern with policy change over the medium term'.

In order to strengthen the analytical potential of the ACF for sport policy, Houlihan (2005) draws on Benson (1979, 1982) in extending its potential application. Benson conceived of 'layers of influence', with administrative arrangements at the shallowest end of the spectrum and subject to change, but nonetheless significant for any analysis of policy, particularly as these arrangements can become embedded over time (Granovetter, 1985). In the sport policy area, the local authority policy co-exists with a range of national agencies linked to central government departments, where 'a steady growth in organizational complexity and specialization' has emerged (Granovetter, 1985: 177). These administrative arrangements can be seen as 'nested within an ever-ascending hierarchy of yet more fundamental, yet more authoritative rules and regimes, and practices and procedures' (Goodin and Klingemann, 1996: 18). Thus, relatively stable parameters and preferences congeal within these administrative arrangements, including perceptions of problems, working practices and the choice of policy instruments.

Houlihan (2005) also views the identification of patterns of inter-organisational resource dependencies as important in understanding the 'shallow' end of 'structures of society'. The focus here is the distribution of resources such as finance, expertise, facilities, authority, administrative capacity and political legitimacy. Of note is the introduction of the National Lottery, which sports a 'good cause' and 'has increased markedly the influence of central government and its agencies' in the sport policy area, through enforcing 'modernisation' of National Governing Bodies (NGBs) for sport (Houlihan, 2005: 177) and local authority services with a remit for sport. In other words, the 'extended state' has enhanced its capacity to steer policy through the strategic manipulation of resources.

At the next 'deeper' level of analysis, structural interest groups exist, such as demand groups (e.g. facility users, voluntary sector lobbying bodies), provider groups (e.g. leisure service managers, physical education teachers and sports development officers), direct support groups (local authorities, schools and NGBs of sport) and indirect support groups (funding sources outside of sport, but accessible by sports bodies, including New Opportunities Fund (NOF) and Neighbourhood Renewal Fund (NRF), and non-sport local authority services, such as land-use planning, education and health departments). At this level, the impact of exogenous influences such as socio-economic factors is most acute, in addition to the benefits and costs of government policy priorities. Houlihan and White (2002) argue that structural interest groups have 'significant defensive potential to protect recent resource gains' (in Houlihan, 2005: 180).

At the 'deepest level' are the 'rules of structure formation' (Benson, 1982) or the 'dominant policy paradigm' that consists of beliefs, values and assumptions that influence policy choice and administrative practice. Here, New Labour's dominant policy paradigm can be seen to consist of concepts such as 'social inclusion', 'modernisation' and 'joined-up governance'. Within this paradigm is the 'service-specific policy paradigm' where 'sport for all' has over time been replaced with a greater priority given to elite sport (see Chapter 3) and instrumental uses of sport such as health promotion (see Chapter 8). The 'rules of structure formation' or 'deep structure' (Benson, 1982) therefore sets the parameters and the tone for policy action and inaction. In sum, in assimilating Benson's analysis of the structural context for policy-making and implementation into a 'modified' ACF, Houlihan (2005) seeks to highlight the importance of the historical context in which policy emerges and evolves, and encourages research beyond the level of 'observable behaviour' in line with the core assumptions of neo-pluralism.

This chapter has sought to detail the theoretical underpinnings for the following study of sport policy at the local level. It is concluded that meso-level theoretical frameworks offer significant potential for meeting the aim and objectives of this book, if located within a macro-level theory such as neo-pluralism. A modified version of the ACF appears to offer the greatest potential in this respect. Nonetheless, the study takes account of other theoretical frameworks in undertaking the research and explaining its findings in order to retain its exploratory character, including the related body of literature around local government and governance.

PART 2

Sport Policy in England

CHAPTER 3

The Evolution of National Sport Policy

CHAPTER CONTENTS

INTRODUCTION

This chapter traces, first, the evolution of sport policy in England in order to provide a historical context to contemporary sport policy processes. The chapter draws primarily on analyses by Henry and Bramham (1993), Green (2004a), Henry (1993, 2001), Houlihan (1997), Houlihan and White (2002) and Oakley and Green (2001). The four time periods relate to shifts in policy direction, in part resulting from an incoming government with a specific political agenda. Second, the chapter explores three key themes of sport policy: first, the political ideologies of governments – the core beliefs, values, policy rationales and priorities of policy actors; second, the changing organisation of sport in the UK – its administration and patterns of funding; and third, the changing inter-organisational or network relations between policy actors over time. It is argued that it is critical to analyse these three interdependent dimensions of policy processes for a satisfactory account of sport policy to emerge.

THE EVOLUTION OF SPORT POLICY: 1970–2008

The 1970s

Although post-war government interest in sport can be traced back to Sport and the Community (Wolfenden Committee, 1960) and the establishment of the Advisory Sports Council in 1965 (see Coghlan and Webb (1990) for details of this period), it is from the early 1970s that a distinct area of public policy emerged around sport, given policy concerns regarding international sporting success, social problems such as youth 'disorder' and electoral pressure to expand state-funded sport facilities (Houlihan, 1991, 1997). A broad agreement on the focus and direction of public policy for sport existed at the time around building new facilities and promoting mass participation or *Sport for All* following Council of Europe guidance (COE, 1976) and the Cobham Report (1973). Houlihan (1991: 98–99) concluded that in the 1970s, 'There was little discernible tension between the interests of the elite and of the mass, [and] there was a consensus … that an increase in facilities was the first priority.' In practice, Coalter, Long and Duffield (1988) observed that *Sport for All* was little more than a slogan. In reality, *Sport for All* became 'sport for the disadvantaged' and inner-city youth in particular (Houlihan, 1991).

The establishment of the Great Britain Sports Council in 1972, an arms-length government organisation, raised the profile of sport and provided an organisational infrastructure around which sports interests could lobby. The appointment of Dennis Howell as the Minister of State for Sport and Recreation (1974–1979) further raised the profile of sport within government, providing leadership and direction to sport as it became embedded within a government department [the Department of the Environment (DoE) at the time] and the Sports Council.

The evolution of sport policy needs to be located into the political, economic and social context of the era where sport was perceived by government as an element of the welfare state. More specifically, in this period, the government rationale for involvement in sport became a matter of citizen rights in a period typified by Henry and Bramham (1993) as one of *welfare reformism*. For example, the White Paper on Sport and Recreation (DoE, 1975) placed an emphasis on universal access and described recreation as 'one of the community's everyday needs' and 'part of the general fabric of social services', and symbolised 'the new thrust of "provision for all as a right", analogous to other welfare rights' (Henry and Bramham, 1993: 117). However, the White Paper, apart from being a 'watershed' in establishing sport as a 'need' and a 'right', also 'reiterated a conventional rationale for intervention, namely a concern with social order, international prestige, and individual wellbeing' (Houlihan, 1997: 93). Further, a rationale associated with diverting young people away from crime is evident in the White Paper's claim that 'By reducing boredom and urban frustration, participation in active recreation contributes to the reduction of hooliganism and delinquency among young people' (DoE, 1975: 2).

The White Paper also introduced the concept of Regional Councils for Sport and Recreation, so as to 'devolve' power to the local and regional levels and maintain a relationship between government and the voluntary sector for sport. Within the regions, the White Paper directed the Sports Council to focus funding on 'recreational priority areas'. With this shift towards increasing government intervention in sport, a related decline in the 'voluntarist' administration of sport occurred (Coalter, 1990; Henry, 1993). Thus, a planned and coordinated approach to sport evolved alongside sport provision in the voluntary sector. In practice, the landmark paper was too broad and too vague to be enacted and recommendations were not delivered due to public expenditure cutbacks in response to changing economic circumstances at the time.

In respect of the increasing role of local authorities in sport policy, Henry and Bramham (1993: 116) note that 'the measure which most significantly influenced the provision of leisure [including sport] opportunities through the public sector ... was the reform of local government [in 1974]'. Leisure Service departments, with relatively large budgets, were established 'generating a need for a new kind of liberal welfare professional' (Henry and Bramham, 1993: 116). Subsequently, in the period 1972–1978, the number of municipal sports centres multiplied tenfold and the number of swimming pools increased by around 70%. In sum, local authorities were placed at the heart of local sport policy, planning and provision, and despite significant change to local government from the 1970s to date, sport and recreational provision remains an important dimension for delivering national policy objectives and is the largest single financial contributor (Henry, 2001; Lord Carter of Coles report, 2005).

By the late 1970s, however, 'welfare reformism' began to decline in influence and was replaced by a period characterised by Henry and Bramham (1993) as *new economic realism*. A series of research reports initiated by the Sports Council (e.g. Grimshaw and Prescott-Clarke, 1978) undermined the claims of welfare professionals regarding the capacity of leisure programmes to tackle social ills. Whannel (1983) suggested that welfare professionals could not identify the needs of disadvantaged social groups. Further concerns related to the growth of state intervention in sport and the perceived 'budget maximisation' of its bureaucrats. Thus, in this period, a re-structuring of the welfare framework (Gough, 1979) began to emerge, under the incoming Conservative government, although spending by local authorities on leisure continued to increase until the mid-1980s despite reductions in other areas of welfare provision. This was due to the utility of sport as a tool of social policy, as identified in the White Paper *A Policy for the Inner Cities* (DoE, 1977) that proposed directing funding to areas experiencing urban unrest, in line with the government's Urban Programme that targeted deprived, mainly inner-city, areas, for example in Toxteth, Liverpool, following the riots in 1981.

To précis, sport policy in this period needs to be located in the context of broad political consensus surrounding the role of the welfare state albeit punctured by economic crisis, rising unemployment and civil unrest in inner-city areas. Also of note in this period are the growing professionalisation of the public policy area for sport and recreation and the slow decline of voluntary sector influence over sport policy (Henry, 1993; Horne, Tomlinson and Whannel, 1999). A summary follows in *Table 3.1*.

The 1980s

Henry and Bramham (1993) identified the 1985–1991 period as one of *State Flexibilisation and Dis-investment*, where New Right interests within the Conservative government held sway. Policy initiatives included the introduction of market principles into the management of public sector leisure provision through CCT (see e.g. Henry, 1993, 2001); the sale of public sector assets (e.g. playing fields); the politicisation of policy areas previously regarded as autonomous or quasi-autonomous of government policy

Table 3.1	Sport Policy: The 1970s		
Key Political/ Policy Event	**Organisational and Administrative Implications**	**Funding Implications**	**Implications for Sport**
1972: GB Sports Council established	Created a 'buffer' between the voluntary sector for sport and government. Focused on mass participation and building new facilities	Grant-aid to NGBs rose considerably – from £3.6m in 1972 to £15.2m in 1979	Rhetoric of *Sport for All* – in practice targeted programmes aimed at specific social groups and areas
1973: House of Lords Report, *Sport and Leisure* (Cobham Report)	Sets the agenda for subsequent debates regarding links between social policies and sport	Funding to be directed less at 'identified demand' and more at 'latent demand'	Emphasised broader category of 'recreation' as against narrower conception of 'sport'
1975: White Paper, *Sport and Recreation*	Confirmed sport and recreation as a legitimate element of the welfare state.	Funding increasingly diverted to areas of deprivation, principally, inner cities	Sport becomes a tool to meet social policy goals, but other rationales underpinning sport policy are retained
1977: White Paper, *A Policy for the Inner Cities*	A context of economic decline sees sport utilised as a means to an end	Funding allocations increasingly directed at wider social objectives	Growing congruence between government and Sports Council policies (e.g. Urban Programme objectives)
1979: 'New Right' Conservative Party elected	Accountability and corporate planning required of sport bodies	Funding for welfare objectives begins to be questioned	Sports Council increasingly directed by government

Source: Adapted from Green (2004a), based on Coalter, Long and Duffield (1988), Coghlan and Webb (1990), Henry (1993, 2001), Horne, Tomlinson and Whannel (1999), Houlihan (1991, 1997) and Roche (1993).

including sport; and a priority awarded to economic as opposed to social policy goals. For example, sport was increasingly utilised as an economic tool in urban regeneration projects (Bianchini et al., 1993; Gratton and Henry, 2001).

Arguably, this policy shift from welfare to economic priorities led to a decline in responsiveness to local sport needs, where spending on inner-city social regeneration initiatives declined. Henry and Bramham (1993: 122) note a 41% spending reduction between 1987 and 1990 in inner-city areas. Further, the Action Sport programmes (McIntosh and Charlton, 1985) established to alleviate urban unrest were scaled down. For Prime Minister Margaret Thatcher, 'mass participation [in sport] was a service for which the user should pay while elite sport, especially soccer, was more a source of problems than a source of pride' (Houlihan, 2000a: 196). Thus, public expenditure on sport was viewed as consumption and a cost, as opposed to an element of a productive economy and an investment. Moreover, in this period, the Sports Council, although retaining a focus linking government social policy with sport policy, as expressed in *Sport in the Community: The Next Ten Years* (Sports Council, 1982), allocated the largest funding commitment to elite-level sport, given government concerns around national sporting success (Coalter, Long and Duffield, 1988: 73–74).

Despite government attempts at developing the administrative structures for sport, this period can be characterised as one of fragmented organisation (Roche, 1993) where a coherent 'voice' for sport was absent, in part because of the tensions between Sports Council and voluntary-sector interests and in part due to the shifting location of 'sport' within central government, at times linked to education, with school sport to the fore, and at times linked to local government through the DoE. Subsequently, the government sought to ensure compliance with national policy aspirations through direct intervention at the local level via the regional sport councils and greater control of local government. For example, government appointments to quangos in the 1980s 'increasingly reflected political leanings sympathetic to the New Right' (Henry and Bramham, 1993: 123). Further, the role and remit of the Sports Council was called in question although the status quo remained in practice (Rossi Committee, 1986: cited in Oakley and Green, 2001).

Thus the period under Prime Minister Thatcher can be characterised as one of increasing state intervention in policy impacting on sport both nationally and locally in the context of a gradual reduction in resources available to local authorities and the Sports Councils. Nonetheless, the Sports Council continued to place an emphasis on widening participation in sport through targeting certain social groups in inner-city areas, as highlighted in *Sport in the Community: Into the '90s* (Sports Council, 1988) and in the DoE (1989) review *Sport and Active Recreation Provision in the Inner Cities* following Treasury White Papers of 1986 and 1987 that allocated resources to the inner cities (see *Table 3.2*).

The 1990s

Following the replacement of Thatcher by the new Conservative prime minister, John Major (1990–1997), the political salience of sport increased, in a period that 'marked a watershed' for sport (Houlihan, 2000a: 196). Importantly, John Major, and a number of his cabinet, placed a value on sport-specific policy concerns, unlike Thatcher, and this was made tangible with the establishment of the Department of National Heritage (DNH) in

Table 3.2	Sport Policy: The 1980s		
Key Political/Policy Event	**Organisational and Administrative Implications**	**Funding Implications**	**Implications for Sport**
1982: GB Sports Council strategy, *Sport in the Community: The Next Ten Years*	Wide-ranging strategy reflected changes in the late 1970s towards increased accountability, specific target groups and increasing links with government policy (e.g. Action Sport)	Acknowledged that despite growing rhetoric of welfarism, grant-in-aid had been weighted towards elitism	Elite sport in receipt of major proportion of Sports Council funding
1986: Rossi Committee Report	Examined the basis of, and justification for, the GB Sports Council's existence	Debates regarding funding centred on how grant monies were to be used	Representing NGB interests, the CCPR argued for more influence as to how funding allocations were spent
1986 and 1987: Treasury White Papers, The Government's Expenditure Plans	Confirmed links between sport, recreation and government policy in inner cities	White Paper expenditure plans frequently stressed how funds should be used	Funding concentrated on broader social policy objectives
1988: Sports Council strategy, *Sport in the Community: Into the '90s*	Major focus on women and young people (primarily the 13–24 age group) as target groups	Targeted funding priorities	Increasing tensions between elite and community sport policy goals

Source: Adapted from Green (2004a), based on Coalter, Long and Duffield (1988), Coghlan and Webb (1990), Henry (1993, 2001), Horne, Tomlinson and Whannel (1999), Houlihan (1991, 1997) and Roche (1993).

1992, where sport was a key component. The DNH was an organisational infrastructure permeated with the values of 'one nation Conservatism', or the notion of a single, unitary, national heritage. Specific sport policy concerns centred on reinvigorating traditional team sports in schools and nation-building via elite sport success. The DNH also brought together policy areas with little history of working together, such as sport and tourism, to act as a tool for city marketing and economic growth.

In 1994, Ian Sproat (then Conservative Minister for Sport) stated that the Sports Council should 'withdraw from the promotion of mass participation and informal recreation, and leisure pursuits, and from health promotion, instead shifting its focus to services in support of excellence' (cited in McDonald, 1995: 72). Lentell (1993: 147) had already noted a shift in Sports Council policy away from the 'dangerous liaison' with the 'community' and community development through sport. McDonald (1995) noted the demise of *Sport for All* not only at the national level, but also at the local authority level, where although responsibility for grass-roots sport and sport as social policy was being devolved to the local level, local authorities were not, in practice, actively engaging in promoting *Sport for All*.

The following year witnessed the publication of the first major policy document on sport in 20 years, namely *Sport: Raising the Game* (DNH, 1995). This policy statement provided an unambiguous indication of government priorities, with its focus on the development of elite sport and specifically Britain's 'national sports'. Further, Green (2004a: 371) argues that *Sport: Raising the Game* 'abandoned any pretence of an integrated and multi-dimensional approach to sports development' as previously represented by the Sports Development Continuum (Houlihan and White, 2002: 41–42). Moreover, the statement signalled the withdrawal of central government administration of welfare objectives for sport, with responsibilities for mass participation to be transferred to local authority leisure/sport services. Houlihan (1997: 95) also notes the introduction of conditional funding arrangements for governing bodies of sport in a bid to steer policy towards elite objectives and the requirement for schools that 'traditional' team sports feature in the National Curriculum.

This 'undoubted change in the government's approach to sport' (Houlihan, 1997: 94) was coupled with the inclusion of sport as a 'good cause' in the newly established National Lottery in 1994, where Jackson and Nesti (2001b) view this development as the single most significant factor in developing the infrastructure for sport, and as Green (2004a) observes, this was particularly the case in respect of elite sport. Oakley and Green (2001) observe important structural changes and new initiatives in sport policy administration and governance up until the year 2000, concluding that the period 1995–2000 represents a period of 'selective re-investment' in British sport. Green (2004a,b) also views the mid-1990s as the time when a policy community emerged around elite sport – one that bound government and voluntary sector bodies through conditional funding linked to unambiguous policy goals and strategic targets. Thus, an organisational, administrative and funding framework was established that supported elite sport development (see also Green and Houlihan, 2005a).

Despite the distinctiveness of sport policy in the Major era, a degree of policy continuity between the Thatcher and Major administrations can be identified that impacted on the role of local government sport/leisure services, notably in respect of the reduction in inner-city social policy spending, promotion of local management of schools, the process of competitive tendering to manage local government leisure and sport facilities, and the emphasis on economic rather than social regeneration. *Table 3.3* summarises this period.

Table 3.3	Sport Policy: The 1990s		
Key Political/Policy Event	**Organisational and Administrative Implications**	**Funding Implications**	**Implications for Sport**
1990: John Major replaced Margaret Thatcher as prime minister	Major's appointment heralded a change in government's approach to sport	Major supported a National Lottery; sport one of five good causes to benefit	Support for role of sport in furthering national heritage and national team success
1992: DNH established	Reflected personal commitment of John Major; attempt to bring together a fragmented policy area	Further centralised control of funding allocations to sport	Raised status of sport at Cabinet level
1994: National Lottery founded	Crucial impact on sport and recreation, largely for capital projects in early years	Sport to benefit from estimated additional £200m to £250m per annum by 1999	Arguably the single most important factor underpinning sport policy at both the elite and welfare ends of the continuum
1995: policy statement, *Sport: Raising the Game*	Two key themes: (i) development of elite athletes and establishment of an elite training centre and (ii) youth sport and schools	Grants to NGBs now conditional upon support for government objectives	Substantial support for elite level, although funding implications were a concern; local authorities to address mass participation/ welfare goals
1997: New Labour elected	Introduction of Best Value initiative aimed at modernising local government services, including sport and leisure; social inclusion becomes key policy concern; DNH renamed DCMS	Increasing policy rhetoric linked sport funding to social inclusion objectives	Continued support for elite sport institute network (UKSI) operating from 1999; UK Sport Council created as part of re-organisation of Sports Councils – Sport England formed and becomes distributor of lottery funding from 1999
1999: Sport England produce Lottery Fund Strategy, 1999–2009	Twin objectives: local projects for all and to improve medal-winning chances at international level	Two key strands: Community Projects Fund (£150m) and World Class Fund (£50m)	Further confirmation of support for elite level

Source: Adapted from Green (2004a), Henry (1993, 2001), Houlihan (1997), Roche (1993), DNH (1995), Green and Houlihan (2005).

2000–2008

In contrast to Conservative government priorities, Labour in opposition re-asserted its commitment to *Sport for All* in its pre-election policy statement (Labour Party, 1996) and in the post-election statement *England, the Sporting Nation* (English Sports Council, 1997c). Further, there was a re-engagement with sport having a role in social policy, through the vehicle of the social inclusion agenda (DCMS, 1999). However, the early years of New Labour can be characterised as a period of 'muddle and retreat' (Houlihan, 2002: 198), in part given the incoming government's 2 year commitment to the spending plans of the prior administration.

It was not until the policy statement *A Sporting Future for All* (DCMS, 2000) and subsequent strategic plans (DCMS, 2001a,b) and delivery report (DCMS, 2004) that Labour found its own voice for sport. In effect, this policy and strategy is the embodiment of New Labour beliefs, values and policy preferences. New Labour sought a path between New Right market-oriented policy and 'old' Left welfarist objectives, or a 'third way' (Giddens, 1998). In respect of welfare, the government sought to coalesce 'recreational welfare' (re-distributive justice by targeting disadvantaged groups) and 'welfare as recreation' (using sport for social benefits or reducing social costs) (see Coalter, Long and Duffield, 1988). Houlihan (2000a: 176) concluded that 'The present government's broad ideological orientation is best reflected in the promotion of social inclusion and best value.'

In terms of social inclusion, defined as a combination of linked problems such as low income, poor health and high crime, it is claimed that 'Sport and recreational activity can contribute to neighbourhood renewal and make a real difference to health, crime, employment and education in deprived communities' (DCMS, 1999: 8). The Best Value agenda reflected a concern with the effectiveness of policy delivered through local authorities (Sport England, 1999a). In sum, *A Sporting Future for All* (DCMS, 2000) identified four instrumental uses for sport: to further social inclusion; to promote healthier lifestyles; to boost national identity and international prestige via elite sporting success; and to utilise sport for economic gain, for example sports tourism. Hence, the policy statement largely represents a continuation of prior government rationales for intervention in sport.

A Sporting Future for All (DCMS, 2000: 7) also persists with changes to school sport introduced under Major, such as establishing specialist sport colleges (DfEE, 1998a, b; Henry, 2001; Houlihan, 2000a; Houlihan and Green, 2006; Penney and Houlihan, 2001; Penney, Houlihan and Eley, 2002), although greater weighting is given to community and educational objectives than under the prior Conservative administration. Nonetheless, specialist sport colleges can be viewed as having a significant role too in securing elite sport policy objectives (Green, 2004a). Finally in respect of school sport, a greater emphasis was placed on protecting playing fields from disposal than under the prior Conservative administration (see Chapter 7).

In terms of policy implementation, New Labour strategy can also be viewed as a continuation of social policy programmes that originated under Major in 1996, such as the Priority Area Initiative (PAI) and Community Sport Initiative (CSI), that aimed to stimulate applications for lottery funding from disadvantaged regions, although due to inequities in the bidding process, New Labour modified the legislation to allow Sport England to 'solicit' bids in 'deprived areas'. The creation of Sport Action Zones (Sport England, 2001b) followed the creation of 'action zones' to tackle social exclusion for other policy areas such as in education, employment and health (see Chapter 9). Further, funding such as the NOF and NRF has to an extent reinvigorated areas of sport policy that relate to educational and social policy goals, within the broader 'regeneration agenda' of central government.

It was *Game Plan* (DCMS, 2002), however, that made explicit the relationships between sport and policy for health, education and youth justice. This document is more than a statement of intent in setting out a clear strategic direction and components of an action plan to deliver core objectives. Government sought once again to re-organise the sport sector to facilitate effective policy implementation. Under Labour, regional bodies were re-introduced replacing the Regional Councils for Sport and Recreation that were disbanded by the Conservative government in 1996. Regional bodies, such as the North-West Regional Sports Board, were required to plan and facilitate national policy objectives and work in partnership with County Sport Partnerships (CSPs), such as the Merseyside Sport Partnership, local authorities and the regional offices of Sport England. Recommendations of *Game Plan* included simplifying fragmented funding arrangements as part of a 'root and branch' review of finance in the sector and encouraging partnership-working between the diverse range of organisations with a remit for sport. Apart from furthering the relationships between sport and non-sport bodies for social policy purposes, *Game Plan* attempts to set the parameters for the relationship between government and governing bodies for sport in line with elite sport development objectives (Green, 2004a).

Green (2004a) characterises the period 1995–2002 as one of increasing support for elite sports development, as demonstrated in policy goals and actions including the National Lottery funding strategy (Sport England, 1999b). Moreover, McDonald (2000: 85) contends that non-elite sport objectives are either peripheral or exist to support this fundamental strategic objective. Given an emergent elite sport policy community, Houlihan (2000a: 175) observed that 'there has been far greater progress in addressing the issues associated with the elite end of the sports continuum' than other policy concerns. McDonald (2000: 84) goes further in arguing that 'a qualitative shift in the sports-participation culture away from the egalitarian and empowering aspirations of community-based sporting activity to an hierarchical and alienating culture of high-performance sport' has occurred. As Green and Houlihan (2005a: 184) conclude, 'state agencies have been crucial in specifying, constructing and maintaining through resource control and dependency the pattern of values and beliefs supportive of elite achievement.' The government priorities around elite sport may become further embedded into policy processes as the organisational and funding structures mature. Moreover, clear strategic goals now exist across the policy community for elite sport following the award of the Olympic Games 2012 to London and relative success of the Great Britain squad at the 2008 Olympics in China.

Since 1997, an increasing element of coercion is evident in sport policy under New Labour. The 'modernisation' of local government and voluntary sector sport bodies is characterised by the features of new managerialism: a 'private sector style' of policy and management that has replaced the 'pluralist' arrangements of the 1970s and 1980s. This takes the form of requirements on organisations to enact corporate planning, managerial efficiency, financial constraint and partnership with the commercial sector. Taylor (1997), in regard to the DNH, identified four types of resources available to government in shaping policy processes: finance; legislation, policy guidance and review; systematic scrutiny; and ministerial activism. Arguably, the DCMS, on replacing the DNH in 1997, retained these powers in shaping sport policy. Thus, even though *A Sporting Future for All* states that the government (via its agencies) should not run sport, it nevertheless has established, in part, an organisational and funding framework that facilitates consensus with central government priorities.

For example, NGBs of sport are required to meet both sport-specific indicators of success and equity targets in their sport in order to access funding. In sum, the directive approach to policy of the New Right administrations has arguably been retained if not extended under New Labour, where pressure from central government on quangos, local government and voluntary sector sport bodies has increased (Green and Houlihan, 2005b). Further, a government review of Sport England in 2004 resulted in a re-definition of the organisation, its funding powers and policy focus, with greater powers awarded to regional sports boards, and in 2008, the powers of the regional bodies were removed and devolved to CSPs.

What is certain is that from the mid- to late 1990s onwards, sport has gained a far greater degree of political salience than prior to this period. Oakley and Green (2001) concluded that the sport policy area has experienced increasing government intervention irrespective of the political administration holding office. As Scambler (2005: 179) observed,

'New Labour from its election in 1997 not only sought to capitalize on sporting success, in line with prior political convention, but was innovative in using mass sport as an instrument of social and health policy, namely, as a way of combating social exclusion and promoting public health respectively. This is an example of ... governmentality,' where the state uses its power to colonise 'civil society'. Moreover, in terms of conditional funding arrangements, the Sport England Strategy for 2008–2011 clearly states that NGBs must engage with priorities around social inclusion and 'If any sport does not wish to accept this challenge, funding will be switched to those that do' (Sport England, 2008: 4). *Table 3.4* summarises the period 2000–2008.

Table 3.4	Sport Policy: 2000–2008		
Key Political/Policy Event	**Organisational and Administrative Implications**	**Funding Implications**	**Implications for Sport**
2000: Policy statement, *A Sporting Future for All*	Reiterated much of rhetoric in *Sport: Raising the Game*; linked to Best Value objectives	NGB funding now directly linked to performance targets	NGBs required to produce national talent. performance plans identifying pathways from grass-roots to international level, and equity targets
2002: *Game Plan: A Strategy for Delivering Government's Sport and Physical Activity Objectives*	Major government review at all levels, structures and financing of sport; symbiotic links between sport, education, health and crime emphasised	Recommendations included 'simplifying the fragmented funding arrangements' for sport	Thematic working to establish mutual benefits across policy sectors encouraged, with a specific focus on sport and health
			Further prioritisation of funding to NGBs recommended
2004: Review of Sport England	Rationalisation of the service. UK Sport to lead elite sport, whilst Sport England lead	Funding powers reduced. Greater powers to regional sports boards	Further severance of elite sport and mass participation and social policy goals
2005: Award of the Olympic Games 2012 to London	Greater focus on rationalising sports administration	Funding increasingly linked to targets/medals – further control of NGBs	Reinforces the emerging elite sport policy community; sport's role in economic regeneration strengthened

(Continued)

Table 3.4	(Continued)		
Key Political/Policy Event	**Organisational and Administrative Implications**	**Funding Implications**	**Implications for Sport**
2006: CPA replaces Best Value	Greater thematic working across local authorities encouraged. Sport's role in the 'regeneration' agenda is extended	Funding linked to performance indicators	Further pressure on local authorities to meet government objectives; the status of sport raised in local authorities
2006: Government streamlines the organisation and funding of sport	Regional sports boards gain influence. Sport England to focus on grass-roots sport and UK Sport to focus on elite sport objectives in line with the 2012 Olympics. Local authorities to link in with widening participation agenda. Greater cross-departmental working within central government	Funding directed at grass-roots sport and elite sport through separate streams	Further rationalisation of Sport England with powers transferred to regional sports boards
National Sports Foundation (NSF) established		Greater involvement of the private sector in grass-roots sport via the NSF – Olympic success a target	The Olympics has acted as a 'focusing event'
New Sport England strategy document for 2008–2011 published	CSPs to take a more prominent role in strategy and NGBs placed at the centre of policy implementation	Conditional funding arrangements reinforced	Sport-specific goals emphasised in the run-up to the 2012 Olympic Games; greater support of grass-roots sport proposed
	The role of Sport England is re-defined		Abolition of Sports Boards with funding re-allocated to NGBs
Success of GB at 2008 Olympic Games	Successful NGB roles and status consolidated	Funding for elite sport secured, particularly for successful sports	Strengthening of elite sport priorities

Source: Adapted from Green (2004a), Green and Houlihan (2005); Collins and Kay (2003), DCMS (2000, 2002), English Sports Council (1998b), Oakley and Green (2001), Houlihan (1997), Houlihan and White (2002), McDonald (2000), and Sport England (1999b, 2008).

POLITICAL IDEOLOGIES AND RATIONALES UNDERPINNING SPORT POLICY

Coalter, Long and Duffield (1988), Henry (1993; 2001) and Roche (1993) relate sport and leisure policy to different political ideologies. Bramham (2001: 9) states that 'Political ideologies are best described as reflections of

Table 3.5	Political Interests in Sport			
Sports Interest	**Political Ideology**	**Political Party**	**Dominant Interests**	**Dominant Sector**
Gentlemanly amateurism	Reluctant collectivism	Traditional Conservatism	Elite development	Voluntary
Corporate welfarism	Fabianism/ collectivism	'Old' Labour	Welfare	Public
Market	Anti-collectivism	New Right/ Thatcherism	Commercial	Private
Market-led welfarism (Best Value)	'Third Way'	New Labour	Social inclusion and elite development	Public–private

Source: Adapted from on Horne, Tomlinson and Whannel (1999: 197).

the world and reflections on the world. They offer a prescription of how the world ought to be and subsequently a guide or mandate for political priorities and action'. Roche (1993: 102) suggests that sport in the early part of the twentieth century was largely dominated by an 'amateur ideology' that emerged out of the Victorian era of public-school sport, when class and sport were most closely related and a distinction between amateurs and professionals emerged.

By the mid-twentieth century, an ideology of 'welfarism' emerged that brought about a more politicised, professional and bureaucratic approach to sport, in, for example, the establishment of the Sports Council – a characteristic of Fabian or 'Old' Labour policy (Horne, Tomlinson and Whannel, 1999: 196). Roche suggests that late-twentieth-century sport policy has been dominated by the twin ideologies of global capitalism and consumerism, which can be related to the anti-collectivism of the New Right or Thatcherism. Horne, Tomlinson and Whannel (1999: 197) link political ideology and political party with 'sports interest'. The author has added 'dominant interests' and 'dominant sectors' in sports/leisure policy to create *Table 3.5*.

However, Henry (1993, 2001) provides the most comprehensive account of political ideology and sport policy. Henry (2001: 52) relates political ideologies to central government sports policy, along a political continuum, from structural Marxism to Liberalism. Each of the six ideologies embodies a view as to the utility of sport. Arguably, in the period 1970–2008, three of the ideologies have at times dominated the government's approach to sport policy, namely Traditional Conservatism, Labourism and neo-conservatism (see *Table 3.6*). Since 1997, the Labour government's 'Third Way' (Giddens,

Table 3.6	Political Ideology and Sport Policy					
	Structural Marxism	New Urban Left	Utopian Socialism	New Labour	Conservatism	New Right
Values Core beliefs	Oppose capitalism	Extend provision for minority groups	Equality, social control	Equity, inclusion, stake-holding	Elitism, heritage, social order	Negative freedom, individualism Meritocracy
The value of sport	Reinforces dominant values; intrinsic value lost in institutionalised sport	Challenge racism; promote positive self-image, multi-culturalism	Reduce inequality of access, support collectivism in sport	Economic, social – education, health, crime reduction, elite sporting success	Social and personal value; character, competition, national unity	Promote personal choice
Policy priorities for sport	None	Use sport to raise political awareness, challenge hegemony	Maximise opportunity for specific social groups, *Sport for All*	Support elite-level sport and extend opportunity for youth	Support elite sport, 'national sports'; use sport to address social order problems	Market-led, no subsidised provision
Role of the State, government	None	Organise leisure locally, resist central state provision	Support non-profit-making provision and subsidise	Strong central lead; responsibility devolved to voluntary sector	Arms-length but strong central lead; support voluntary sector	Limited state role; extend private sector role

Source: Adapted from Henry (2001: 58–59).

1998) has underpinned policy processes impacting on sport. The 'modernisation' of local government around the concept of Best Value is at the core of this 'ideology' (Henry, 2001). In sum, policy actors with the sport policy area are likely to hold core beliefs and values that are instrumental in the shaping of sports policy.

Houlihan (1991, 1997) states that governments have perceived sports policy as a means to an end, rather than an end in itself, with the instrumental uses of sport having increased in number over time – in particular, in relation to the use of sport to address social policy 'problems'. In this regard, Henry and Bramham (1993: 105) observe that 'The state's interest in intervention in leisure [including sport] is most clearly associated with periods of high social and political tension.' In effect, successive governments have invested in sport more for the potential extrinsic benefits (e.g. national prestige, social order, economic development, reducing health costs, reducing crime, 'rational recreation') than simply encouraging citizens to participate in sport 'for its own sake'. Houlihan and White (2002) make a distinction between 'development through sport' (extrinsic benefits, e.g. sport in social policy) and 'development of sport' (the intrinsic benefits of participation and sport-specific objectives).

Arguably, the two persistent policy concerns of government have been the youth 'problem', from the 'Wolfenden gap' to the current focus on 'social inclusion' (Collins and Kay, 2003), and elite sport, where national sporting achievement has emerged as the dominant policy concern in the last decade (Green, 2004a). In respect of young people and sport policy, the Wolfenden Report (1960) states that 'if more young people had opportunities for playing games fewer of them would develop criminal habits' (cited in Houlihan, 2000a: 193). The government has been concerned with both 'too much leisure' for youth, with, for example, the emergence of affluent youth in the 1960s and potential social disorder, and 'too little' active leisure and sport, as with the current concerns about the health of young people and the 'crisis' of obesity (see Chapter 8). The association between sport policy, youth and social integration is demonstrated in the 1980s 'Action Sport' initiative (MacIntosh and Charlton, 1985) following a series of inner-city riots and more recently with the social inclusion agenda, as reflected in the Policy Action Team 10 report (DCMS, 1999).

In relation to elite sport, the rationales for government intervention have included nation-building, international recognition and the use of sport as a diplomatic resource (Houlihan, 1991). Further rationales of increasing significance in sport policy include the utilisation of sport as a component of economic development and city re-imaging to boost tourism, particularly from the 1980s (Gratton and Henry, 2001). Houlihan (2000b: 195) concludes that the state treats sport 'as a convenient and malleable instrument for the achievement of non-sporting goals [and a] relatively inexpensive policy instrument'. In sum, the changing rationales for state involvement, or absence from involvement, reflect fundamental concerns about rights of citizenship, the state and the individual (cf. Henry and Bramham, 1986).

THE REPRESENTATION, ORGANISATION AND ADMINISTRATION OF SPORT

As noted, attempts at founding a planned and coordinated approach to sport policy began with the establishment of Advisory Sports Council in 1965, following the recommendations of the Wolfenden Report (1960). This was the precedent to the founding of the Sports Council in 1972. Further, the Cobham Report (1973) on *Sport and Leisure* pointed to the weakness in the fragmentary nature of government responsibility for sport and suggested the appointment of a 'Minister for Recreation' as an essential step towards a greater measure of coordination. However, the representation of sport within central government has subsequently proved problematic. The portfolio for sport has been moved within central government on a number of occasions, from 1962 to date, through departments responsible for education, housing and local government, prior to a lengthy period in the DoE (1974–1991) that oversaw local government and land-use planning, back to education in 1990 and amalgamated with the arts, tourism, broadcasting and film within the DNH in 1992.

In 1997, Labour replaced the DNH with the DCMS with the aim of creating synergy between sport and other policy areas within the DCMS remit, but it is questionable whether this has proven to be of value to sports interests. Horne, Tomlinson and Whannel (1999: 210) concluded that as a result of the changing locations for sports policy within government, 'a coherent and systematic policy towards sport has never been produced in Britain'.

Further, in this time, 12 ministers have assumed the role, with Dennis Howell (1964–1970 and 1974–1979) widely acknowledged as the minister who initially raised the profile of sport within central government. Also of significance is the increasing activism (Taylor, 1997) of ministers for sport, perhaps most notably since the mid-1990s. Despite this, the role carries relatively little influence. Some commentators (e.g. Pickup, 1996) argue that the sports minister has the only portfolio in government with no budget, limited authority and little or no power, and yet is accountable for Sports Council policy failure. It can also be argued that ministers for sport have been selected on the basis of having an interest in sport rather than in the interests of sport. The ministers chosen to represent sport tend to enter and exit the role on a frequent basis, which hardly furthers the sustainability of policy direction, although a recent incumbent, Richard Caborn, held the post for more than 5 years.

Moreover, Houlihan (1997) argues that there has been considerable uncertainty over the status and location of sport within government as a result of a diversity of policy objectives to which sport has been linked and the lack of a parent department that encapsulated such a broad and amorphous range of policy objectives. This uncertainty arose as both major political parties were reluctant to bring sport into the mainstream of parliamentary debate and also due to a lack of civil service expertise in this policy area. Moreover, both inside and outside of government, Roche (1993: 91) observes, the 'structural disorganisation and internal conflict are at least long-standing and probably endemic in … British sport policy-making.' In fact, Roche (1993) refers to the organisation of sport as a 'disorganised shambles'. Arguably the policy area has recently exhibited further 'organisational pluralism' with the creation of new bodies such as the Youth Sport Trust [YST (in 1994)]; bodies dealing with new funding sources (e.g. Foundation for Sport and the Arts in 1991); and a plethora of regional-, county- and local-level policy actors across over 100 recognised sports in England.

Key actors and relationships in the sport policy area

A number of government departments have become involved in sport, PE, recreation and leisure. The Home Office addresses issues connected with anti-doping, hooliganism and crime in sport, and the Department of Health (DH) promotes physical activity for health, for example, in schools. However, three central government departments have most responsibility for sport and physical recreation. The DfES oversees sport in schools; the Department for Communities and Local Government addresses local authority spending controls and land-use planning; and the DCMS oversees both the UK Sport and the English Sports Council (ESC) (Sport England). Sport England is accountable to parliament through the Secretary of State for Culture, Media and Sport who appoints members of Sport England. Essentially, the role of Sport England is twofold: to develop and maintain the grass-roots infrastructure of sport in England and to distribute Lottery funds via its LSF. The UK Sport takes a lead among the Sports Councils in all aspects that require strategic planning, administration, coordination or representation for elite sports development. For example, UK Sport heads the UK Sports Institute (UKSI) regional network.

Schematic representations of the organisation and administration of sport in the UK demonstrate the complexity of the policy area (Lord Carter of Coles report, 2005; Oakley and Green, 2001: 78). However, with frequent changes in government responsibilities, schematic representation of the sport policy area dates quickly. Nonetheless, the key departments with a remit for sport remain (as of 2008) the DCMS and departments for education and for local government. Additionally, in the last decade, as argued in Chapter 8, the department responsible for health has increasingly been concerned with physical activity, inclusive of sport. *Table 3.7* identifies the various government responsibilities for sport.

Local authorities

In respect of the role of local authorities, sport and recreation emerged as a discrete service in the early 1970s, although sport tends to be a policy concern within broader departmental policies and competing priorities, where

Table 3.7	The Pattern of Government Responsibility for Sport and Recreation in England					
Central Government Ministry	DCMS	DfES	DCLG	DH	Home Office
Main responsibilities related to sport	Sport England, after-school sport, national lottery	Sport in the National Curriculum, community use of sports facilities	Local government organisation and finance, land-use policy	Health promotion and education (physical activity focus)	Crime, drug-use
Examples of national and regional government agencies and key partnerships	Sport England, UK Sport, regional sports boards	LEAs	Leisure/Sport Services within local government; government offices for the regions, Regional Development Agencies	Regional health authorities, primary care trusts	Youth Justice Board, Youth Services within local authorities
Examples of national non-government organisations	CCPR, NPFA, governing bodies of sport	YST, voluntary sector school sport organisations, teaching unions, CCPR, NPFA	NPFA, CCPR	Various voluntary and community sector bodies	Youth organisations in the voluntary sector

Source: Based on Houlihan (1997: 97).

in terms of departmental boundaries, sport is usually located within leisure services, itself aligned to either education, community services, youth services, cultural services or combinations of these. In recent years, departments such as Leisure and Community Services, which oversaw sport, have been phased out, with sport transferred to departments with a remit for regeneration objectives such as health promotion and social inclusion, in line with key central government priorities. Within 'leisure', sport may share a budget with services such as libraries and/or the arts or tourism. 'Sport' itself may be divided into different units such as sports development, leisure facility management, indoor and outdoor recreation, and parks.

Capital and revenue expenditure for leisure services grew in the 1970s, levelled off in the 1980s and has steadily declined in absolute terms since the early 1990s, although capital expenditure has fallen more so than revenue expenditure (Houlihan, 1997: 133). The relative stability of funding can be explained in terms of central government concerns regarding urban unrest (most notably in the 1980s); leisure (including sport) as elements of economic regeneration (from the 1980s onwards) (Bianchini et al., 1993; Gratton and Henry, 2001); and social exclusion, youth crime, educational standards and the health of the nation (since 1997 in particular). It is also noteworthy that despite the impact of the lottery funding for sport in the last decade, local government expenditure on sport and recreation far exceeds that of both UK Sport and Sport England combined (Henry, 2001: 115–116; see also the Lord Carter of Coles report, 2005; and the report of the Independent Sports Review Group, 2005: 69–76).

The impact of legislation, budgetary pressure, re-organisations and private sector management practices on the public sector, from the mid-1980s to date, has arguably weakened the autonomy of local authorities in establishing and implementing sport policy independent of central government intervention. *Sport for Whom? Clarifying the Local Authority Role in Sport and Recreation* (Audit Commission, 1988) favoured the marketisation of leisure services given the view that local authorities lacked a strategic vision, policy direction, planning and financial accountability. An increasing focus on the 'financial imperative' followed in the early 1990s given economic recession and factors such as the changing demographic profile for sport, with community sports development the hardest hit area of sport services, where a local authority preference existed for activities that generated a more rapid return on investment.

The 'modernisation' of local government since 1997 (Henry, 2001) has again impacted on local sport policy via Best Value (Sport England, 1999a), which replaced CCT and which required greater accountability, efficiency and effectiveness of local services (recently replaced by the CPA framework that extends the 'auditing culture' into leisure services). (See Chapter 4 for a focus on Liverpool local authority sport and recreation services.)

In terms of influence, representative bodies for leisure services include the Chief Leisure Officers' Association and representation within the Local Government Association. However, the voice of these bodies and the professional bodies in the policy area is arguably relatively weak. For example, successive governments have rejected the idea of introducing a statutory duty on local authorities to provide sport and only the local education authorities (LEAs) must provide facilities for PE. Sport remains a marginal concern with its budget relatively unprotected (again, see Chapter 4). In sum, sport interests are weak within local government and increasingly subject to central government pressures to 'tailor' programmes to best fit central government key policy priorities. As Houlihan (1997: 46) observes, 'the powers, finances and responsibilities of local authorities in the UK are determined by parliament. Consequently, although local government is a major provider of opportunities for sport and recreation, the scope for variation and discretion has become increasingly limited.'

Whereas Henry and Bramham (1986) observed how leisure professionals mediated state policy at the local level in an urban context, more recently, Lowndes and Wilson (2003) argued that under the current Labour government, there has been a progressive shift from commitment-based to control-based strategies for change, where local government has been subject to the principle of 'earned autonomy'. As Houlihan (1997: 132) states, 'The period since 1974 has been characterised by continual tinkering with the structure, the powers of local authorities and the method of funding.' A number of tensions have existed between central and local governments, where the role, remit and relative autonomy of local authority sport and recreation services were a persistent concern. Local government was notable for its absence in *Sport: Raising the Game* (DNH, 1995) but reinstated as central to delivering community sport in *A Sporting Future for All* (DCMS, 2000), where the contribution to community objectives through facility provision and programme delivery is recognised by the current Labour government. Finally, Houlihan and White (2002: 220) observe, 'it is easy to overlook the significant contribution that local authorities make to excellence ... through the provision and subsidy of specialist training and competition venues'.

The voluntary sector

As Houlihan (1997: 165) observes, 'Among the defining features of British sport is the extensive network of governing bodies and their influence on the character of competitive sport up until the mid-1980s.' However, in the last 20 years, the influence of the voluntary sector for sport has waned, although the 'extensive network' continues. This decline in influence can be attributed to the relative growth of state power underpinned in part by the substantive resource dependency on government grants and lottery monies attached to conditional funding arrangements. Roche (1993: 78) stated that 'While sport authorities have some power, most financial power lies outside their hands in the control of various other agencies and sectors ... (hence) a basic gulf between the rhetoric of authority and the power to act, to control and to produce intended outcomes.'

The antipathy of the voluntary sector towards professionalism, commercialisation and state involvement in sport has gradually receded, whilst the fragmented organisation of the voluntary sector has only partially been addressed and a coherent 'voice' for voluntary sector sport interests remains an issue. At the hub of the voluntary sector is the CCPR, which was formed in 1965 with the objectives of providing a unified voice for a disparate group of governing bodies of sport and other organisations and facilitating a strategic approach to decisions and actions affecting sport. Initially it was highly successful in attracting political and media support for its policies and campaigns (Jackson and Nesti, 2001a).

However, with the establishment of the Sports Council, ostensibly to replace the CCPR, 'high level political support resulted in the continuation of this body albeit in a much more emaciated form' (Jackson and Nesti, 2001a: 22). The tensions surrounding this transfer of responsibilities and resources were arguably exacerbated as government extended its focus on sport, particularly in respect of utilising sport to meet welfare objectives, where significant resistance from the voluntary sector to such objectives remains today. Garrett (2004), for example, observed how voluntary sector sport bodies mediated state sport policy in the acquisition of lottery funding. Jackson and Nesti (2001a) add that government-sanctioned organisations have in effect attempted to remove the voice of the CCPR from the sport policy arena.

Houlihan (1997: 169) concludes that the CCPR 'has dissipated its resources in an ultimately fruitless squabble with the ... Sports Council', and the British Olympic Association, although identified as 'a potential alternative focus for collective lobbying by the voluntary sports sector [has] deliberately maintained a peripheral role'. Therefore, the effective representation of the voluntary sector for sport remains problematic, given the expansion of state influence over sport policy, particularly in the last decade. Further tensions between the voluntary sector and government, which have shaped the sport policy area, have materialised around issues such as playing fields policy, in respect of which the National Playing Fields Association (NPFA) has proved to be a key voluntary sector body of national policy significance (see Chapter 9).

Arguably, a more formal and selective relationship has developed between the government and voluntary sector for sport than existed in the 1970s and 1980s (Houlihan, 1997). Houlihan (2000a: 200) observes that 'the major NGBs are involved in an increasingly close and prescriptive relationship with the Sports Councils where grant aid is predicated on compliance with Council (and government) policy objectives.' Relationships between government and governing bodies of sport have also experienced significant tension where the recent 'modernisation' of governing bodies has raised issues to do with voluntary sector autonomy from government intervention, particularly in respect of elite sport policy priorities (Green and Houlihan, 2005a).

With the increasing focus on elite sport (Green, 2004a), a lack of policy coordination and consensus has been viewed as hindering international sporting success. As Pickup (1996: 172) stated, 'the provision of crucial support services such as top level coaching; elite training facilities ... or of opportunities for competitive experience are seen to be uncoordinated, inconsistent in quality and financially wasteful, [and] it is time to take seriously the need for reform.' A decade later, that 'reform' is taking shape as voluntary sector bodies adapt to government policy priorities. In the 'new world order', resource-rich NGBs that have had elite-level success are set to benefit most.

Sport England

The existence of Sport England is based on the government being reluctant to intervene 'directly' in sports matters, as direct involvement may result in an 'overload' of government administration, as well as 'politicising' a policy area where there is much 'electoral danger' and relatively minimal political capital to be gained (Coalter, 1990). Houlihan (1991) suggests governments use quangos to administer policy solutions that have a high public profile, promise an immediate impact and are inexpensive. Most commentators do not perceive 'clear blue water' between the interests of central government and the actions of Sport England. In other words, a 'hands-on' rather than 'arms-length' metaphor perhaps better characterises the relationship between the government and its lead agency.

Since its inception in 1972, the Sports Councils have been 'squeezed' between two frequently oppositional coalitions of interests, one in the voluntary sector representing sport-specific interests and one predominantly in the public sector representing sport as an instrument of social policy. Sport England's location at the 'hub' of the sports community has regularly been challenged by the CCPR since the Council's inception and its policy guidance has habitually been ignored by local authorities in respect of certain issues (see Chapter 9 on playing fields policy). Nonetheless, the government agency, although widely criticised in the sport policy area for producing a plethora of short-term programmes with little account taken of the local capacity to implement them, has negotiated mutually beneficial relationships with a number of local authorities.

According to Taylor (1997), McDonald (2000) and Oakley and Green (2001), power has increasingly shifted towards the central government department with the responsibility for sport (the DCMS since 1997), and away from Sport England. The arms-length government agency has been subject to many government reviews since the 1980s related to its role, responsibilities and authority, including the Rossi committee's review (1986) which examined the justification for the Sport Council's very existence (but recommended maintaining the status quo), and seven other government reviews between 1989 and 2000 (Oakley and Green, 2001). Further reviews in 2004 and 2006 resulted in changes to the remit of Sport England, giving it a grass-roots development focus and further reducing its powers.

The regional organisation of sport

The regional organisation of sport has been subject to many changes over the last 40 years. The 1975 White Paper set up the Regional Councils for Sport and Recreation and gave them the task of producing Regional Recreational Strategies. Until the 1990s, Sports Council regional offices operated alongside Regional Councils for Sport and Recreation. These councils represented a composite of specific sports interests at the regional and sometimes county and local levels. Under the Conservative administrations of the 1990s, the government sought to create 'clear blue water' between the Sports Council and the voluntary sector by abolishing the Regional Councils for Sport and Recreation in 1996, as these were serviced by the regional offices of the Sports Council. The key motivation for doing so, however, was to increase central government steering of sport policy, as the regional bodies effectively had access to decision-making processes. Central government was concerned that interest group pressure would influence the government agency, creating an 'internal lobby'.

Although regional bodies were re-introduced under a Labour government in 1999/2000 in the form of sports boards, central government has retained control over policy by appointing members of the boards whose representation is largely made up of public sector professionals, with limited direct input from the voluntary sector. The sport boards work with, were intented to and increasingly direct, the Sport England regional offices, with sports board policy mediated by the objectives of Regional Development Agencies (RDAs) and Government Offices for the regions (GORs), which were established in 1994, arguably to extend central government influence at the regional level. These agencies put pressure on local government to deliver policy via a cross-cutting approach where 'sport' is one component of wider economic and social policy goals. As of late 2008, the powers of regional sports boards are being downgraded and the strategic focus has shifted to the role of the CSPs.

Arguably, at the regional level, sport has a limited voice mediated if not subsumed by broader government objectives. Wilson (2003: 317) concludes that 'while there is extensive interaction between actors at sub-national level, this should not be seen as a proxy for policy influence.... Sub-national actors participate but they are rarely major players in shaping policy outcomes: the plurality which characterises sub-central governance does not reflect a pluralist power structure.'

Patterns of interests

In terms of patterns of interests, a cluster of organisations work with one or more government departments in respect of sport policy issues and these have changed over time. A series of issue networks (see Chapter 2) can be identified that share a concern with, for example, the use of sport in addressing social issues. Some issues are addressed by interested parties on a regular basis and involve a specific government department and an administrative framework through which organisations negotiate policy inputs, outputs and outcomes. In other words, a policy community (see Chapter 2) is to some extent discernible. This community may have a relatively stable membership over time, with 'barriers to entry' to 'outsiders'. One such emerging community has been identified as consisting of those concerned with elite sports development, sharing similar interests, policy preferences, values and beliefs (Green and Houlihan, 2005a).

Arguably, there is competition between 'clusters of interests' for recognition and scarce resources. These are elite sport; school sport/youth participation; community development/regeneration; and a range of other issue areas (see *Table 3.8*).

Resources for sport

The funding of sport in England is complex on account of the fact that a number of government departments are stakeholders in a policy area

Table 3.8	Patterns of Interests in the Sport Policy Area in England	
Cluster of Interests	**Policy Formulation**	**Policy Implementation**
Elite sports development	DCMS, UK Sport	UK Sport, sports medicine organisations, sports science organisations, BOA, Sports Coach UK, sport-specific coaches, CCPR, some NGBs, UKSI network actors, SSCs (provisionally), Sports academies, sport-specific SDOs in local authorities
Grass-roots sports development/widening participation	DCMS, DfES	Sport England, local authorities, voluntary sector sport bodies, schools, YST
Education (PE and sport)	DfES	Schools, FE, Higher Education, local authorities, LEAs, YST
Public health issues	DH	PCTs, HAZ, SAZ, schools, local health authorities
Social inclusion/community development	DCMS, DfES	Sport England, local authorities, Youth organisations, some SDOs
Crime, drugs, hooliganism	Home Office	SAZ, NACRO, local authority youth services, voluntary sector bodies
Economic regeneration	DCLG	RDAs, local authorities, PPPs/private sector, Cultural Consortia
Land-use planning, for example Playing Fields	DCMS, DCLG	NPFA, Sport England, local planning authorities and leisure services

characterised by multiple organisations operating at national, regional, county and local authority area levels. *Figure 3.1* highlights the complexity of the funding dynamics within the sport policy area.

As can be ascertained from *Figure 3.1*, the Office of the Deputy Prime Minister (ODPM) [now Department of Communities and Local Government (DCLG)] provides more than the DCMS and all Lottery funding to sport combined (Independent Sports Review Group, 2005: 71). As recognised by Sport England (1998a: 3), 'The Lottery Sports Fund has given a great boost to sport, but we must not forget that it does not and will not equal and should never replace public and private investment in sport. Local government spends considerably more on sport than central government and the Lottery Sports Fund combined, and this investment is key to continued development at grass-roots level'.

However, despite this insight, Oakley and Green (2001: 85) state that 'Any study of contemporary sport policy should perhaps start with a consideration

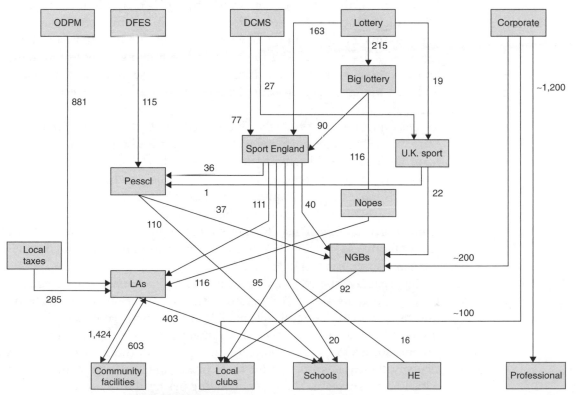

FIGURE 3.1 *The funding of sport in the UK. [Source: Lord Carter of Coles report (2005: 22). Figures in millions of pounds per annum.]*

of the policies adopted in directing Lottery grants, since this now dominates the "power" structures of British sport'. Referring to *A Sporting Future for All* (DCMS, 2000), Jackson and Nesti (2001b: 149) also note that the success of sport 'appears closely connected with the effective use of National Lottery capital and revenue monies'. Oakley and Green (2001) concluded that central government influence on sport policy and practice has increased through the use of legislative and financial power, with the lottery a significant instrument of this power.

The National Lottery was introduced under the Conservative administration of the 1990s, where *The National Lottery Act 1993* detailed five 'good causes' of which sport was one. Conservative priorities for lottery funding in sport included specific 'national sports' such as cricket and tennis. Sport England was charged with administering and distributing lottery grants. Arguably, the lottery funding arrangements favoured wealthier and better organised sports clubs as well as specific regions of the country. Under New Labour, the *Lottery Act 1998* modified aspects of the original legislation. Further, the focus of funding priorities changed under Labour. In 1998, the former DCMS Secretary of State Chris Smith wished to 'establish a completely different framework for Lottery funding' (Lottery Monitor, 1998: 8). This included shifting the focus of funding away from buildings and towards people and activities, a focus on 'sustainable development' and a greater emphasis on using Lottery monies for tackling economic and social deprivation.

Subsequently, in 1999, the Sport England Lottery Fund Strategy was introduced. Two billion pounds was to be spent on sport up to 2009, where Sport England (1999b) claim that 'This will help to create a nation of champions, give access and opportunities to all, and help address key social issues in urban and rural communities'. *Investing in Our Sporting Future* (Sport England, 1999b) aimed to divide the estimated £200m per annum into a Community Projects Fund (for grass-roots sport and community development objectives, securing 75% of the annual sum) and a World Class Fund (for elite sport objectives, claiming 25%).

Increasingly, however, non-sport lottery sources have become accessible to sports organisations. For example, the introduction of the NOF (now known as the Big Lottery), responsible for the new 'good cause' supporting health, education and the environment, has provided a further lottery funding source for organisations linking sport with these areas. This is particularly the case as funding for sport in England has non-statutory status which in part explains the lower spending per head on sport than in neighbouring Scotland, whose spend on sport per head is more than double that of England. The Lord Carter of Coles report (2005) also highlighted a steady reduction in funds to sport since the 1980s, with resources diverted to education and social services in particular. The impact of the national funding context on local-level sport policy is explored more fully in Chapter 4.

CONCLUSIONS

Sport as a policy concern has gained in political salience although largely due to its potential to meet elite sport objectives and for social policy purposes, most notably of late in relation to health policy goals. In the last decade, a plethora of government documentation has been produced impacting on sport, including a series of policy statements, strategies and guidance instruments. Attempts have been made to 'modernise' both local authority leisure/sport services and voluntary sector sport bodies, with central government devolving responsibilities and limited authority but retaining, and increasing, control of policy priorities.

The idea of a unified sport development continuum linking *Sport for All* with elite sport appears to have receded over the last 30 years as distinct areas of policy have evolved. McDonald (2000: 86) concluded that 'it is hard to avoid the conclusion that elite sport development and achievement on the one hand and mass participation and club development on the other are deeply incompatible functions within [sport] ... policy'. This in part highlights the deep-seated divides that remain, most notably, between development *of* sport and development *through* sport objectives (Houlihan and White, 2002).

With increasing organisational and administrative complexity being one characteristic of the sport 'sector', arguably the policy area has witnessed increasing demarcation, compartmentalisation and specialisation. Houlihan and White (2002: 220–221) identify four 'clusters of interests' that have emerged: elite sport, school sport/young participation, community sport/recreation and performance sport. The authors argue that as resources become more constrained, the coalitions associated with elite sport and school sport will be 'better able to fulfil an effective defensive and advocacy function than those for performance and participation' (Houlihan and White, 2002: 221).

Houlihan and White (2002: 231) conclude that sport policy lacks the systemic embeddedness that exists in other policy areas such as education and health, where 'organisational and professional roots are multiple and go deep into the infrastructure of political parties, the government and the state'. In this context, elite sport policy priorities, assuming state support continues, may become institutionalised, which is arguably the key prerequisite for acquiring and sustaining influence, recognition, resources and autonomy.

Finally, although the influence over sport policy of central government has increased, Houlihan and White (2002: 230) note that 'the growth in specialist expertise … might offer some counter-balance to the increasing centralisation of policy influence'. For example, policy actors operating at the local level are needed by government for policy implementation, and as Jackson and Nesti (2001b: 152) observe, 'policy statements and strategies cannot effect a change without the concerted efforts of those closest to the point of delivery.' This accounts for the importance of local authorities to sport policy and practices, and it is to the local level of policy that this book now turns.

PART 3

Sport Policy in Liverpool

The Policy Context in Liverpool

INTRODUCTION

This chapter highlights the key dimensions of the policy context in the city of Liverpool that serves to shape decisions and actions in the sport policy area. These inter-related dimensions include the local socio-economic, political, organisational and funding contexts. A short case study fore-grounds the role of sport in the economic and social regeneration of the city through the vehicle of *European Capital of Culture 2008*.

SOCIO-ECONOMIC CONTEXT

The city of Liverpool sits on the east bank of the River Mersey, spanning approximately 11,000 hectares and being predominantly urban in character.

Liverpool was a wealthy seaport that entered a period of post-war economic decline with the collapse of its shipping and manufacturing base leading to large-scale unemployment in the 1980s (Parkinson, 1985, 1989, 1990). Murden (2006: 435) identifies the 'complex interplay between the macro-economic pressure at national and international levels and factors unique to the locality itself' in explaining the economic decline in Liverpool. Post-war, Liverpool had sought to diversify the local economy by expanding manufacturing, rather than remain resource dependent on shipping, but Liverpool lost control of its own economic destiny as both economic drivers went into recession as multinational companies demonstrated little loyalty to the city when the negative effects of globalisation emerged.

Compounding this dilemma was the political conflict of central and local government, where a Conservative government regarded Liverpool as 'expensive, inefficient and badly run – incapable of responding adequately, politically or administratively, to the scale of the problems it faced' (Murden, 2006: 438). The 1980 *Local Government, Planning and Land Act* provided the powers to establish urban development corporations that effectively bypassed the local authority in the policy process. The MDC sought to encourage private sector investment in the city with subsequent attempts at regeneration through service sector industries, including the leisure and cultural sector, replacing the dependence on the 'traditional' industries (Bianchini and Parkinson (eds.) 1993; Couch, 2003; Couch and Dennemann, 2000; Jones and Wilks-Heeg, 2004). In relation to sport and recreation, the International Garden Festival and the Tall Ships Race of 1984 were the first initiatives to generate investment through tourism where the economic benefits of sports tourism are now an established component of the regeneration portfolio in the city.

Murden (2006: 473) observed that 'Ironically, while Liverpool's economic difficulties had been an unforeseen outcome of the "geopolitical turn towards Europe" ... economic decline made the city eligible for support from the European Commission's Structural Funds Programme.' Liverpool qualified for Objective One funding in 1993, until 2008–2009, which supported Strategic Investment Areas and Neighbourhood Partnerships in areas of 'significant deprivation'. The city has a history of being targeted by central government urban policy, via a number of national funding streams and initiatives within the 'regeneration' remit such as 'Community development' projects, a health action zone (HAZ; now disbanded) and others for education and employment. Arguably, these initiatives have failed to tackle the city's underlying problems given that the schemes 'concentrated on the symptoms of economic decline rather than structural issues' (Murden, 2006: 447). A SAZ was established in recent years following the same policy principle of targeting specific problems in specific communities (see Chapter 10). In a sense, the story of urban policy is the story of sport policy locally, characterised by under-investment, ad hoc experiments, weak coordination between agencies responsible for policy implementation, political expediency, short-termism and government intervention without regard to the existing delivery infrastructure (See forthcoming chapters).

Largely as a consequence of economic decline, the city has experienced extensive outward migration from a city with over 845,000 residents in the pre-war 1930s to approximately 445,000 in 2007 (ONS, 2007). Importantly, the population size has stabilised in recent years as the economic fortunes of the city slowly improve. The recent regeneration of the city via the vehicle of *European Capital of Culture 2008* has encouraged investment and an expansion of the leisure sector, the arts and tourism to couple the economic benefits of an expansion in Higher Education although the beneficiaries of the ongoing regeneration of the city are undetermined at the time of writing.

Despite recent improvements in the economic fortunes of the city, the 2007 indices of deprivation statistics (LCC, 2008b) demonstrate that Liverpool is the most deprived local authority area in England where over half of residents live in the most deprived 10% nationally. In fact, Speke/ Garston in the south-east of the city and most areas to the north of the city, particularly Anfield and Everton/Kirkdale, are especially deprived given high unemployment, poor health and education, and low levels of engagement in physical activity and sport (Sport England, 2006). Large areas of the city therefore suffer from social exclusion (Collins and Kay, 2003; DCMS, 1999). However, there are pockets of relative wealth in the south-east of the city characterised by relatively high levels of employment, university campuses, independent schools and voluntary sector activity including a number of active cricket, golf and tennis clubs.

POLITICAL CONTEXT

Liverpool has an exceptional political history that has had a significant impact on local sport provision, policy and practice. Pre-war, it was the Conservative Party that held the balance of power locally, given the strength of support from the protestant working class by comparison with catholic working-class support for the Labour Party, in a city once characterised by sectarianism (see Murden, 2006: 448, for a fuller account of this era). In these circumstances, socialism as a political force did not take hold within Labour, whose pragmatism and statecraft resulted in the 'boss politics' that characterised the Labour group in office during the 1950s, with policy control based on personal authority and the use of patronage. In fact, by the late 1960s, an autocratic style of governance was deeply embedded with the council, with limited space for debate and critique. With falling support for Labour in the early 1970s, the Liberal Party took office albeit with no overall control (NOC), between 1974 and 1983. 'In office but not in power', the Liberal group was ineffectually benign, in a period of political uncertainty, including for the under-resourced area of leisure services.

Liverpool City Council is perhaps best known for the period between 1983 and 1987 when the Trotskyite Militant wing of the Labour Party controlled the council during the Thatcherite era of Conservative central government (Crick, 1986; Lansley, Goss and Wolmar, 1989; Parkinson, 1985, 1989; Taafe and Mulhearn, 1988). Since 1979, Labour-controlled local authorities such as Liverpool had experienced significant central government reductions in grants that compounded the local economic crisis. In this context of rapid economic decline, the ideological certainties that Militant appeared to offer proved attractive to voters seeking political leadership in a crisis. On being elected in 1983, using the threat of an illegal budget and possible council bankruptcy, Militant were initially successful in raising additional resources from central government and set about a programme of spending, predominantly on new housing, but resources were also allocated to an expansion of sport facilities, and a park, in areas of core voter support. Arguably, the economic and political events of the 1980s had a significant impact on sport locally, and to understand sport policy today, the legacy of 1980s must be accounted for (see Chapter 5 for details of this period).

With the demise of Militant and the local Labour Party, a period of NOC in the 1990s preceded a brief resurgence of Labour support in 1996–1997, before the city rejected Labour in favour of the Liberal Democrats who have been in office since 1998 (see *Table 4.1*). However, Liverpool remains a Labour 'stronghold' in general elections.

Table 4.1	Local Political Control in Liverpool: 1973–2008		
1973: NOC	1975: NOC	1976: NOC	1978: NOC
1979: NOC	1980: NOC	1982: NOC	1983: LAB (Militant)
1984: LAB (Militant)	1986: LAB (Militant)	1987: LAB	1988: LAB
1990: LAB	1991: LAB	1992: NOC	1994: NOC
1995: NOC	1996: LAB	1998: LD	1999: LD
2000: LD	2002: LD	2003: LD	2004: LD
2006: LD	2007: LD	2008: LD	

LAB, Labour; LD, Liberal Democrat; NOC, no overall control.
Source: Liverpool Central Library documentation.

As the chapters to follow demonstrate, political control of LCC has been a factor shaping local sport policy, as is the relationship between the local political regime and central government policy priorities. A change in political leadership of LCC can impact on the value placed on sport and level of support for the service area. For example, a change in council leader and chief executive in 2005 intimated that sport would make gains in political salience, particularly as the former council leader and chief executive had minimal empathy with sport, and the incoming council leader previously oversaw the culture portfolio within which sport was located and took an active interest in its promotion. However, although the former executive member overseeing sport has had considerable influence over decisions directly affecting sport services, difficulties were experienced in locating sport into broader LCC portfolios, especially within the Culture Company that oversaw the European Capital of Culture programmes (see the case study in this chapter).

Also of importance in understanding the political context for local sport policy is the relationship between members (councillors) and officers. To a significant extent, it is the officers who formulate a strategic approach to sport policy. Councillors tend to be a benign influence on sport policy but only a minority are pro-active in seeking to influence policy. Members with a remit to oversee sport within a broader education or culture portfolio tend to follow the lead of officers, lacking in the experience needed to challenge policy priorities and resource allocations. By contrast, members outside of sport have strong professional backgrounds in specific disciplines and work to influence officers. Education, for example, is directed by elected members.

Further, it has been observed by senior personnel within LCC that the quality and impartiality of the discourse in select committees and other venues is questionable where officers set the agenda and in effect steer the discourse away from issues that might raise debate or concern. One such concern might be the increasing levels of subsidy that supports the service area (see *Table 4.2* in the section The Funding Context) , or as one councillor noted, within LCC, 'sport is seen as a drain on resources' (by other departments) in part as 'subsidy is a lot higher than other services'. Although the relationship between officers and members is susceptible to change on account of personnel turnover, and this may provide 'checks and balances' on influence in decision-making, it can be observed that core LCC Sport interests are embedded, in part due to long-serving officers, by comparison with frequent personnel change in councillors overseeing sport. In this context, the strategy of LCC Sport is therefore one of actively seeking member support for sport whilst retaining control over decisions affecting policy direction and resource allocation.

To a large extent, the core characteristics of local politics in Liverpool have resulted from the geographical, socio-cultural and turbulent economic history that the city has experienced. These characteristics include an oppositional character and sense of self-determination that underpins a politics of resistance to national identity and central government authority. Whilst evading central government control, the local authority has struggled to devolve a centralisation of power locally. The local authority's self-image is one of 'direct provider' as opposed to 'enabler' or 'facilitator', and there is a deep-seated suspicion of organisations that 'facilitate' policy delivery through partnerships. This is visible in the policy and practices of LCC Sport. For example, as of 2008, LCC remains one of the few larger local authorities to retain direct management control over all leisure and sport facilities, and there has never been the 'political will' to change this. In sum, the political character of the City Council cannot be separated from the organisational culture of its departments. Nonetheless, outside of leisure/sport services, components of the local authority have retreated from direct control over service areas in favour of public, private and community partnerships, although arguably not through choice, but as a result of central government intervention.

ORGANISATIONAL CONTEXT

Within LCC Sport emerged in the 1970s and has traditionally incorporated event organisation, sports development and the direct provision and management of leisure/sport facilities, parks and playing fields. Alongside the service area are a number of other internal departments with a stake in issues central to sport policy, such as Education and Planning. Further, a number of semi-autonomous government agencies and public – private partnerships (PPPs) in Liverpool have an impact on sport policy. These include the Liverpool Partnership Group (LPG) – originating from the city's Urban Programme in the early 1990s – that oversees the regeneration of Liverpool and includes members from the local authority and Liverpool Health Authority; the city's local strategic partnership, Liverpool First, which is responsible for the Sustainable Community Strategy (SCS) and Local Area Agreements (LAAs) that all local authorities are required to put in place. Of note is that neither the LPG nor Liverpool First boards have members specifically representing the sport and recreational interests, although, to an extent, sport is treated as a component of 'culture' (see the case study). Parallel to public-sector-led regeneration are the activities of the city's private sector economic development company *Liverpool Vision* that has local authority, regional and national development agency membership. In this policy venue, the benefit of sports events to showcase the city can feature in discourse around city marketing and economic growth (Gratton and Henry, 2001).

The location and representation of sport within the organisational structures and policy processes of LCC is arguably a key factor shaping the influence of sports interests. Prior to 1992, the service area for sport and recreation was located in the Education department. However, between the years 1992 and 2000, sport was integrated into Leisure and Cultural services. In 2000, sport was re-located into Education (known as Children's Services from 2005). The location of sport within Education has not been viewed favourably by the LSF membership: the LSF minutes (2005a) state that 'The association of the sport and recreational service with Education is not thought to be of any advantage placing the sports service as the poor relation.' However, other policy actors view sport to be best placed within education rather than assimilated into culture, where interests around the arts tend to dominate.

As of 2007, sport was re-located again into a DCMS-type model of organisation in alignment with culture within the *European Capital of Culture Framework* for regeneration. A draft of the Sport and Recreation strategy for 2008–2012 notes that the 'latest restructure creates opportunities for sport and recreation to integrate more effectively with the wider cultural and leisure services' (LCC, 2008a: 14). This move was short-lived, when following a re-structuring of the local authority aligned to core service spending priorities in 2008, the decision to align sport with culture was reversed, resulting in sport becoming a component of Education once again. However, in late 2008, sport was re-located yet again, this time into Community Services, alongside Library Services.

In terms of the governance structures, it is at City Council meetings and via executive board that key policy-related decisions are made. At executive board level, sport has a 'small voice' outside of the 'showcasing agenda' underpinned by economic discourses. In terms of the select committee structures established to scrutinise policy, sport has over time been re-located on a number of occasions. A particular concern to both LCC Sport and voluntary sector sport advocates is the regular re-locations of sport in service area and governance processes that compromises both longer-term strategic decisions by officers and the scrutiny of decisions by councillors. In practice, sport tends to be subsumed within leisure, culture, tourism, education or, since late 2008 community development concerns.

Further, the select committee structures and processes tend not to foreground sport unless it is a financial issue impacting on other service areas or there is public objection to facility closures, for example. Until the most recent re-organisation of the portfolios, a *Sport and Recreation Panel* acted as a sub-group of the select committee structure but its status was not permanent, further indicating a weak status in LCC policy priorities. Moreover, select committee members observe that, unlike other committees, sport-related items tend to be subject to lengthy delays and tracking issues over time is problematic where issues can 'fall off the agenda'. As observed by members, scrutiny needs an immediate response from the Executive or it 'disappears out of view'.

Arguably, the scrutiny role of the select committee is questionable where events tend to overtake select committee actions and further, there is no 'clear blue water' between executive board and its scrutinisers. Although executive board decisions can be 'called in', as was the case for the recently built 50 metre pool (see case study in Chapter 5), the 'powers' of the select committee have little impact in practice. Arguably, as the Liberal Democrats have controlled LCC for the last decade, their interests are entrenched in policy processes.

A re-structuring of LCC political structures in 2003 into the 'cabinet model' similar to that of central government appeared at first to favour sport interests as the political salience of sport increased in line with central government policy priorities. Despite this structural change, however, the location and representation of sport within local structures and processes remains relatively weak and this is compounded by the fact that many key decisions impacting on sport are made outside of the City Council structure and processes altogether via largely unelected bodies with control of independent resources. For example, the Liverpool Partnership Group (LPG) is responsible for the NRF and Objective One funding for city regeneration and 'sets the tone' and policy direction. A senior officer noted that 'Sport is not pulling its weight at LPG level,' adding that 'Sport in Liverpool [has] not properly proven itself ... (or demonstrated) its significance to all LPG concerns' that can be identified as employment, education, health and crime. Arguably, sport needs skilled policy brokers in positions of influence within the local authority if the 'case for sport' is to be heard.

Internal relations between departments are also important in understanding sport policy processes and change in Liverpool. A number of tensions have been apparent in relationships between LCC Sport and the service areas for Education, Planning and Youth Services, for example. Senior personnel within Education identify the tensions as arising out of LCC Sport's focus on specific sports whereas Education has a 'grass-roots' or participation-based focus (see Chapter 7 on School Sport). Health services respond positively to discourse around physical activity, but less so 'sport' (see Chapter 8 on Sport, Physical Activity and Health Policy). Within Planning, personnel cite disputes as emerging from land-use priorities (see Chapter 9 on Sport, Land-Use Planning and Playing Fields Policy). Internal departments concerned with community regeneration do not necessarily value sport's role in tackling social exclusion (see Chapter 10 on Sport and Community Regeneration). Moreover, each of these service areas does not consider the level of subsidy for sport to be appropriate for a non-statutory service.

Tensions around competing agendas in the context of scarce resources can be exasperated by changes in the funding context where, as one officer stated, 'Funding always has an influence on relationships.' For example, significant central government funding of Education since 1997 has impacted on LCC Sport. Internal redistribution of funding from sport, within Leisure Services, to Education impacted negatively on service area relationships. Moreover, sport-based programmes, supported by the Leisure budget, that have roots in schools, can create the potential for overlap and conflict. LCC Sport is therefore engaged on an ongoing struggle to secure resources and find consensus for its core priorities and policy objectives.

It is argued, in summary, that the organisational structures and processes within and external to the local authority and the relationships between components of these structures, in the context of changing political priorities, have served to shape sport policy and practices. As is demonstrated in the following section, locating sport within 'culture' did not advantage sport interests. Whereas culture is considered to be a core component of city-wide regeneration and, in terms of governance, located within the Regeneration portfolio, sport is located at the periphery of policy processes.

CASE STUDY: Sport in the European Capital of Culture Framework

In 2003, Liverpool won the title of *European Capital of Culture 2008* within which was the *Year of Performance* in 2006 (inclusive of sports events and originally conceived of as a 'year of sport'). Despite featuring heavily in the bid documentation for city marketing purposes (LCC, 2003b), it can be argued that sport has had limited representation within *Capital of Culture*. First, a number of factors appear to have led to a shift away from a *Year of Sport*. Arguably, the weak lobby for sport in the city did not mobilise a 'case for sport'. LCC Sport appeared to wait on events elsewhere, such as delays in the establishment of the Culture Company that oversaw delivery of *Capital of Culture* events, before deciding on a course of action. Further, LCC Sport awaited a steer from the DCMS as to whether sports events were to be generic or specific. In fact, there is evidence of the DCMS directing the local authority towards delivering a *Year of Performance* rather than a *Year of Sport* indicating the level of influence central government has over local government sport policy in matters concerning 'culture'.

The *Year of Sport* was also changed by senior officers at executive board level operating 'outside of sport', leaving officers within Leisure Services to present it as something they agreed with. If LCC Sport had little control over key decisions in this area, the ineffectiveness of the poorly resourced and fragmented sports lobby outside of the local authority can also be noted, by comparison with the effective lobbying by arts and business interests for a *Year of Performance*. It can be noted that one key component of the successful advocacy of arts interests is the access of major arts organisations in the city to mainstreamed grant funding.

Moreover, Sport England, which funded the Culture Company post for sport, were perhaps more supportive of the Commonwealth Games in Manchester, where the remit for sport was clear, by comparison with *Capital of Culture* where the government agency was slow to respond. For example, the length of time it took to appoint a representative for sport within the Culture Company is indicative of the relatively low value placed on sport both within LCC and external to it. Not until 2005 was a former leisure facility manager appointed to lead in respect of sport's developmental role in the themed year of 2006 and other activities until 2009. A number of interviewees questioned whether the successful applicant would prove to be effective in this role, given the inexperience in brokering the diverse and

THE FUNDING CONTEXT

Data from CIPFA (2006) (see *Tables 4.2 and 4.3*) only provides a general guide on income and expenditure, as what is included as 'sport and recreation' is defined differently across local authorities. Also of note is that statistics were recorded differently up until 2001–2002 financial year, hence not all data is available. Nonetheless, it is clear that Sport and Recreation Services is resource-dependent on internal budget management where expenditure exceeds outcome and income itself has decreased. The 'deficit', however, represents only a tiny proportion of the Council budget and by comparison with Education, Social Services and Housing, spending on sport and recreation is modest. Capital spending and borrowing in the major policy areas has had a significant impact on recent budgets where Education and Social Services are labour-intensive, and Housing is capital-intensive. Liverpool has always struggled to provide decent housing, competing interests in the local sport sector. Further, the post was poorly resourced given the size of the task.

A further reason for the limited engagement of sport in *Capital of Culture* is found in the voluntary sport sector that resisted involvement in the enterprise, where few organisations have perceived the event as an opportunity to showcase their sport and most perceived their organisations to be disconnected or even marginalised by public sector interests on account of limited consultation. Also of note is that few sports bodies are involved in delivery outside of LCC. As a result Sports Development Officers (SDOs) within LCC questioned how new initiatives or events can be included given capacity issues.

Interviewees concluded in late 2005 that LCC Sport have 'still got a lot of work to do to prepare for the *Year of Performance*' in 2006 and 'perhaps they [LCC Sport] will be forced to focus on the 2008 celebrations instead'. Indeed, this was the outcome. A programme of events for the *Year of Performance* was finally to be announced in late January 2006 (LCC, 2006a) that included events that were, in the main, part of an existing calendar of sports events. Moreover, in preparation for *Capital of Culture*, the events section within sport and recreation services was reduced in size to accommodate cultural events, leaving minimal staff to oversee and organise the existing sport-related events programme. In practice, the Culture Company fitted in LCC-run sports to a programme of events.

In sum, although it can be argued that prior to *Capital of Culture*, sport's location and influence within LCC was even more tenuous than it is currently, sport remains at the margins of *Capital of Culture*, which indicates its weak organisational embeddedness within LCC and an inability of sport bodies external to LCC to exact pressure on key policy actors. The draft Cultural Strategy 2008–2012 (LCC, 2008a) includes reference to sport as a contributor to raising the profile of the city, but the contribution of sport to the diverse cultural fabric of the city and in terms of strengthening civic society is a secondary consideration. Arguably, an overcrowded agenda has existed in the *Capital of Culture* year, and concerns around sport, particularly at the grass roots, have been peripheral to the core discourse of economic regeneration and the contribution of 'culture' to a programme of events to showcase the city. Further, as noted, the organisational infrastructure and policy processes within the city council do not enable a voice for sport to be heard.

and major housing programmes have resulted in a significant financial legacy. In this context, sport and recreation services (LCC Sport), as a non-statutory service area, assimilated within wider service area concerns such as Leisure Services, is a minor player.

The national average spend per head in local authorities was £19 in 2003–2004 (Independent Sports Review Group, 2005: 71), indicating that LCC spent above the average on sport although many local authorities do not have the financial commitment to facilities that LCC has or the investment priorities awarded to showcasing the city through events. The CIPFA (2006) data raises a number of questions. First, the data illustrates that expenditure is almost twice the levels of income over a 7-year period resulting in a significant dependence on subsidy from other service areas. Given this data, it is evident that maintaining and expanding sport services is dependent on other service areas such as Education valuing sport and its externalities and on the local authority raising funding from external sources.

| Table 4.2 | Financial Data for Sport and Recreation Services, Liverpool City Council: 1997–2008 |

Financial Year	Total Income £'000s	Total Expenditure £'000s	Deficit (Net Expenditure) £'000s	Net Expenditure per Head of Population £p
2007–2008	11,522	22,895	11,373	25.93
2006–2007	10,429	20,491	10,062	23.45
2005–2006	7,745	14,499	6,754	15.29
2004–2005	9,752	19,469	9,717	22.01
2003–2004	7,339	19,388	12,049	27.43
2002–2003	11,218	19,501	8,283	18.20
2001–2002	12,188	20,564	8,376	18.54
2000–2001	–	–	10,279	–
1999–2000	–	–	9,349	–
1998–1999	–	–	9,001	–
1997–1998	–	–	9,115	–
Average	**10,027**	**19,544**	**9,487**	**21.55**

Note: This data should be treated with caution as comparison across years is subject to changing accounting conventions. Further, there are inconsistencies in respect of what constitutes income and expenditure for the category 'sport and recreation', and this varies across local authorities. Source: CIPFA, 2006.

| Table 4.3 | Net Expenditure per Head of Population by Sport and Recreation Services, Liverpool City Council: 2001–2008 |

Year/Spending Area	Indoor Facilities	Outdoor Facilities	Sports Development and Community Recreation
2007–2008	19.64	3.68	2.64
2006–2007	17.38	3.50	2.57
2005–2006	11.80	3.12	0.54
2004–2005	15.44	3.81	0.84
2003–2004	17.30	3.91	4.48
2002–2003	10.35	3.42	3.31
2001–2002	11.89	3.44	2.75
Average	**14.82**	**3.55**	**2.44**

Source: CIPFA, 2006.

Compounding the difficulties of maintaining service levels is the decreasing annual budget for sport with a non-statutory service area always subject to cuts, particularly where pressures exist on social services and education. For 2008–2009, severe budget cuts have for the first time in many years led to job losses, and community facilities have been closed during off-peak times to reduce costs or in one case, closed permanently. In the context of a deepening national economic recession at the time of writing (late 2008) and reductions to local authority spending, it is unlikely that sport services will be able to maintain its current commitments and this may undercut the policy objectives as set out in the most recent sport and recreation strategy (LCC, 2008a). It can be added that only 2 of the leisure/sport facilities of the 15 in Liverpool and the use of synthetic pitches (used for 5-a-side and 6-a-side football primarily) provide a revenue surplus.

Second, the CIPFA (2006) data reveals that where the deficit expenditure increases, so spend per head increases. This dependence on subsidy leaves the service area exposed to periodic cuts in spending, as in 2005–2006, following a period of 'over-spending' in the context of decreasing income. However, spending patterns need to be located in a context of changing central government spending reviews, impacts from unfavourable Audit Commission reports, changing spending priorities and rising costs in other local authority service areas, the increasing costs associated with maintaining an aging facility base, external events that exert financial pressure on service areas, such as Liverpool acquiring *Capital of Culture* status, and other factors.

Of note in a study of local sport policy priorities is the amount per head spent on the category 'sports development and community recreation' by comparison with 'indoor and outdoor sports and recreation facilities' (see Table 4.3). In the seven financial years (2001–2008) since the breakdown of these figures has been available, the average spend per head (per annum) that relates to facilities is £18.37 and has been steady, which compares with £2.44 for 'sports development and community recreation', a category of spending that has varied, with spend on community-related sport reaching a low point in 2005–2006, when spend per head on was 54 pence per annum, although this did subsequently increase again between 2006 and 2008. It is clear from this data that a spending commitment has been made to maintaining indoor facilities over time by comparison with the minimal allocation to development objectives at the community level.

In respect of local government financing, the fundamental issue is the non-statutory status of sport that underpins the funding framework, as a consequence of which LCC Sport must actively seek funds or 'chase the money'. In the context of non-statutory status, longer-term service area planning has been constrained. Raising additional monies through local taxation has never been a palatable option for political parties seeking to retain office, leaving LCC Sport to 'muddle through' on a year-by-year basis and hope that annual budgets remain stable. As one senior LSF member observed, the local authority 'seems totally focussed on reducing council tax, and sport which is not a statutory service suffers badly' (LSF, 2002c). In this context, accessing external funding has become a core concern of LCC Sport.

In terms of external funding sources to support service area policy, planning and provision, of note is that approximately 30% of lottery funding goes to local authorities (DCMS, 2002) who are therefore a major beneficiary. In terms of sport-specific lottery funding, LCC Sport had been successful in raising monies, with over £100m of lottery monies brought into sport for capital schemes from 1997 to 2002. As a result of this investment much of LCC Sport's facility-related strategy could be implemented. Further, the significance of the lottery funding via the Football Foundation has impacted on local authority pitch improvements (see Chapter 9).

However, there has been a shift from capital to revenue funding, following the re-structuring of Sport England in 2004, where it had been recognised that spending on capital projects nation-wide has not increased participation levels. Nonetheless, funding already committed through 'legacy projects' was guaranteed, and the £4m allocated to LCC towards the construction of a 50 metre pool in Liverpool could be released (the facility is reviewed in Chapter 6). In respect of revenue monies, reductions in sport-specific funding through the National Lottery, since 2004, for example, have been offset to some extent by new funding sources (e.g. NOF and NRF) that require local authority sport services to recognise the social policy agenda for sport. In recent years, LCC Sport has demonstrated a high success rate in acquiring monies from non-sport funding streams in particular from the health sector (see Chapter 8).

The use of external monies by local authorities has proved to be a contentious issue. In practice, as one senior officer noted, in the context of reductions in mainstream budgets, NRF monies are used to 'prop-up sport budgets ... [and NRF] ... was not created for this purpose ... it's used to fill the gaps because of reductions in mainstream budgets ... [and] ... used to maintain existing service levels'. Although NRF monies were allocated to local authorities on the condition of being 'ring-fenced', in practice, local authority sport services have been creative in re-distributing externally sourced funding into maintaining core service priorities. For example, local programmes that sit outside of the mainstream budget such as *Sportslinx* became dependent on NRF. Subsequently, the distribution of NOF monies, for example, has become increasingly conditional.

Moreover, a number of examples can be identified where local authorities have not spent the funding assigned to sport and 'claw-back' by funders has taken place, including the NOF, PE, School Sport and Club Links (PESSCL), Football Foundation monies, the *Active England* initiative and for the *Space for Sport and the Arts* (SfSA) programme. Components of the problem of 'claw-back' include the planning application process, management agreements and methods of procurement. However, there are also difficulties associated with spending monies allocated to sport. As a senior councillor noted, 'if sport was statutory they [central government] would passport funds through, there would be a capital strand'. Further, the structures and processes within funding bodies are often a problem, with infrastructures not in place to release the monies, and conditional funding arrangements are a disincentive to risk-taking and innovation by policymakers and service area managers.

In part, this context explains why the majority of development officers within LCC Sport have been 'caretakers' of services rather than engaging in developmental work, that might in turn put pressure on budgets and other aspects of the service area. Although there has been internal support for sports development over time (see Chapter 6), there has been little emphasis on building local capacity in part due to the problems with sustaining core funding. Moreover, in allocating monies, external funding bodies have rarely taken full account of the local capacity to deliver policy goals. It is, however, difficult for the service area to plan for the mid- to long term, given the status and funding of the service and competing agendas for sport within LCC. For example, the budget for leisure and sport facilities varies year on year as priorities change and the costs of maintaining services change; budgets for specific projects are removed and then reinstated; and savings made are not spent on some occasions. Given the fragmented nature of the service area, communication channels can break down and consultation across the different aspects of Sport and Recreation Services in respect of financial management and resource allocation has been limited.

Given that national funding criteria and objectives are re-interpreted locally, with flexible understandings of funding guidance and conditions employed by local authorities, an increasing trend has been for central government to bypass local authority control over resources where at all possible (see Chapter 7 on school sport policy). It can be argued that LCC accommodate national policy out of expediency and for funding acquisition in a bid to evade central government control over how the funding is spent locally. On the other hand, localism has a strong tradition in Liverpool and the very purpose of local authorities was originally conceived as applying discretion in resource allocation relative to local circumstances and need (see Wilson and Game, 2006: chapter 18).

Critically, the funding context is mediated by a lack of trust between central and local government, compounded by a party political divide where both the Liberal Democrats in Liverpool and Labour in central government have held office for over a decade. This is most evident in high-profile disagreements over large-scale capital projects since the inception of *Capital of Culture* (such as the Mersey Tram system). A senior officer observed that due to minimal trust between government departments and funding agencies, central government is 'losing faith in organisations responsible for delivery' and 'calling-in' projects, in the context of government departments themselves being increasingly accountable to financial constraints and timescales of the Treasury.

In the last decade, discretion in local authority spending priorities and resource allocations has decreased as central government departments have increasingly established conditional funding arrangements tied to government policy priorities. LCC Sport is both resource dependent within the local authority and in respect of external funding bodies. Consequently, LCC Sport is, as one interviewee noted, 'under a cloud of worry about the budget' where instability year to year militates against strategic development. Given the restructuring of LCC in 2008, LCC Sport has experienced significant budget reductions for 2008–2009, for example. In this context, LCC Sport has demonstrated a high level of skill in accessing funding and negotiating funding support, particularly from the local Health Authority and its partners.

Since 1997, LCC Sport has taken a pro-active stance in order to protect itself from reduction in budgets, with one senior officer stating that 'We've tagged ourselves to the Health group,' in part because the Culture group is 'dominated by the arts … [who] look down on sport'. Moreover, established arts interests have funding stability by comparison with sports interests (see the case study in this chapter). Officers in LCC Sport have therefore had to act as 'entrepreneurs' in securing funding and retaining the service subsidy particularly given that external funding rarely extends beyond 3 years.

Looking to the future, although the leisure/sport service subsidy 'is not considered a problem by other departments' according to a senior councillor, where the 'Education [department] recognizes the value of sport', it is questionable whether sport policy priorities can be maintained given budget reductions and rising costs of service maintenance, coupled with increasing pressure from central government to deliver across a raft of agendas. Sport has in part retained support through the priority given to the Education budget in Liverpool unlike other areas of the North of England, where Social Services is 'bleeding the Education budget' and this impacts on sport when 'sport' is located within Education services. In the short term, the sport development programme, for example, may be relatively unaffected by budget reductions, with 'reserves covering the loss', but reserves cannot be relied on indefinitely (as highlighted in the 2008 Audit Commission report into the LCC's finances).

The move from a 1 year to a 3-year funding cycle of local authorities in 2008–2009 arguably provides improved scope for planning. However, even in a favourable context for planning, organisations in other policy sectors are working to different agendas, funding frameworks and timescales. Finally, for capital projects, timescales for completion tend to be extended resulting in escalating costs which in turn can end in a dependence on unsupported borrowing, as in the case of the 50 metre swimming pool (outlined in Chapter 6).

In this context, one option in an increasingly pressured financial context for LCC Sport is the use of capital receipts (e.g. sale of land) or simply to close community facilities. Both options, however, are politically sensitive, as is raising location taxation to pay for services. Increasingly, therefore, there is resource dependence on external funding sources through capital grants in the case of new sports facilities, but acquiring such funding ties LCC to conditions that arguably give central government greater control over local authority policy direction. Alternatively, LCC can, and on occasion has, raised charges for services. This course of action may, however, impact negatively on participation, and indirectly increased the costs associated with social exclusion, including poor health. Recent initiatives promoting 'free usage' of facilities to young people across Liverpool is clearly a policy direction that does not sit easily with raising charges (see Wilson and Game, 2006: chapter 10, for a detailed account of local authority financing).

It has not been the intention of this section to provide a detailed analysis of the financing of LCC Sport, or funding mechanisms across central and local government, but to highlight the financial issues that influence sport policy. The strategy and actions of LCC Sport need to be understood within a resources-driven context, where weak status and limited funding continuity within LCC compromise sport policy, planning and provision. An Audit Commission (2002) report stated that Leisure Services was 'too resource based', with the response from the Head of Resources being one of proposing the closing of older municipal swimming pools, hence a focus on 'cost cutting' and the short term. In the absence of statutory status, senior managers arguably allocate too much time to 'chasing the money', which compromises resources for ensuring effective use of monies, programme monitoring and evaluation, research, staff development, negotiating successful actions and outcomes with partners, and other components of best practice in building the capacity to deliver services.

The Evolution of Sport Policy in Liverpool

This chapter traces the evolution of sport policy in Liverpool from the 1970s to date, with a particular focus on the role, remit, priorities and actions of the key policy actor, LCC Sport. Sport policy at the local level is understood within changing political, economic, socio-cultural and institutional contexts. The chapter is divided into time periods that broadly reflect shifts in local policy direction. The chapter concludes with a summary table of the significant policy outcomes for the period 1971–2008 and looking to the future, an overview of the new Sport and Recreation Strategy for Liverpool (LCC, 2008a).

Sport Policy and Governance: Local Perspectives

THE 1970s

In the late 1960s and early 1970s, when 'sport and recreation' emerged as a policy concern in the city, and nationally, 'sport' was organised via three separate departments in Liverpool, namely Parks and Gardens, Baths and Laundries, and the Town Clerks Department that oversaw the Liverpool Show which included sporting events. It was in the internal re-organisation of LCC in 1971 that the Department of Recreation and Space (now known as Sport and Recreation Services) was formed and became the first department of its type in the UK, subsequently influencing the Bains Committee on Local Authority Management, whose report recommended that in the local government re-organisation of 1974, separate recreation departments should be established 'to provide a strong organisational and policy focus' (cited in Houlihan and White, 2002: 21). Interviewees noted that there were minimal resources for sport-specific provision in the 1970s with greater focus on historically embedded interests around municipal parks and swimming pool provision, and to date LCC retains a management remit for parks, swimming pools and a timetable of sporting events. However, no public sector sport or leisure centres existed at the time in Liverpool.

In outlining the gradual emergence of sport as a policy concern in the 1970s, a former head of Sport and Recreation Services highlighted the struggle for recognition and resources. The first strategic document was written in 1971, which proposed the construction of new indoor sports facilities. However, LCC priorities for housing development in the Everton area at the time constrained implementation, and frequent changes in local political control of LCC further impeded plans. It was not until 1976 that the Liberal leader of the Council, under NOC at the time agreed to allocate monies towards establishing three dry sport centres, which were 'little more than games halls in practice', but again, with a change in local political control to a Labour leadership (again under NOC) late in 1976, plans were scaled down and the monies were directed into two new sport centres at Everton and Picton (both 'Labour areas' of the city) that subsequently opened in 1979. With the Liberal Democrats (formerly Liberal) gaining local political control in 1979 (under NOC), plans were supported to extend sport centre provision with new centres planned for Garston, Speke and Walton. However, these plans were again put on hold, given competing spending priorities, until a favourable political climate for sport re-emerged in the 1980s, when this period of NOC ended.

Apart from capital projects, the policy priorities that continue today, based around elite sport and linked to the existing organisation of sporting events to promote the city, emerged in the mid-1970s. For example, in 1976, the first sport-specific Sports Development Officer (SDO) in the UK was created by LCC, in swimming, following the Canadian model of sports development. This emphasis on performance and competition in six sports grew out of the priorities and preferences of its former head of Sport and Recreation Services, who chose in part not only to build on existing strengths in the city, where a grass-roots infrastructure existed to support the development of a certain sport, but also to develop other sports that would 'put Liverpool on the map' and win favour with politicians. This approach was in sharp contrast to most other local authorities who emphasised generic rather than specific sports development in this decade. A current senior officer observed that the performance-related success of six 'priority' sports has facilitated political leverage and access to internal funding support.

THE 1980s

The 1980s can be characterised both as a period of facility expansion and as a period in which elite sport priorities became embedded as the dominant policy concern of LCC. This is despite two major events in the city in the 1980s that invigorated a focus on community sport in areas of socio-economic deprivation. First, the 1981 Toxteth riots can be described as the 'watershed event' (Chalip, 1995) for sport in the city, as it acted as a catalyst for sports development and the sought-after facility expansion. The building of the SASH centres, based on the model of public facility expansion in France, was intended to be a national programme, but of the few that were actually built, most were in Liverpool. The preferred sports centre model of Sport and Recreation Services was rejected due to local financial constraints, with the newly built facilities being relatively inexpensive sports halls (approximately £1m each).

It was former Conservative MP Michael Heseltine who was charged with establishing the MDC that recommended the construction of Toxteth Sports Centre, opened in 1983. Further, the MDC's flagship project, the 1984 International Garden Festival, contained plans to use the main building as a sports arena and a public park, post the event. (however, its development was stopped by Militant) The riots also acted as a catalyst for the founding of the Unemployed Football Leagues, managed at the time as a separate section of LCC Sport by an existing senior SDO.

Second, the rise of the Militant wing of the Labour Party (see Chapter 4) that controlled LCC between 1983 and 1987 saw comprehensive leisure and sport facility development for 'Labour areas' of the city, with the building of four new sport centres in Croxteth, Garston, Speke and Walton, three of which were already at an early stage of development under the prior administration. It was the former head of Sport and Recreation Services who negotiated the building of these indoor facilities, in a policy climate that favoured investment. A strategic document was used to lobby for the facilities in 1984.

However, by contrast, pitch sports organised through the voluntary sector and schools were not actively supported, given the sale of playing fields, to raise capital receipts for other policy priorities. In recreation, the orchestration of the closure and disposal of botanic gardens was not the local authority's finest hour. As observed by Murden (2006: 457) 'the Militant ruling elite had little ideological sympathy for the voluntary sector' including voluntary-aided schools, community housing associations and local sports organisations. Sports that were not aligned to ideological priorities, based on 'class politics', such as cricket and tennis, were out of favour. As a former senior officer stated, 'the local authority [the politicians] destroyed cricket in schools.'

On balance, the Militant era brought benefits and costs for sport as a whole in the city. Arguably, the new sports facilities were much needed in poorer wards of the city and initiatives started in the period, such as the Unemployed men's football leagues would run for many years to come. Critically, for the local authority department responsible for sport, the mid-1980s provided an opportunity for service expansion and has served as a foundation for career development for many existing staff that had been recruited at the time. More negatively, the era also resulted in tensions between the local authority and the voluntary sector leaving a legacy that has not been fully resolved nearly 30 years later. The demise of Militant in 1987 did not constrain the momentum towards facility expansion across the city, with two more leisure centres built in the late 1980s. In the early 1990s, an athletics and tennis centre were built at Wavertree and a soccer centre at Walton. In sum, the 1980s is described, by a former senior facilities management officer, as 'a productive era for facility provision'.

Apart from facilities, the expansion of sports-specific development within LCC also emerged from concerns of the local politicians following the period of urban unrest. However, as stated, its focus was neither generic nor community based. In fact, by the mid- to late 1980s, sport-specific SDOs were in place for athletics, boxing, football, gymnastics, swimming and tennis, each having a dedicated facility for developing performance-related sport (LCC, 1997). A former head of Sport and Recreation was pro-active in 'buying in' the Great Britain gymnastics squad who would represent Liverpool, which led to the city becoming a 'centre of excellence' in this sport, supported by the construction of a gymnastics centre at Park Road Leisure Centre in 1983. The subsequent success of specific sports has been used to lever support within LCC for the continued focus on elite sport, as noted in the LSF minutes (LSF, 2002e) where the utility of hosting high-profile award ceremonies in the city is noted. It is claimed that sporting success sends 'a tangible message to senior officers and politicians of the value of investing in sport and sports development in Liverpool'. The six sports remain the priority sports today, with the SDOs, in post from the 1980s until recently, providing continuity and policy stability.

In terms of service area management, the late 1980s witnessed increasing central government intervention in sport and leisure with the introduction of CCT (see Henry, 1993: 97–102 for an analysis of CCT in leisure services). Locally, implementing CCT was divisive in terms of both meeting the goals of sports development and facility management simultaneously and impacting on relationships with the education sector. Where previously schools used the dry sport centres at no cost, under CCT full cost subsidy could no longer be provided. However, LCC did continue to subsidise school sport to an extent and as a former head teacher observed, although CCT was 'a disaster for school sport' nationally, in Liverpool, the actions of the local authority acted as a buffer against the potential impact of CCT.

Arguably, the 1980s were a defining decade, both positively and negatively, for sport in Liverpool in the context of socio-economic and political crisis. Murden (2006: 463) observed, 'In the midst of economic meltdown, social malaise and political controversy … the city was always able to take pride in its sporting endeavours.' The revival of the Grand National, boxing success, and the domestic and European dominance of the two professional football clubs provided an escape from the socio-economic and political realities of life in Liverpool. However, the confidence and positive image of the city associated with football was to be almost completely dissipated by the spectator deaths at Heysel in 1985 and Hillsborough in 1989.

The 1980s also witnessed a re-structuring of local secondary education and the teachers' strike that impacted significantly on school sport (see Chapter 7). The 1980s also saw the fortunes of some sports rise and others fall, with, for example, the revival of the Liverpool Marathon (since disbanded) in a boom era for road running, and less positively, the demolition of the Liverpool Stadium that hosted boxing events, although boxing thrives in the city today (see Chapter 6 for case studies of specific sports).

THE 1990s

A notable development in the 1990s was the publication of the city's first sport policy and strategy document following discussions between LCC and voluntary sector sport representatives (LCC, 1997). One recommendation identified in *On the Right Track* (LCC, 1997) was the establishment of the Liverpool Sports Forum (LSF) to represent sport interests across the public, voluntary and commercial sectors. LSF was primarily intended to broker the interests of the local authority and voluntary sector for sport. The policy statement also embeds the core priorities of the service at the time around investing in six priority sports, although the role of sport in the community and in the health agenda was also highlighted in line with central government priorities of the incoming New Labour government.

The 1990s and early years of the twenty-first century can be characterised as a period where the focus on community facilities began to decline parallel to an emerging growth in private sector leisure and sports facilities in Liverpool. By the mid-1990s, a number of aging facilities had been closed or refurbished as maintenance costs increased. Moreover, in terms of usage, most facilities in areas of high socio-economic deprivation have not attracted participants in large numbers as the concept of *Sport for All* declined (McDonald, 1995). All indoor leisure facilities were and are still managed 'in house' by a Direct Service Organisation (DSO), including specialist centres for athletics, football, gymnastics and tennis. This placed significant funding pressure on Leisure Services. Given budgetary pressures and falling usage of facilities, local authorities at the time took note of declining participation in the traditional sports and increasing participation in fitness- and health-related exercise; the growth in private sector gym memberships; and a growth in casual and individualised forms of participation in leisure services planning. LCC have responded to these trends by converting areas of many of the city's dry indoor sport facilities to health and fitness areas, known as *Lifestyles* centres.

These changes were not met with universal approval as those with sport-specific interests within the LSF, a cross-sector body lobbying for sport, expressed concerns over this shift in policy, noting 'an over concentration on providing health suites in sports centres and little attention to sport itself ... why compete with the private sector when health is well provided for?' (LSF, 2002d). Moreover, one LSF member 'felt that the proposals were the most damaging proposals of their kind ever made. The effect was extremely wide-ranging, had implications for local communities and should be opposed in every way and everyone should make their objections known' (LSF, 2002d). Nonetheless, in financial terms, the *Lifestyle* gyms have improved the income levels of the service area for sport where the other growth area in service provision has been astroturf usage for football, and female usage of local facilities has increased significantly.

Perhaps the key event in the late 1990s that has subsequently impacted on sport policy was the resignation of the former head of the service at a time when the new Labour government sought to extend greater control over local government through a 'modernisation' programme. The significant influence of the former service head was noted by all interviewees, as it was his priorities, largely based around performance sport, in gymnastics and swimming in particular that became key sport-specific priorities of the department. From initiating a focus on specific sports in the 1980s to bidding for a British Academy of Sport in Liverpool (replaced by the UKSI regional network for elite sport development) to lobbying for establishing the SAZ (see Chapter 10), the former service area head has been highly influential in local sport policy and practice. Importantly, the former head 'was working in a time of greater flexibility' than today, where the incumbent head of department works within a framework based on central government priorities. As one senior officer noted, 'the culture of LCC has changed … it is less favourable to innovation' and has been replaced with an 'auditing culture'.

2000–2008

A re-structuring of Sport and Recreation in 2003 followed a *Best Value* review (Audit Commission, 2002), with a single-entity Sport and Recreation service created that 'offered the capacity to find a consensus on strategic direction and facilitate economies of scale' and 'allow for greater flexibility in responding to a rapidly changing local, regional and national picture' (LCC, 2003a). The *Best Value* review (Audit Commission, 2002: cited in LSF, 2002c) had been critical of many aspects of the service, notably finding that the heads of Sport and Recreation, and Leisure Management, were responsible to two different executive directors making coordination difficult and policies divisive. Further, the review found that there was a lack of 'joined-up thinking' between national and local levels and no local strategic overview; and 'a lack of investment in capital terms in the older buildings and even the more recently built buildings'. Unfortunately, the Audit Commission (2002) report concluded that the service had poor prospects for improvement.

The re-structuring has not favoured all components of the service area, however. In 2006, senior officers observed that although the audit had criticised the facility management component of Sport and Recreation services for operating in isolation, little had changed in practice. Arguably, the 're-structuring' favoured some elements of sport services and marginalised others. These intra-departmental tensions signify internal debates, such as whether to replace DSO with the private sector management of public facilities. More generally, in respect of audits, senior service personnel observed that *Best Value* had 'an impact at the time… [and] will have some residual effect', but recommendations 'quickly disappear from view… once the audit has passed' and by implication, audits have a limited impact on working practices and departmental priorities, where a weak sense of ownership of the recommended changes appears to exist. Another officer states that *Best Value* was 'not held in high regard' and 'has had little impact in practice'. Nonetheless, there is general agreement that *Best Value* is more advantageous to sport services than CCT, where CCT placed an overemphasis on costs.

With the demise of *Best Value* came its replacement: the CPA framework. CPA is intended to link resource allocation to performance in leisure/sport (within a 'Culture block') with performance indicators coming on stream in Liverpool in 2006. A former head of Leisure Services stated that pre-1997, 'we took the wider benefits [of sport] for granted ... now we have to justify actions and clearly identify the benefits,' but admitted 'sport has pushed for it,' although it can be noted that advocacy was 'a defence mechanism' given the non-statutory status of sport within local government. Whether CCT, *Best Value* or CPA, the core tension remains around localism or centralism (Wilson and Game, 2006) in the priority-setting and resourcing of sport-related services. A senior officer observed that government 'modernisation' is in effect a search for a context in which central government strategic decisions can be realised rather than being endlessly thwarted by the competing interests of local government.

Possibly the key event in Liverpool in recent years was the announcement in 2003 that Liverpool was acquiring the status of *European Capital of Culture 2008*, as part of the wider economic regeneration of the city. In this context, Sport and Recreation Services sought to highlight its focus on elite sport and high-profile event organisation, particularly within the planned *2006 Year of Sport* (replaced by a *Year of Performance*). Within this framework, Sport and Recreation Services sought to secure projects that had stalled, for example the 50 metre swimming pool, and secure sport's place in the planned multi-events arena planned for Kings Dock. Elite sport priorities elite sport priorities received a boost through sport's inclusion within *Capital of Culture* as up until this event, it was accepted that Liverpool lacked venues suitable for national events that in turn compromised elite sport objectives (e.g. LSF, 2002e).

A further significant development in recent years has been the emergence in Liverpool of the 'development through sport' agenda (Houlihan and White, 2002), where sport is treated as an aspect of social policy (DCMS, 2002). This agenda can, however, be traced back to the early 1990s where discussions took place between LCC Sport and the former Merseyside Sports Association. Arguably an embedded policy focus on performance sport and elite sport events within LCC resulted in the 'development through sport' lobby gaining little influence at the time. This alternative view of the value of sport subsequently gained ground in some schools (see Chapter 7) and other areas where central government objectives have an impact such as the SAZ in Liverpool (see Chapter 10).

Critically, however, it is within local authorities themselves that the 'regeneration agenda' has recently gained a foothold, where in recent years, sport and leisure has been viewed as a 'sub-set of regeneration'. Nonetheless, questions are outstanding as regards the 'diminished status' of sport-specific interests within a 'regeneration' remit. In 2006, central government introduced LAAs that steer local public sector bodies such as Primary Care Trusts (PCTs) and local authorities towards allocating resources into core national policy priorities. For Liverpool, the challenge for sport is to incorporate local policy into four areas of policy concern around economic development, health, community safety and services for children and young people. Nonetheless, within LCC, elite sport and events programme to 'showcase' the city is defended as a specific policy concern. The current social policy of central government priorities for sport have put pressure on the traditional focus of LCC Sport, but the elite sport events focus remains 'a jealously protected programme'. In fact, Liverpool can be considered one of only a few local authorities where sport-specific objectives are embedded, particularly at the elite end of the continuum.

LCC Sport had, until recently, a long-standing Community Sports section although it had decreasing influence in departmental priorities, indicating a hierarchy of priorities within Sport and Recreation Services, with community sport being the poor relation. The community sport section of sport/recreation services was reduced in size over time, in terms of human and financial resources, having its 'heyday' in the 1970s when *Sport for All* was centre stage. The community section was eventually dissolved as was its Youth Sport component in 2007, given the growing autonomy of school sport where schools have acquired greater resources to underpin self-determination in sport policy (see Chapter 7). In *Game Plan* (DCMS, 2002), participation is targeted to increase from 32% to 70% in 'moderate physical activity' including sport, by 2020, and although this target has been revised to 50% in the North-West by Sport England [Sport England North-West (SENW), 2004], the priorities for sport in Liverpool may need to change if this aspiration is to be realised.

In terms of local political leadership and sport, the appointment of the former executive member for the leisure and culture portfolio (inclusive of sport) as Council Leader in November 2005 was widely welcomed by LCC Sport and lobbyists in the voluntary sector, particularly as the Council Leader was identified as 'a big supporter of sport' and notably *Sport for All*. In fact, whilst acting as executive member for sport interests, the elite focus of each of the

SDOs has been challenged. For example, personnel changes had been made in athletics and tennis where an elite focus existed, and the appointment of a Boxing Development Officer (BDO) with a grass-roots remit also signalled a greater emphasis on participation. Further, a post was created with a partial remit to develop running groups in areas of low participation. In sum, from 2004, a re-emergence of community sport priorities has slowly taken place.

The role, remit, autonomy and policy priorities of LCC Sport services have therefore been under increasing pressure from central government in recent years. One outcome is that, Sport and Recreation Services has shifted its focus and role from one of direct service provider across all areas of the service to a combination of delivery and facilitator through partnerships and, given the increasing costs of DSO, may eventually become a facilitator across all areas. However, as a former head of Leisure Services in a neighbouring local authority noted, 'The commissioning and partnership model cannot guarantee increasing participation' and therefore argues that local authorities will need to retain a provider role, if only to protect a 'sport for all' rationale.

Nonetheless, as stated, the engagement with community sport objectives and 'development through sport' policy goals are not currently embedded within the organisational culture or structure of the service. Grass-roots sport and social policy–related objectives are largely dependent on external sources of funding and little in the LCC Sport portfolio that could be included as 'community sport' is mainstream funded. Although young people can access leisure facilities for free across the city, for health rationales (see Chapter 8), the strategic impact of the council leader on the political salience of sport, its internal representation and its significance for the city has been buried beneath economic regeneration agendas, financial crisis and political party concerns around re-election.

FUTURE DIRECTIONS: THE SPORT AND RECREATION STRATEGY FOR 2008–2012

In late 2008, LCC published the *Sport and Recreation Strategy for 2008–2012* (LCC, 2008a). Within a broad set of aims and objectives, sport has a clear social policy remit to link with national policy priorities. There is an emphasis on SPAAs to deliver these objectives in partnerships with SSCs. As stated in the draft document, 'Crucially Liverpool SPAA has clear links to key agencies at a strategic level and is able to influence both policy and the allocation of resources' (LCC, 2008a: 14). Key strategic partners are LPG , Liverpool First (via Liverpool First for Health), the PCT, LCC Executive

Board and Select Committee, LSF and, at the county level, the MSP. However, organisational links do not necessarily translate into influence.

At the level of implementation, the five SPAAs will link to the five Neighbourhood Management Areas (NMAs) to deliver the LAA priorities. The success of the former SAZ and the alliance of regeneration agencies with Cardinal Heenan SSC known as the Eastern Link Sports Alliance provide a foundation of good practice and scope for policy learning. The *Active City* strategy (see Chapter 8), supported by NRF, is also an important partnership for the sport service area linked to health-related objectives set out in *Game Plan* (DCMS, 2002).

The new strategy also aims to strengthen the role of the LSF in order to create an effective partnership between LCC and local voluntary sector associations and clubs. Building the capacity of the voluntary sector to deliver objectives is a core policy concern as demonstrated in the employment of a dedicated officer by LCC. The six priority sports are to be retained in the new strategy with new development officers appointed in other sports, part-funded by NGBs and part-funded by NRF through the SPAA structures, including basketball (that has long-standing presence in clubs and schools in the city and was a priority sport, albeit briefly, in the 1980s), cricket and rugby league (see Chapter 6).

The status of elite basketball has been raised locally through a partnership between LCC, Everton FC and the long-standing community club Toxteth Tigers. Everton Tigers basketball club subsequently entered the UK league and generated the highest attendance for a basketball game using the recently opened Echo Arena. Handball may also become a secondary priority given that the first two governing body accredited clubs are based in Liverpool. The emerging model of LCC–NGB partnerships may be extended further to include other sports with a presence in the city where 'the increased focus on Olympic sports in the lead up to London 2012 will also be a factor in considering future sports specific programmes' (LCC, 2008a: 17). For each sport, a forum or development group will be instrumental in bringing together club, school, governing body and LCC interests. Existing development groups have had utility in talent identification and development and attracting events to the city. The strategy proposes retaining this focus alongside developing the grass roots at neighbourhood level.

In summary, the new strategy seeks to retain existing elite sport policy priorities and build capacity at the grass-roots level. These goals are in addition to utilising sport as a social policy instrument. Attempting to meet all of these goals will prove to be a significant challenge. Unfortunately, the new strategy remains unpublished as of early 2009, with its content currently under review. A summary of the significant sport policy outcomes for the period 1971 to 2008 is documented in *Table 5.1*.

Table 5.1	Overview and Commentary of Significant Policy Outcomes in Liverpool: 1971–2008	
Year	**Policy or Focusing Event**	**Commentary**
1971	Creation of Recreation and Space Department	First UK department in local government to focus on sport and recreation
1970s	Facility expansion from the mid-1970s in Liverpool, but city in economic decline	Emerging concern to widen participation: first priority to expand facilities and related to this, widening participation
1980's	Economic decline of the city and mass unemployment. Urban unrest including the Toxteth riots of 1981	First SASH centre built. Unemployed men's football leagues established. The introduction of Sports Development Officers (sport-specific). Significant expansion of inexpensive facilities in areas of socio-economic deprivation
	Rise and fall of Militant control of LCC. First policy statements for sport	
	National teachers' strike and re-organisation of secondary education at the local level	Impact on teacher volunteering in schools. Impact on some school sports such as swimming – loss of pools
Early 1990s	Introduction of CCT – introduction of the private sector into local authority service provision	Leisure Services remains as DSOs, but LCC – secondary schools relationship affected
1994–1995	Introduction of the National Lottery – with sport a 'good cause'	Significant impact on sport in Liverpool 1995 – to date. LCC funding control over sport diminished
1995	Policy statement *Sport: Raising the Game* – first statement since 1975	Withdrawal from local government focus on mass participation – LCC retain sport-specific priorities
1997	*On the Right Track* (LCC, 1997) – first Sport and Recreation Strategy published by LCC. Resignation of the long-serving head of sport/recreation. Change in local political control	Response to *A Sporting Future for All*
		Establishment of the Liverpool Sports Forum to reduce LCC–voluntary sector tensions
Late 1990s	Growing concerns around health – a role for sport identified	Sportslinx established
Late 1990s– to date	Modernisation of local government – introduction of *Best Value. A Sporting Future for All* – social inclusion focus	Local government again given the remit of widening participation – limited impact on sport/recreation priorities within LCC
1999	Growing focus on regeneration through sport objectives – PAT Report into sport and social exclusion	SAZ in South Liverpool established – 100% lottery funded – targets 50,000 people
2000	Sport service area moves from Leisure and Culture to Education	Alignment with school sport re-established
2001	New 50 metre swimming pool agreed – but changing Sport England focus to revenue-based projects in 2004	Construction of the swimming pool delayed – eventually completed and opened in 2008
2002–to date	*Game Plan* (DCMS): Focus on increasing participation and national sporting success. Local authorities' core remit is to utilise sport to tackle social exclusion, promote health, further lifelong learning, reduce crime and economic regeneration	Sport/recreation services ill-equipped to meet these policy priorities. The 2003–2008 sport strategy delayed and eventually abandoned. Poor performance identified by the Audit Commission

(Continued)

Table 5.1	(Continued)	
Year	**Policy or Focusing Event**	**Commentary**
2004	Liverpool awarded title of *European Capital of Culture 2008*	A themed year (2006) for sport, later 'downgraded' to *Year of Performance*
2004–to date	Sport England NW plan for sport; creation of the NW Sports Board; review of Merseyside Sports Partnership – NWSB and MSB to receive devolved powers, Sport England to lead strategically in line with DCMS priorities	Reduced role for LCC sport/recreation in the county/region. Strategic aims linked to region, not the city. Three schools gain specialist sport status. Community section of sport development closed
2005–2006	Significant budgetary cuts for Sport and Recreation Services. Rising costs of DSO (facilities) – increasing reliance on subsidy	Greater central government control of policy priorities linked to conditional funding arrangements
2007	LCC Sport and Recreation Services transferred to newly created Culture, Media and Sport portfolio, mirroring the central government organisational framework *Active City* strategy brings together existing health-related programmes	The potential impact on relationships and resources remains undetermined as sport was transferred back to the Education portfolio in 2008 Emerging relationship with health sector around physical activity (inclusive of some sports)
2008	Sport and Physical Activity Alliances established across five neighbourhood management areas based on the success of the SAZ and Eastern Link Sports Alliance	Potential impact on social exclusion–related objectives underpinned by external funding
	European Capital of Culture year	Events programme delivered to showcase the city
	50 metre pool completed and opened	Opportunities to elite training and competition increased
	The Echo Arena opened to host middle-sized events including sports events	Opportunities for those sports with commercial backing to host events
	New LCC strategy for sport 2008–2012 published	Signals the retention of elite sport priorities; building capacity at the grass-roots level; and utilising sport as a
	NW Sports Board to be disbanded. Merseyside Sport Partnership to assume greater responsibilities	social policy instrument through the SPAAs, particularly for health. Joining-up schools and SPAAs
	Re-structuring of LCC financing following poor Audit	Regional tier replaced by greater emphasis on County
	Commission report. Budgetary cuts to sport services. LCC Sport and Recreation Services transferred to Education (children's services) then transferred again to Community Services (including Libraries)	Sport Partnerships in a further re-structuring of the sector Diminishing influence of Sport and Recreation Services. Indecision as to the role of sport in strategic priorities for the city.

CONCLUSION

In sum, in tracing the evolution of sport policy within LCC, the key themes to emerge relate, first, to the changing role and remit of Sport and Recreation Services, partly as a result of central government pressure and partly as a result of local political influence. Second, tensions between competing priorities within LCC and Leisure Services itself and between LCC and external bodies mediate policy and practice. Third, the influence of key individuals such as the head of Sport and Recreation Services can and does make a difference to policymaking although there may be less autonomy for senior management to 'steer a course' than in past decades.

Fourth, in analysing sport policy in Liverpool, it is clear that many factors shape policy, including the location of sport interests within LCC; changes in the organisational, administrative and funding context; the dynamics of local politics; inter-organisational relations; and 'focusing events' requiring policy responses. More broadly, in the local sport sector, changes in resource dependencies have resulted in a growth of public sector influence, particularly central government and its agencies, and a weakening of voluntary sector influence over decisions affecting sport in Liverpool. These themes are explored further in Chapter 11, following the case studies.

Local Case Studies

Sports Development

This chapter will describe and analyse sport-specific policy and practices in one local authority area. Since the inception of Leisure Services Department and service area for sport was founded in the 1970s, the local authority has been the key driving force in sports development. This is demonstrated in the significant investment in a number of specific sports, namely, athletics, boxing, football, gymnastics, swimming and tennis. These sports are classed as 'priority one' sports in Sport and Recreation Service policy and strategy (LCC, 1997, 2003a, 2008a), where for each sport a local public sector infrastructure has emerged over time including facilities directly managed by LCC and dedicated human resources, notably sport-specific development officers.

This chapter foregrounds three of the six priority sports (boxing, gymnastics and swimming) and due to the limitations of space, athletics, grass-roots

Table 6.1	The Status of Five Sports in Liverpool			
Relationships Sport	Status within Local Authority	Representation in Local Schools	Local Voluntary Sector Activity	Relationship between LCC and Governing Body/Bodies
Boxing	Priority	Emerging	Extensive	Integrated
Cricket	Secondary status	Poor, outside of independent and grammar schools	An established network of clubs and competition	Limited
Gymnastics	Priority given to elite gymnastics	Poor	A network of recreational clubs	Integrated at elite level
Road running	Weakening	Poor	Weak apart from high-profile events	Poor
Swimming	Priority given to elite swimming	Weak	Active clubs and associations	Integrated at elite level

football and tennis are not included. Additionally, a short case study centring on the building of the newly opened 50 metre swimming pool is included. The chapter also provides an overview of two sports that are located outside of LCC priorities (cricket and road running). A comparison between sports is therefore possible where the extent of local authority involvement is the constant variable (see *Table 6.1*). The five sports have varying degrees of embeddedness within Liverpool schools, either in the National Curriculum for PE (NCPE) or in extra-curricular sport activities or both, and varying levels of voluntary sector provision and development.

BOXING

Liverpool has a long history of participation and a strong track record of sporting success in boxing and is arguably Britain's amateur 'boxing capital' (Physick, 2007). The establishment of LCC Sport in the early 1970s coincided with a peak in interest in boxing when Liverpool could be described as a 'hotbed' for the sport. Building on voluntary sector enthusiasm for the sport, boxing became a local authority priority sport with its own BDO in the mid-1980s. This was the first local authority role of its type and until very recently, Liverpool was the only local authority in England employing a BDO. The former BDO was in post for 19 years (1986–2005) facilitating a continuity of service that has resulted in LCC boxing development today being located at the core of an extensive club network and elite events programme where LCC Sport plays an active role in providing financial and human resource support in addition to the organisation of competition.

As indicators of the strength of the sport locally, expanding participation and competition can be cited with three new boxing clubs being established in 2008–2009. At county level, there are 42 clubs on Merseyside, which represents almost 20% of all clubs in England. Liverpool alone has 15 boxing clubs mainly situated in poorer areas of the city to the north and centrally with two clubs designated centres of excellence, namely Rotunda and Salisbury. Clubs are generally inclusive in their approach to gender and disability, where, in terms of equity in boxing, women's participation is increasing, particularly in non-contact boxing and boxercise and disability boxing is expanding with links established between LCC Sport and Greenbank Sports Academy (a fully inclusive facility for disabled and non-disabled people) and non-contact boxing is escalating in local schools.

Since the 1990s, boxing within LCC centred on performance and the organisation of an expanding elite events programme jointly organised by LCC and the Amateur Boxing Association (ABA). For example, LCC was a key partner in the delivery of the European Championships in 2006 and the city hosted the first UK event featuring Cuba in 2005. LCC has also brokered media support for many of the 50 events held per annum. During *Capital of Culture* year, the city is to host the European Championships at the newly built Echo Arena at Kings Dock, and the refurbished St Georges Hall can now host events alongside the use of municipal sport centres and hotel venues. To gauge the size of the operation locally, in the first half of the financial year 2007–2008 alone, 37 events were conducted with an approximate total attendance of 16,000. Moreover, spectator demand exceeds supply. Alongside events, Liverpool has the strongest coaching base for boxing in the UK with LCC Sport investing in upskilling coaches, organising international coach exchanges and organising a residential camp infrastructure. LCC activities are linked to the Sports Coach UK national coaching framework with 40 local coaches at level 3 as of 2008. Further, LCC is the only English local authority directly training boxing officials.

As of 2006–2007, following the incoming council leader signalling a policy shift towards community sport, the BDO's role and remit changed to place greater emphasis on developing the grass roots of boxing. The current BDO has a revenue-based budget to develop coaches, events and for equipment and responsibilities for the organisation of delivery of club events; provide financial and human resource support to clubs; establish new clubs; and attempt to embed boxing in schools. As a result of this focus, the infrastructure has started to knit together where previously organisation at community level was fragmented. In respect of continuing the elite boxing programme of events and development, an increasing dependence on external funding sources has emerged in partnership with the ABA. The value of boxing in *Capital of Culture* and in the forthcoming 2012 Olympic Games should retain the elite focus, and the recent community focus may also be sustainable given the strength of the sport at club level.

Playing a pivotal role in boxing development was the former BDO who oversaw the development of boxing through a sea change in government attitudes towards the sport. Whereas SDOs in the local authority are traditionally 'caretakers' of a service, the former BDO adopted a developmental focus in, for example, brokering the interests of LCC Sport, the ABA, Sport England, commercial sector stakeholders, schools and clubs in the development of local plans that have existed for boxing since the early 1990s. Critically, to underpin boxing development, the BDO was instrumental in establishing reciprocity between LCC Sport and the ABA. Parallel to this developmental approach within a local authority, the voluntary sector governance of boxing in England has arguably not embodied an agreed direction, aims, targets and outcomes until recently, when the former LCC BDO took a senior role within the ABA with responsibilities for establishing a *Whole Sport Plan* that represents the first comprehensive strategy for boxing in England. A component of the strategy involves expanding the number of local authority BDOs nationally.

In understanding policymaking, implementation and change for boxing, the role of the policy entrepreneur or policy broker has been central in policy processes. However, the actions of policy actors need to be contextualised and it should be noted that, as one senior officer stated, 'It took twelve years to start to manipulate funding towards the sport' and it was only in the late 1990s that boxing became fully embedded in the portfolio of local authority sport priorities. In practice, it was changes in the exogenous context that were required before boxing could move from the margins to the centre of LCC policy priorities, indicating that policy actors often require structural changes to occur, before windows of opportunity open and skilled brokering can take effect.

It can be argued that, in the last decade, the strength of amateur boxing in Liverpool has increased partly as a result of a number of exogenous influences. These include, first, boxing acquiring legitimacy within central government, particularly since the election of New Labour (1997–date) where sport has taken on a social policy role, most clearly articulated in the social exclusion agenda (DCMS, 1999, 2000, 2002). Boxing is viewed as delivering a raft of related agendas from building citizenship, improving education and health and contributing to reducing crime and anti-social behaviour. Partnerships between the police, probation service, the *Positive Futures* initiative, the local authority and boxing clubs have therefore emerged and boxing development now works with health agencies locally in addressing the 'obesity issue' via the 'Make the Weight' scheme.

The change in central government thinking regarding the sport may not have had any significant impact at the local level if it were not for the fact that, in Liverpool, the social role of boxing was already embedded, prior to the recent government emphasis on sport as social policy. This is manifest in the fact that clubs are a feature of the socio-cultural fabric of areas of socio-economic deprivation within the city; embody a very strong local volunteer base, thus contributing to civic engagement and play a significant role in charity fundraising, thus building social capital. However, the intervention of central government and its agencies and partners across the regeneration spectrum has arguably strengthened the capacity of the local delivery infrastructure. For example, LCC can now more readily support clubs through grants such as the Community Club Development Fund.

Second, it is widely recognised at the local level that National Lottery funding has had a significant impact on boxing development. Funding for boxing has followed the core concerns of government across social policy objectives via the former NRF and *Awards for All* to elite sport objectives via *World Class Performance* monies. Not only has Liverpool been best placed to draw-down funding for boxing given its prominence in the city and in England, but it has been pro-active in accessing funding streams through skilled brokering by the former BDO. Importantly for amateur boxing, club facilities have been improved and the lottery has helped some amateur boxers delay turning professional. Moreover, private sector sponsors and trusts have been increasingly supportive for the sport. In terms of funding commitment, Sport England has ring-fenced monies for boxing development as the sport 'ticks every box' from welfare goals to elite-level success. The local authority too has a dedicated budget for boxing, for coach development, equipment purchase and delivering events.

Third, the image and perception of boxing has changed where, for example, the British Medical Association (BMA) has moved from a position of viewing the sport negatively to one of recognising the value of boxing. Subsequently, boxing is now adopting a pro-active rather than a reactive or defensive stance. This is most tangible in the success of boxing's advocacy in the education sector – an area resistant to the sport for many decades. Teacher resistance to boxing in local schools has diminished and children are increasingly receptive to a non-contact adaptation of the sport, with

30 primary schools having placed boxing into their sport provision (a quarter of primary schools in the city), supported by the NOF, and 80 primary schools having completed at least one taster session since 2007. Further, Cardinal Heenan SSC has built a boxing-specific gym and may form an affiliated boxing club, and Childwall SSC has established an after-school boxing club.

Moreover, the differences in recreation and competitive boxing are more fully understood in schools, teachers are gaining relevant coaching qualifications in SSCs, Sports Leaders Awards for pupils have been linked to boxing and locating boxing into the General Certificate in Secondary Education (GCSE) curriculum is emerging. Although intervention to introduce boxing into schools can be traced back to the 1980s when LCC piloted the skills-based *Kidgloves* scheme that subsequently was rolled out nationally, since 2000, boxing development has been underpinned by education for the first time. In higher education too, John Moores University (JMU) has established a student boxing team – the first of its kind in England.

Fourth, at the local level, the political and personal support of councillors, many of whom have a personal or family history connected to the sport, from Derek Hatton in the 1980s to the current Council Leader, Warren Bradley, has proven important in retaining the profile and priority assigned to the sport. Boxing events are widely perceived as helping the city re-position itself for city marketing purposes in an international context and boxing features within the *Capital of Culture* events programme. However, although councillors remain supportive, in practice, they have little direct engagement in boxing development. It has been the advocacy of officers who have sought and secured councillor support and investment from key agencies such as Sport England that has expanded LCC's contribution to the sport.

Nonetheless, despite the successful entrenchment of public sector involvement in boxing in the city, a number of challenges face the current BDO in developing voluntary sector provision. For example, most club facilities, owned by the local authority, are in need of refurbishment and quality-related issues remain around delivery. In order to facilitate club development, LCC has recently founded a Liverpool Boxing Clubs Forum to improve coordination and cooperation between clubs and address issues around pooling resources, longer-term planning and the development of boxers. The forum also has a role in promoting effective partnership-working where sharing information/expertise and facilities is mediated by inter-club competition and elements of short-termism. The forum can also offset the danger of clubs perceiving LCC as a 'cash cow'. A related issue is the challenge for clubs in attaining Clubmark status, without which access to PESSCL monies, for example, has not been possible. LCC has responded by supporting Clubmark applications with a target of achieving the award for at least one club in each of the five NMAs by late 2008 and it is anticipated that a third of local clubs will gain Clubmark in 2008–2009.

The other issues and challenges facing boxing are similar to those affecting sport development as a whole and include resolving tensions between the professional and amateur components of the sport, the recruitment and retention of volunteers given long-standing resource dependence on unpaid support (although volunteering is relatively high currently), sustainability of school–club links, pathway development from schools to the elite performance squad given dropout at age 16 and 17 (development squad), the potential impact of the LCC preferred long-term athlete development (LTAD) model on relationships and resources within boxing, and establishing evidence-based data to support the anecdotal evidence which indicates the positive impacts of the sport in tackling components of social exclusion.

In respect of crime-reduction objectives, boxing in Liverpool is linked, as stated, to the *Positive Futures* programme, which builds on a youth and young offenders programme that has operated for 10 years with dedicated staff. In this respect, Liverpool shares good practice with similar programmes in Manchester and Bolton, demonstrating evidence of policy learning. One further challenge for the local authority is managing the expectations and the aspirations of clubs and their members in a service area experiencing high demand to participate and spectate. Although the sport has recently experienced the 'Amir Khan effect' in participation, and a further boost via a successful Olympic Games in 2008, boxing in Liverpool has needed little promotion.

Understanding local authority policy processes and practices for boxing therefore requires an appreciation of the dynamic relationship at the macro-level between a number of influences on policy, including, the changes over time in the perceptions and attitudes towards the sport among the general public, health and education policy communities and central government. At the meso-level, a research focus on relationships and resources serves to highlight how changes in the national and local funding context can impact on relationships and create opportunities for those organisations in the local boxing networks to pursue their interests. A central government focus over the last decade on utilising sport for social policy purposes, with the associated funding opportunities, further re-enforced the location of boxing within core sport priorities within LCC and has acted to legitimise a local sport policy priority. The local policy network around boxing can mobilise its interests effectively through the local authority and its key partners such as Sport England, the ABA and private sector supporters. This is not to suggest that the coalition of local boxing interests is a collective entity with shared objectives as there have been tensions between the grass roots and the local authority around the prominence of the elite aspects of boxing and events to showcase the city.

At the micro-level, the role of the policy broker, particularly given continuity in employment over two decades, has proved significant in driving policy and practice although the actions of individuals need to be located in the socio-cultural, economic and political context in which boxing has evolved. As the case study demonstrates, without changes in the macro-level context, it proved difficult, even for a skilled broker, to adopt a pro-active rather than a defensive stance. In short, structural and cultural changes mediate agency. Policy change therefore appears to result from the interplay between both brokering and exogenous change in the sporting/boxing landscape. Further, the local context is critical, in the case of boxing, for understanding policy given its entrenchment in the history and psyche of the city and the high value placed on the sport by the local authority and a number of its senior politicians.

Finally, despite local budgetary constraints, LCC Sport has demonstrated a commitment to the sport through the pro-active pursuit of both sport-specific and non-sport external funding streams and in seeking permanence in relationships with key partners, in addition to recent investment in capacity-building at the grass-roots level. Conversely, with the former BDO taking a senior ABA role in late 2005, and the current LCC BDO not holding the post until early 2007, due to an unfortunate accident to his predecessor, development simply stalled for a year, indicating the importance of continuity in human resource support. These insights offer possibilities for the development of a theoretical framework for explaining sport policy processes at the local level and are explored in Chapter 12.

SWIMMING

This section highlights national and local policy concerns around elite-level competitive swimming, the role of swimming in public health and the decline of school swimming. It also includes a description of the historical development of the infrastructure for recreational and competitive swimming in Liverpool; an analysis of relationships between the local authority, schools and the voluntary sector in the context of shifting government and governing body policy priorities; and a short account on the making of the aquatics centre in Liverpool that incorporates a 50 metre swimming pool, in order to underscore the key themes of the case study and illuminate aspects of sport policy processes.

Physick (2007) charts the historical association of both bathing and swimming in Liverpool, where a network of baths existed as early as 1900. Although facilities were originally only accessible to the wealthy, the City Council set a precedent in becoming the first local authority to build and fund public baths – an action that pre-dates the *1846 Baths and Wash-houses Act*. Concerns about the population's health and the high rate of drowning rather than swimming per se, prompted the authorities to expand provision with a spate of pools built in the late nineteenth century. The association of bathing with health also led to Liverpool hosting the World Health Conference in 1903. The local authority also has a strong historical association with subsidised swimming, with free bathing to all schoolboys established in 1900 – a policy that produced a significant increase in participation. By the mid-1930s, the local authority operated 18 public baths and approximately 25 school pools. Post-war, Liverpool's aging stock of pools suffered from a lack of investment given the slow economic decline of the city and rising costs of maintenance, health and safety concerns, changing social trends, population decline and competing priorities for public monies. Most of the pre-war pools have now been closed and the once popular network of open-air pools have also been lost with the last to close being in Stanley Park in 1960.

The reinvigoration of swimming provision and development emerged from the establishment of sport and recreation services in the early 1970s and the period of facility expansion that followed in the late 1970s to the mid-1980s (see Chapter 5). A number of pools have been constructed over the last 30 years from Everton Park pools built in 1985 to the new aquatics centre at Wavertree playground, opened in 2008. Of note is that LCC has retained direct management of its pools where many local authorities use contractors to deliver services following the introduction of CCT (Henry, 1993: 97–102). The pools are mostly housed within leisure/sport facilities branded as Lifestyles centres to emphasise the health benefits of sport and physical activity, on account of the 'health crisis' in the city (see Chapter 8).

Apart from recreational and health-related swimming, Liverpool has a strong tradition of performance-related or elite swimming that pre-dates local authority priorities. In fact, as early as the 1920s, Garston Swimming Club provided swimmers in the Great Britain Olympic squads. In fact, there are eight voluntary sector clubs in 'Greater Liverpool' (four in the local authority area), most of which originally focused on teaching swimming as opposed to competition and some retain this focus, such as the Bridgefield Club that originated in a comprehensive school. Others, such as Liverpool Penguins (formerly Speke Swimming Club), shifted their priorities to competition. Due to pool closures, many clubs have been forced to relocate on at least one occasion. In recent years, most clubs have responded to the demands of accreditation and have acquired *Swim 21* status.

Unlike the majority of local authorities in England, LCC has allocated significant public resources into elite swimming development. In fact, performance-related swimming has been a 'priority sport' from the early 1980s and had employed a swimming development officer from the mid-1970s. The existing development officer has been in post since 1992 with strategies established to develop both competitive and public use from the year 2000. LCC has also demonstrated its commitment to elite swimming through investment in the City of Liverpool Swimming Club (LSC). The importance of LSC to the local authority and city is evidenced in the fact that it receives an annual grant from the LCC Sport and Recreation Services budget, in addition to staffing and pool hire prioritisation, with the club now based at the newly built aquatics centre. The investment has generated high-level competitive success for the club in the national league and the junior development programme is recognised as the premier programme in the UK.

The 2000–2005 strategy (LCC, 2000c) intended to create a seamless progression from foundation to elite-level swimming and was formulated with the construction of a 50 metre pool central to the decision-making process as it creates an opportunity to host elite swimming events in the city and provides a training facility for competitive swimming. In part, the focusing of resources on elite swimming has been one component of a broader strategy to showcase Liverpool as a 'city of sport', thus enhancing the marketing of the city and the economic value of sports tourism (Gratton and Henry, 2001). In recent years, Liverpool has acted as a satellite city for smaller-scale swimming events, whereas Sheffield is located at the hub of British swimming. The construction of the 50 metre pool therefore offers the potential to host higher-profile swimming competitions to compete with other cities, including Manchester.

In terms of key partnerships, LCC has a close working relationship with the governing body, the Amateur Swimming Association (ASA) and its regional representation, *Swim North West*; with voluntary sector county and regional bodies including Liverpool and District Swimming Association and Lancashire County Swimming Association; and, further, with the UKSI network, MSP and local universities. Key relationships were born out of the intervention of the former head of LCC Sport where practitioners observe that relationships have been weaker since his retirement, highlighting the importance of policy brokers in steering policy processes. A senior voluntary sector representative observed that LCC Sport 'have been superb in support of swimming' adding that 'it is unheard of in the North of England to get local authority support of clubs and competitive swimming'.

Recently, relationships with the voluntary sector have been formalised through the *Swim 21* framework given the 'modernisation' of swimming (Green and Houlihan, 2005b: chapter 6). 'Modernisation' has had an impact on local-level swimming, where, for example, a restructuring of the ASA North-West regional body, following the NGB policy direction, resulted in the production of the *Swim North West* regional strategy for 2009–2013 that centres on improving performance, participation and health-related objectives. Prior to the recent 'modernisation' of the sport, clubs in Liverpool engaged primarily in organising competitions as opposed to developmental activities and lacked a strategic direction. There were attempts to rationalise competition earlier, most notably through a local authority swimming plan for Merseyside in the early 1990s, based on pooling resources to underpin competitive progression. However, local authorities apart from Liverpool, particularly Wirral Borough Council, resisted the proposals.

Political intervention at both central and local level has therefore been a significant factor in shaping the sport. Further, the introduction of the club accreditation requirements is slowly re-shaping swimming policy and practice at the local level, despite resistance from some clubs and county bodies. Critically, LCC Sport will only support *Swim 21*-accredited clubs and as a result, in the last 3 years, most clubs in the city have acquired accreditation. Strategically, LCC Sport has membership of a swimming clubs forum for the city and region that has played a role in encouraging clubs to change policy positions. As of 2008, clubs are generally supportive of LCC plans for swimming development. The opening of the new 50 metre pool, however, provides both an opportunity and a threat for clubs as not all Liverpool-based clubs have regular access for training, competition and/or teaching purposes, apart from City of Liverpool Club that has arguably strengthened its location as the hub of competitive swimming in the city. It can also be noted that some club members have expressed concern regarding the limited seating capacity in the 50 metre pool area for hosting larger-scale events.

In respect of school swimming, over the last 25 years, the city has experienced a rapid decline. Notably, school swimming was re-organised in the restructuring of education under the Militant Labour control of the City Council (1983–1987). Post-war, approximately 50 schools had pools of varying standards and sizes, but few remain, given the restructuring that led to school closures with the introduction of larger comprehensive schools and the costs for schools and the LEA of maintaining pools. Schools, therefore, inherited transport and pool hire costs in offering swimming in the curriculum, and given health and safety legislation, there are increasing insurance costs associated with provision. In sum, a lack of water space to meet the needs of the school curriculum exists across most of the city. Schools must therefore use local authority facilities. However, although pool hire costs have been mid-priced in Liverpool, compared to other cities, many schools have simply not offered swimming to pupils, particularly given time constraints in an already crowded curriculum and in some cases, teachers are not trained as swimming instructors.

Today, only two SSCs, namely Archbishop Beck SSC and Cardinal Heenan SSC have pools – the latter being small-sized – and four other state schools and one independent school (Bluecoats) have a pool. Further, not enough learner pools exist in the city and the highest quality facility for learners, Austin Rawlinson pool in Speke, is located in an area of the city that is least accessible for most young people. Moreover, there is no requirement for schools to adhere to the ASA *Learn to Swim* programme and it is the responsibility of individual pool managers to deliver teaching swimming programmes and the quality therefore varies. Further, very few 'improver group' structures exist in the city for talent identification and development purposes. Until very recently, the difficulties of delivering school swimming locally is compounded by the LCC school swimming programme not being centrally coordinated with schools hiring instructors who work differently. In practice, schools use teaching assistants to deliver swimming which can compromise standards and there has been little monitoring of quality in delivery. A number of inter-related issues therefore compromise policy and practice.

In 2007, Department of Education statistics revealed that only 50% of Liverpool children could swim 25 metres by the age of 11 compared with a national average of 83% or 77% for inner-city areas (Hunt and Lamble, 2007). The policy response to this 'crisis' that was widely reported in the media was multi-faceted and included allocating exclusive use of selected community pools for schoolchildren; subsidised swimming for young people within the *Active City* strategic framework (LCC, 2005) that facilitated access to health sector monies but sustaining this policy direction will be challenging for the local authority; and a partnership with a commercial operator, *Total Swimming*, that builds temporary pools in schools to deliver swimming lessons and locate 'future champions'. The national PESSCL strategy has also been introduced at the local level, linking schools with swimming clubs, but there are similar implementation challenges for extra-curricular swimming provision as there are within school curriculum time. Critically, the 'crisis' in swimming also opened a 'window of opportunity' for LCC Sport to acquire support for the 50 metre pool among councillors.

In 2008, with the aquatics centre built, including the 50 metre pool, and following an internal review, the disparate facets of swimming were brought together under the *Swim Liverpool* programme. The new structures attempt to strengthen core swimming objectives around hosting events and training elite swimmers, with the LSC at the hub, and meet objectives around learn to swim, community, schools and club use. In effect the new facility provided an opportunity for LCC Sport to embed its priorities for swimming in the city. The organisational restructuring was also a policy response to the crisis in levels of young people learning to swim, whereas additional human resources have now been put in place for developing school swimming.

Balancing the competing uses of water space and competition for peak times in the city has been an enduring issue where tensions have existed between performance-related swimming, school and community use. A further issue is which water-based sports have access to the space available. Apart from swimming, where clubs compete for adequate space for teaching and competition purposes, both diving and water polo have sought space in the city, with diving experiencing particular difficulties in finding a location given the unsuitability of most existing venues for the sport, including the new aquatics centre.

In conclusion, the original rationales underpinning local authority investment in swimming have persisted over time. Given the local authority endorsement of performance-related swimming over the previous two decades, LCC Sport is best placed to react to the recent national emphasis on elite sport (Green and Houlihan, 2005a). Moreover, an established and constructive relationship between LCC and the ASA has retained the continuity of the policy focus, with the recent 'modernisation' of the voluntary sector serving to formalise the relationship around the *Swim 21* framework. Clubs have been sceptical of these changes, but combined LCC and ASA pressure has gradually lessened resistance. Delivering a wider range of elite swimming events is also possible now, given the opening of the 50 metre pool in 2008 where, arguably, the poor quality of the existing pools for elite training and competition purposes, and for general use in most cases, coupled with closures, assisted the advocacy for a new pool.

In terms of implementing policy priorities around recreational swimming, the goal of increasing participation, in part for public health purposes, is problematic, in part because of a dependence on subsidy to finance an aging stock of pools that experience below-capacity usage. The ownership and direct management of a number of pools has provided LCC with control over the direction of policy and practice but at a significant financial cost. Further, the closure of community pools is likely, and some would argue, necessary, as older pools are replaced by modern facilities that residents will use. Nonetheless, closures will prove to be politically sensitive. Finally, despite swimming being a 'priority sport' within LCC, advocates of the 50 metre pool for Liverpool were initially unsuccessful in securing the facility. As the following case study indicates, only a change in local political leadership in the lead-up to *Capital of Culture*, within the national focus on building pools for elite swimming purposes, secured the construction of the pool.

CASE STUDY: The 50 metre Swimming Pool

A 50 metre pool was sought by swimming advocates in Liverpool for many years on account of the closure of Westminster Road pool (that was in part suitable for training purposes because of its large size) and the outdated pools at Everton Park leisure centre. The capital project can be traced back to City Council discussions in 1999 and later at Executive Board level (LCC, 2001) with a view to being 'on site by October 2001'. However, delays in the construction were a concern in early 2002 (LSF, 2002a). Minutes of meetings of the LSF include a reference to the two issues that 'would impact on sport in the city and which the forum had and would continue to play a significant role were the 50m pool and the *Capital of Culture* particularly the themed years aspect' (LSF, 2004d). Subsequently, advocates lobbied for the opening of the pool to take place in early 2006 to coincide with the planned 'Year of Sport'. In fact, the aquatics centre including the 50 metre pool was opened in April 2008, and therefore its opening and usage completely bypassed the *Year of Performance* (that usurped the proposed year of sport) and what could have been a showcase year for swimming and sport itself.

A number of reasons appear to exist for the significant delay in constructing the new pool, and provide insights into the sport policy process in Liverpool. First, the lobby for the pool has proved ineffective. Although the former chair of LSF noted in a letter to members that progress with the 50m pool is 'a very positive reflection on the relationship which the forum has established with both elected members and senior officers' (LSF, 2004e) and a written agreement with LCC was eventually acquired stating that construction would begin on 1December, 2005, agreement at LSF level clearly has little impact on key decisions regarding capital projects. Second, the absence of a consensus at executive board level within the City Council compromised progress where some senior officers and members have questioned whether the pool was needed given that there are 50 metre pools for competitive use in nearby Manchester, Stockport and Wigan. However, some politicians have advocated a pool on the basis of inter-city competition, where competition with Manchester in particular has permeated policy debates in Liverpool.

Third, disagreement over how the pool should be funded was a critical issue in its delay. Specifically, whether the pool should be funded nationally or locally through council tax was an issue, where raising local taxes to pay for the pool could prove to be an electoral liability for the ruling Liberal Democratic Party. In the wider LCC financing context (see Chapter 4), investment in major capital projects such as a 50 metre pool was not a priority, particularly given the non-statutory status of sport. The use of unsupported borrowing or reliance on City Council reserves was not considered to be an option either and the project stalled. Not only were the capital costs of the pool cited as a concern in late 2002 (LSF, 2002d) but concerns arose over revenue funding for operating the pool (LSF, 2002b). LCC therefore sought financial support through the National Lottery. Eventually, Sport England agreed to part-fund the pool (£4m), whilst LCC had to raise £8m (which subsequently escalated to £11m). With a political consensus not achieved and delays continuing, Sport England may have 'clawed-back' the Lottery monies, as it had in other cases, especially as a review and restructuring of Sport England in 2004 resulted in a policy shift from investing in capital projects to revenue-based programmes.

GYMNASTICS

Liverpool has been a 'centre of excellence' for gymnastics with a history dating back to the mid-nineteenth century (Physick, 2007). A purpose-built indoor gymnasium was erected in 1865 that became a hub for British gymnastics. The former Liverpool gymnasium (demolished in the 1970s) hosted events in the Olympic Festivals of the late nineteenth century and in effect became the catalyst for almost 30 private gymnasiums in the

However, the pool was viewed by Sport England as a 'legacy project' and it was given approval.

UK Sport and the ASA also supported the expansion of 50 metre pools at the time for elite swimming purposes given their relative paucity nationwide (Green and Houlihan, 2005a). However, with Leisure Services unable to support the costs of construction, even with Sport England support, and with project costs increasing, the pool development was to be tied in with the Kings Dock facility development (the Echo Arena) to 'make up the shortfall'. These arrangements fell through in early 2006, leaving LCC to cover the rising costs through unsupported borrowing after all (LCC, 2006a).

Fourth, the potential impact on community pools of building the 50 metre pool generated opposition to its construction. As swimming pools tend not to generate a profit, it was argued by community groups and some politicians that building the 50 metre pool will result in closing other 'out-of-date' community pools. Subsequently, construction of the pool was delayed by objections to planning permission, supported by some councillors, where a loss of green space became a core concern, although this space was of poor quality and not used by the community. Eventually the positioning of the building was altered to avoid the 'green space'. A fifth issue concerned the usage of the pool, where competition for a scarce resource exists on account of the shortage of water space locally. As noted, balancing club and community use has been an issue in the city. For example, Everton Park pool was built for performance and was not well used by the community but public opposition successfully secured greater community use. Sixth, as with many capital projects,

delays can result from changing arrangements between local authorities, contractors and utility companies.

A number of reasons therefore exist for the delay in constructing the new pool, which in part highlight the relatively weak influence of sport interests in the city, within a context of competing priorities, funding issues and control of policy. Arguably, the pool would not have been agreed to be built had it not been for the direct intervention of the incoming Council Leader with a 'sport agenda' at a time when the Chief Executive had resigned and weak opposition existed to the pool from the local Labour Party who 'called in' the decision to proceed (LCC, 2006a), expressing concerns over the rising costs of the facility now dependent on unsupported borrowing, whilst privately supporting extending leisure provision in a poorer area of the city. These concerns were again raised in early 2008 (CMS Select Committee, 21st January), when additional unsupported borrowing was acquired from the DCMS in order that the facility could be completed by March 2008. The implications for spending across the sport and recreation service area as a whole are unquantifiable at the time of writing.

Finally, the opening of the new facility has not resolved the long-standing tensions between elite squad, club, school and community use or between different water sports. And if the core idea was the use of the facility for city marketing purposes through high-profile swimming events, then due to limited spectating capacity, it cannot be said to have achieved this goal either. Nonetheless, middle-sized events can be staged at the new venue and it is hoped that the centre will impact on participation and performance in due course.

city. Gymnastics became a local authority priority sport in the 1980s when the elite men's squad, which were previously located across the UK, were brought to Liverpool by the former head of sport and recreation services, to represent the City of Liverpool Gymnastics Club that subsequently dominated elite competition for many years.

The employment of a dedicated development officer for gymnastics with a remit centred on elite gymnastics with recreational gymnastics being supplementary, supported by international coaches and part-time staff, was a further demonstration of the value placed on the sport in raising Liverpool's sporting prowess (volunteers, who are usually parents of gymnasts, also play a vital supporting role). The gymnastics development officer (GDO) has been in place since the early 1990s and therefore provides continuity to core objectives around elite gymnastics development, although increasing participation in the sport remains an important objective too, albeit to underpin elite goals. The GDO also manages a mainstreamed budget for gymnastics within Sport and Recreation Service financial parameters.

A high-performance centre was established in 1984 at the Park Road leisure centre in Toxteth and was extended in 1991 to become two gyms, with a shift in focus from men to girls' and women's gymnastics. In fact, elite gymnastics is female dominated today as are the related activities of trampolining, acrobatics, cheerleading and recreational gymnastics, all of which have expanded in recent years. The facilities were upgraded through National Lottery funding in 2002 and again in 2005, using monies from the Sport and Recreation Services budget. Despite the elite focus, it was not until the opening of the Echo Arena in late 2007 that there was a facility to host major gymnastics events in the city.

However, staging international competition remains problematic given that sponsorship potential is compromised by the lack of television exposure given low levels of spectating and the costs of facility hire are prohibitive. Therefore, the sport remains resource dependent on continued support from LCC budgets. The *Capital of Culture* arm of LCC steered the agenda for 2006–2008, 'fitting in' gymnastics to a programme of sports events. For example, the 2006 *Year of Performance* acted as a catalyst for an annual international event held at Park Road gym named the *Norman Wilkinson Cup*.

The local gymnastics strategy for 2004–2007 was developed within the parameters of the NGB, the British Gymnastics Association (BGA) with Liverpool contributing significantly to BGA objectives around performance and international success. This was strengthened further given the acquisition of the 2012 Olympic Games by London. The local gymnastics strategy for 2008–2011 represents an elite performance plan aligned to BGA targets and guidelines set by the international governing body, the Federation of

International Gymnastics (FIG). In practice, BGA targets put pressure on Liverpool to deliver elite success given that half the Great Britain (GB) team are based on Liverpool. It can be noted that, as with other sports, the recent 'modernisation' of the NGBs has had an impact on the sport. For example, the conditional funding arrangements correlated with the goal of GB team success have created significant demands on the sport locally. In this context, the latest strategy centres on building the capacity of the local gymnastics infrastructure to underpin the elite programme where girls focus primarily on elite and artistic gymnastics and boys on recreational gymnastics.

In terms of funding, pressures exist on retaining gymnastics as a core priority of LCC sport. For example, updating equipment in line with FIG guidelines for competition incurs costs and a recent refurbishment of Park Road was necessary to meet international competition standards. Further, despite prior support from lottery monies, recent national-level reductions in *World Class Performance* monies have resulted in LCC accruing the staffing costs for a coach formerly paid through the lottery. Thus, policy and funding changes at national and international level can impact on local planning and delivery. Nonetheless, a strong partnership is evident between gymnastics development in Liverpool and the BGA and in respect of English gymnastics, the English Gymnastics Union (EGU).

Sustaining this relationship over the longer term may be problematic should LCC gymnastics fail to deliver elite success and in circumstances where funding shifts to other priorities. In respect of implementation of the 2008–2011 strategy, a working relationship exists between LCC and the voluntary sector clubs where some clubs send talented gymnasts to Park Road for specialist coaching. However, it can also be noted that local clubs prioritise recreational gymnastics for revenue purposes as opposed to elite objectives and few clubs have the facilities or the expertise to deliver BGA targets. Further, clubs use different development models, and little information or expertise is shared between them.

In terms of LCC partnerships with education, around half of Liverpool schools include gymnastics in extra-curricular provision. Gymnastics within the NCPE is limited in practice given that school gymnasia became sports halls and few PE teachers can deliver gymnastics despite being a component of KS1 and KS2, and to a lesser extent KS3. As a result, links with Specialist Sport Coordinators were established in 2005 with the aim of upskilling teachers to coach gymnastics. School–club links can be described as emergent where extra-curricular gymnastic activities in schools are generally not linked to recreational gymnastics clubs. The sustainability of these embryonic partnerships is dependent on progress in embedding gymnastics into the school curriculum and after-school clubs. Nonetheless, a clear pathway can be identified from pre-school to recreational gymnastics in schools and clubs and onto performance levels, where the pathway continues to the UK Sport performance structures.

In a bid to create greater permanence of gymnastics in schools, a gymnastics forum for schools was recently established by the GDO, but there has been little active support from partnership development managers (PDMs) and school heads to date apart from Childwall SSC and the PDM for the cluster of schools in south-central Liverpool. In practice, schools tend to operate independently in terms of gymnastics provision, teacher commitment to gymnastics is limited and of variable standards, and schools fear litigation in delivering gymnastics to minors where the standard of the management of gymnastics in local schools varies. Subsequently, in the last few years, there has been a policy shift from expanding participation and identifying talent through schools to an approach based on training staff in the LCC lifestyles centres to deliver and develop gymnastics in order to increase participation, leaving the talent identification objectives to the coaches at Park Road and via LCC's *Sportslinx* programme that has three 'gifted and talented' programmes. This suggests that schools did not perceive elite gymnastics development to be a component of their remit.

In order to retain elite gymnastics as a core policy priority, advocates of the sport have been innovative in lobbying for the sport around major events such as the Olympic Games in 2008. The forthcoming 2012 Olympic Games is a window of opportunity for promoting the merits of the sport and its continued priority funding and status in Liverpool. Apart from elite sporting success, advocates have also identified the sport's contribution to the government's social policy goals, particularly through recreational gymnastics and the potential and actual health benefits of the sport.

It is recognised, however, that this advocacy exists in a local context where there are tensions between the competing goals of competitive and recreational gymnastics. It is also recognised that income from public sports centres (Lifestyle gyms) in the city in effect supports the continued LCC focus on elite-level gymnastics (and the other priority sports), given limited commercial sector support. Nonetheless, Liverpool's strong location within the structures of elite gymnastics in England and GB may guarantee continued support from the governing bodies. The key future challenge will be building the local infrastructure to underpin elite gymnastics including expanding mass participation via the network of Lifestyles centres. The 2008 Olympic Games did result in a surge in interest in gymnastics but retaining interest could be problematic.

This section highlights the resource dependence of elite gymnastics on the local authority, whose decisions around sport policy priorities made in the 1980s have resulted in a legacy for both the sport and the city. The commitment of the local authority to the sport is manifest in the dedicated facilities and human resources and in funding support to replace the loss of external funding, for example. Further, a close working relationship with the governing body, its strategic planning around the 2012 Olympic Games and related access to lottery funding has sustained the focus. However, the elite gymnastics network includes few local schools and clubs, both of which have a different set of policy priorities.

ROAD RUNNING

Currently, a number of bodies organise and deliver road races across the public, voluntary and private sectors, including local authorities, governing bodies, clubs, charities and commercial sector companies. These organisations have different rationales for investing in road running, including city marketing, health promotion, elite competition and simply for recreational or social purposes.

In terms of the governance of the sport, road running has historically been one component of athletics. However, following a major review of athletics (Foster, 2004), significant resistance from the voluntary sector to alignment with the objectives of UK Athletics (UKA) has arisen, foregrounding long-standing juridical tensions between government and voluntary sector athletics bodies. A central tension concerns payments to UKA by road race organisers of a levy for non-club runners (most race participants are not affiliated to a club). In 2006, the Association of GB Athletics Clubs (ABAC) founded a separate Association of Running Clubs (ARC) to provide a voice for road running clubs in opposition to increasing government intervention in sport and the drive towards professionalisation and 'modernisation' given the value placed on amateurism and voluntarism in the sport (Green and Houlihan, 2005b).

Specifically, clubs have concerns over the conditional funding arrangements that is shaping the governance of the sport, resource allocation decisions of UKA favouring elite athletics rather than the grass roots, the 'undermining' of the club structures, the accountability of government agencies and the contention that recreational road running is in effect subsidising elite, professional athletics. Subsequently, in 2007, UKA founded the Road Running Leadership Group (RRLG) that will review the administration-, financing-, marketing- and performance-related goals of the sport, including a new licensing scheme to replace the levy system (UK Athletics, 2007). This context is important as it will impact on the implementation of any local strategy to develop the sport, although of note is that clubs in the north of England are less active in resisting government intervention given their weaker financial status than those in the south. As of late 2008, the beneficiaries of the 'modernisation' of road running are unclear.

In terms of participation, the 1980s were the 'boom years' for road running nationally, with the introduction of the *London Marathon* and *Great North Run* that subsequently became embedded into both the national sporting identity and local cultural fabric of London and the North-East, respectively. This in turn ensured the survival of these major road running events despite the increasing difficulties associated with hosting and staging events in urban areas. These include, first, changes in legislation such as the introduction of the *Road Traffic Regulation (Special Events) Act 1994* and the *Health and Safety at Work Act 1999* that resulted in concerns over liability for accidents and the costs of medical insurance.

Second, the introduction of Sunday trading resulted in busier roads and with most road races traditionally taking place on a Sunday, many police forces discouraged races given that race organisers had to assume the health and safety risks themselves (despite very few accidents historically). Hosting an event without local authority and local constabulary support proved problematic for race organisers and many events were cancelled. Third, rising police, stewarding and traffic management costs acted as a further disincentive to stage races, being up to 60% of the total organisational costs in practice. The cost to local authorities of organising and underwriting their own events also became prohibitive. Fourth, commercial operators often found difficulties in securing sponsorship, given this context, with monies for marketing limited given the high costs of delivery.

In Liverpool, high-profile road races have traditionally been supported by local politicians given the potential impact on the image of the city and the local economy. However, the organisation and delivery of road running has changed from a situation where LCC supported marathons between 1982 and 1994 but subsequently staged only half-marathons and smaller events such as two 10 km events including a women-only event and a 5 km team challenge race, to a situation where, in 2009–2010, five of the seven large-scale races are to be organised and delivered by commercial sector operators, notably the race organiser L1310K. These include a half-marathon, introduced in 1994, a fun-run and another 10 km race, introduced in 2004, that incorporated the use of the Mersey Tunnel. Despite the limited operational involvement of LCC in recent years, the local authority continues to support road running through *Active City* funding on account of the potential health benefits of running.

Nonetheless, outside of these high-profile events, there are fewer road races in Liverpool today than two decades ago. By the early to mid-1990s, the rising costs associated with temporary road closures combined with a drop-off in the number of runners led to some races organised by clubs being removed from the calendar of events. This is despite the fact that Merseyside Police was one of the last police forces to bring in charging at road running events.

A number of factors have influenced the status and delivery of road running in the city. First, the ongoing regeneration of the city centre via the *European Capital of Culture* economic development programme has 'pushed out' race events from the city centre and some races are under threat of survival. Arguably, within *Capital of Culture*, 'cultural' events were given priority over sports events from around 2004, when the city won the bid (see Chapter 3). Second, the founding of a Safety Advisory Group (SAG), which oversees road safety in line with central government policy guidance, has become a key local influence on road races. The body includes the LCC Highways Department, LCC Legal Office, Emergency Services, the Police and the commercial travel operator, Mersey Travel. Arguably, this agency has little empathy with road running per se and road running clubs now need SAG accreditation to participate in race organisation. Third, there are a number of funding issues that include race organisers experiencing difficulties in raising sponsorship monies; a reluctance of public sector funding bodies to support private sector race operators; and the local authority cannot access National Lottery monies for road running, as running events do not meet the funding criteria, unlike athletics development and facility refurbishment, for example.

Fourth, opposition to races has been mobilised by residents, some ward councillors and the church 'lobby' opposed to sporting activities or trading on a Sunday (advocates of the Catholic church in particular have retained a significant influence in the city, notably in schools). In fact, a general decline in public tolerance of races in the city can be observed over time. Fifth, the clubs themselves do not represent a significant body of influence on policy, particularly given that 80% of runners in the major seven events are not affiliated to a club. Moreover, clubs tend to focus on the social and recreational elements of road running as opposed to 'performance' and most clubs operate in isolation and do not assist in race organisation. Sixth, and not insignificantly, the geography of the city poses logistical challenges for race organisers where a myriad of road closures are needed for races to proceed. In recent years, the parks in Liverpool have been used for race events and although some are suitable for events, such as Sefton Park, which is ideal in size, scope, scale and access, by comparison, Croxteth Park is arguably unsuitable for larger events, and numbers of races held at this venue have declined.

In relation to this changing context, LCC's role has shifted over time from provider to facilitator and from delivering events independently to working in partnership. One such partnership was with the London Marathon Company (LMC), which funded a running development officer (RDO) post within LCC in 2005, for 3 years, in part to bring LMC events to the city, such as a half-marathon. However, LMC subsequently withdrew from local race organisation in 2007, claiming it did not receive adequate support from LCC. Commercial sector operators highlight the differences in working practices across the sectors that can compromise race organisation, with weak events marketing expertise cited within LCC, given the absence of strategic links to tourism strategy, for example. It can also be noted that Liverpool events do not attract a national profile or significant numbers of non-residents to race compared with other cities (only a fifth of competitors in large-scale events are non-residents). Recently, LCC Sport and Recreation Services have established a departmental marketing arm as part of a professionalisation of the service area.

At the grass-roots level, the RDO has a remit to raise participation adopting a 'running for all' focus through establishing running groups in areas of low participation as part of an outreach programme, for example in the Speke/Garston area of south Liverpool. The RDO is charged with developing the first road running strategy for the city, independent of athletics development. LCC Sport was to work with the LMC with the aim of using any profits for sport provision as a whole (not necessarily ring-fenced for running). One component of the strategy was to engage residents living on the geographical periphery of the city in events linked to the *Year of Performance* 2006, as part of the 2008 *Capital of Culture* celebrations. The strategy was aligned to health promotion through running in schools, such as establishing after-school clubs, in partnership with *Sportslinx*. In terms of schools, club–school links are sought although acknowledging that schools are limited in what they can provide and lack expertise in delivering running activities and events. The strategy includes targeting primary schools not involved in cross-country leagues (approximately 30% are involved city-wide). However, delivery is problematic given that few teachers hold relevant UKA-accredited coaching qualifications and the availability of club coaches during school time is very limited as is teachers' time. The difficulty of involving young people in running is evidenced in recent events that have not attracted mass pupil participation and have been cancelled. The participation profile of road running remains centred on adults.

In conclusion, the sport of road running and particularly competitive racing has undergone significant changes since the 'golden era' of the 1980s.

As a result of a combination of local influences shaping policy and practice, within the national context as outlined, participation in road running in Liverpool is now on the decline, although some events continue to attract relatively large numbers. Road running events in Liverpool have not acquired a similar embeddedness locally or in terms of national profile to the *Great North Run*, for example. It can be argued that there were too many events within the local market and races are no longer sufficiently attractive to retain mass participation. In 2007, L1310K registered 25,000 entries for six events and in 2008 there were 20,000 entrants across seven events. In sum, legislative, political and economic factors in particular have influenced the staging of events with road running existing today in a less supportive policy environment.

In understanding policy impacting on road running as a sport, this case study, first, highlights the critical role of central and local governments in sport. Second, it serves to foreground the tensions between competing agendas within and between the public, commercial and voluntary sectors. Third, the study illustrates how sport practices are shaped by non-sport interests. Fourth, it can be noted that the core values held by advocates of the sport are not widely shared among authorities who oversee the use of the highways. Nonetheless, the resilience of advocates who continue using the roads to run, despite the increasing set of challenges race organisers face in delivering the sport in urban environments, is highlighted. The potential influence of an emergent governing body for road running, independent of the existing organisational and funding infrastructure, may offer the sport opportunities to extend advocacy and retain a diverse programme of road races.

CRICKET

The history of cricket in Liverpool can be charted from the latter end of the eighteenth century to the early years of the twenty-first century (Physick, 2007). Influences that shaped the development of clubs and competition between them include the expansion of the railways linking suburban areas and dormitory town populated by the middle classes who invested time and financial resources into the sport. Unlike in the south of England where the interests of the landed gentry were invested into cricket, in Liverpool, patronage originated from wealthy businessmen seeking to maximise social advantage. The growth in popularity of the sport across the social classes led to demand outstripping the supply of pitches. This demand underpinned the growth of an organised league, the Liverpool Competition (Walker, 1988) that continues today, with most clubs being members since the 1800s. Of note is the formation of Liverpool Cricket Club in the early nineteenth century that still hosts Lancashire county matches (albeit in the shadow of the rival facilities in Manchester).

Since the 1950s, cricket has gradually declined in terms of participation, spectating, volunteering and school competition. However, as late as the 1970s, many clubs in the city remained rooted within local communities. A few clubs have retained a community profile, with, for example, clubs such as Sefton Park, Bootle and Birkenhead retaining relatively large match attendances compared with the general trend. However, club membership has declined over the last 25 years, for example Sefton Park Club had 1000 members in 1983 and has 480 in 2008. Reasons for this decline include changing lifestyles including patterns of employment and increasing competition for leisure time and the difficulties of creating and sustaining a sense of community around clubs in urban areas. Liverpool Cricket Club is successful as it operates as a multi-sports club and is a satellite for Lancashire county matches, in addition to being historically embedded into the city's sporting heritage. Nonetheless, most clubs are struggling financially as they are expensive to operate. Today, most clubs increasingly depend on secondary sources of income in order to survive.

In terms of schools cricket, the peak of inter-school competition in Liverpool was in the 1970s. In the state sector, cricket was mainly played in grammar schools. Public schools had their own leagues, and competition with state schools was limited, in part because state schools had poor-quality pitches. Independent schools have retained a partial focus on the sport, but little cricket features today in the games aspect of the NCPE in state schools or in after-school clubs. The period 1982–1986 can be identified as the one when local school competitive cricket declined and has arguably never recovered. Reasons for the decline include the teachers' strike in the early 1980s resulting in fewer teachers willing to volunteer their time to deliver sport outside of school hours, the adversarial politics of Militant (1983–1987; see Chapter 4) that opposed voluntary-aided schools and their dominant sports, changes in school hours resulting in fewer opportunities for employed people to volunteer, the cost of maintaining pitches and a growth in health and safety legislation.

LCC has had a significant influence over time on both club and schools cricket. Of note is the considerable initial investment in cricket made by LCC, which in 1881 purchased the land on which the oldest club, Liverpool Cricket Club, still stands and paid for the facilities. However, the club had been searching for a permanent home in Liverpool since its inception in 1807, before the local authority finally entrenched the club into a suburban location at Aigburth. Clubs, once established at a site, sought security of tenure and depending on their financial status, either purchased the land, leased it or sought local authority support (Walker, 1988). Aside from land-use planning policy and practices, the City Council has influenced cricket through its sport policy priorities and resourcing decisions since Sport and Recreation Services was established.

However, when sport development priorities were established in the 1980s, the City Council did not make cricket a core priority and was perhaps reluctant to intervene given the politics of the city at the time and cricket was considered to be effectively managed, participation was high and clubs delivered without the need for direct involvement of the local authority. LCC Sport did briefly have a development remit for cricket from 1987 to 1989 before the introduction of a similar role at county level. A development officer for Merseyside has become an established role with the current cricket development officer appointed and funded by Lancashire Cricket Board. More recently, St Margaret's school has established a cricket academy with some financial support from the local authority. The relationship between LCC and cricket can therefore be characterised as 'arms-length'.

Apart from the City Council, the governing body, the England and Wales Cricket Board (ECB), started to influence club cricket around 1999 given concerns over national standards. The influence of 'modernisation' at the local level can be found in the increasing professionalisation of the sport including the use of overseas players, which has had an impact on club resources and the recreational side of the sport, and the pressure on clubs to acquire Clubmark accreditation, for example. In Liverpool, ECB funding has also been targeted at facility improvements and coaching development with coaching support improving at some clubs as a result. However, there is some resistance to the modernisation of cricket from clubs, for example, in respect of the PESSCL strategy to create school–club partnerships.

The government policy of encouraging such partnerships has been embraced more readily by schools than clubs, where clubs are expected to fill the gaps in school provision. Prior to the formalising of school–club partnerships, arrangements were ad hoc and reciprocity evolved from local need rather than 'top-down' intervention. The formalisation of partnerships can be seen by clubs as an imposition on autonomous status. Further, the Liverpool Competition became an ECB premier league in the year 2000 with two divisions created for the first time. Some clubs resisted the restructuring and joined either the Cheshire County League or the Lancashire County League. Additionally, the ECB policy emphasis on equity, encouraged by government, has met with a limited response locally where the women's game and disability cricket have not been a traditional feature of club provision, although Mossley Hill Club (multi-sports) do have a cricket section for women. Limited expertise exists locally to develop disability cricket.

In sum, the evolution of cricket, which pre-dates association football in Liverpool, is centred on advocates of the sport acquiring and seeking to retain, first, spaces to play in an urban area subject to development pressures, urban sprawl and competition from other sports. Where once Wavertree Playground was used for cricket in the south of the city, it is now used predominantly for athletics, football, tennis and swimming, and Stanley Park, once a site for cricket to the north of the city, is now the site of the planned stadium for Liverpool professional football club. Second, the voluntary sector has sought autonomy and greater control of the sport, avoiding resource dependency on the local authority. Local cricket clubs, too, have not always welcomed the influence of the governing body for the sport. Nevertheless, the ECB's blueprint for cricket development for 2005–2009 has had an impact locally through its funding of facility development, increasing coaching in clubs and schools and through an expansion of performance pathways centred on effective school–club partnerships.

The storyline of cricket at the local level highlights how local authorities can impact on voluntary sector sport. The decline of cricket in local schools is in part a legacy of local authority policy in the 1980s with the 'class-based politics' of Militant, although cricket in Liverpool spans class divides to some extent, with Bootle Cricket Club, for example, having its origins in a working class area of the city. The local decline of club and schools cricket at the time cannot be separated from the national decline given changes in social trends, and the local authority did not or could not defend local cricket from these national trends. For several sports, acquiring priority sport status within the local authority has provided a degree of insulation from external influences. Being outside of core priorities weakened a sport already subject to competition from other sports, football in particular. Further, in state schools, cricket has been squeezed out of provision by sports that are easier to deliver in the context of a crowded curriculum. Nonetheless, despite political and economic influences on the sport in Liverpool, a number of clubs have acquired a level of permanence in the sporting landscape and are largely self-sufficient. Perhaps a more significant influence than the local authority in the last decade has been the intervention of the 'modernised' governing body. However, many clubs remain semi-autonomous from governing body pressures, and the resilience of the grass roots in safeguarding a degree of self-determination cannot be underestimated.

CONCLUSIONS

In summary, each of these storylines highlights how sports at the local level are subject to exogenous influences from government and its agencies, related governing body and local government policy priorities and resources. Endogenous influences include the embeddedness of the sport within LCC Sport policy and provision and within local schools. The changing relationship between LCC and a range of sports is in part related to the resource dependencies for each sport or to what extent a sport is autonomous of public sector influence. *Table 6.1* compares the five sports where local authority policy and practice have been highly influential in shaping the status of each sport.

School Sport

INTRODUCTION

This chapter will explore the relationship between policy for school sport at the national and local levels in order to acquire insight into the influences shaping school sport policy and practice. This chapter relates central government policy during the Conservative administrations 1979–1997 and under New Labour 1997–2008 to changes in school sport in Liverpool during the last 30 years, but particularly in the last decade. Nonetheless, as this book spans the approximate period of 1970 to date, this chapter begins

Sport Policy and Governance: Local Perspectives
Copyright © 2009, Dr. Neil King. Published by Elsevier Ltd. All rights reserved.

with a brief summary of the period 1970–1979. It should also be noted that this chapter is not primarily concerned with policy relating to PE, although there is clearly a relationship between PE and sport policy in schools.

THE EVOLUTION OF SCHOOL SPORT POLICY

1970–1979

As with other areas of policy in the 1970s, such as sport as a component of social policy (see Chapter 3), health (see Chapter 8), social services, youth justice and community 'regeneration' (see Chapter 10), education was a core component of welfarism that prioritised equality of opportunity where the state was the provider. The emergence of comprehensive schools concerned with providing 'progressive education' formed one component of a broader welfare consensus. However, with the demise of the welfare state came the rise of the New Right and the 'fitness for industry' educational philosophy that began to shape state school policy and practice.

The Conservative administrations: 1979–1997

Perhaps, the most significant era for policy change within the education sector was during the period 1979–1997, when successive Conservative governments introduced a range of legislation and policy directives that had a significant impact on school governance, management and curriculum content. In essence, the Conservative administration sought to place market-oriented goals at the heart of education policy and undermine the post-war welfare consensus that had held sway in Britain until the mid-1970s. The main vehicle for change was the *Education Reform Act* (DfEE, 1988) which proposed a National Curriculum (DES, 1991), established a direct funding relationship between schools and central government that gave greater financial autonomy to some schools.

In making these changes, the local management and funding of schools through LEAs were weakened, leaving central government to steer school policy. The New Right challenge to the teaching profession, its organisation and methods, and not least its politics, is the context to the creation of the NCPE (Penney and Evans, 1999). The politics of the NCPE is well documented (Evans and Penney, 1995, 1998, 2005; Houlihan, 1997; Penney and Evans, 1999; Talbot, 1998). In an analysis of the changing policy context shaping school sport and PE, Houlihan (1997: 243) concluded that 'The long-established frame which prioritised matters associated with equity and individual potential was eroded and replaced by a frame that stressed standards and the pursuit of excellence and which sought policy solutions from the "logic" of the market.' This logic also resulted in the sale of school playing fields (see Chapter 9).

A central tension throughout the 1980s for school sport was establishing a policy consensus between the Sports Council (and its attendant government department) and the government department responsible for education. Subsequently, the transfer of 'sport' to the government department responsible for education in 1990 changed the pattern of established relationships, and the Minister for Sport at the time therefore had responsibility for PE within the school curriculum. The Sports Council chairman at the time stated, 'This is excellent news which now clearly acknowledges that school sport must once again become the heart of sports teaching and education' (cited in Houlihan, 1992: 72). However, as Houlihan (1992: 68) observes, policy initiatives requiring the cooperation of two or more government departments have a history of failure, and locating sport within education at the level of central government did not resolve the tension between educational and sport-specific agendas within schools.

Further, sport itself had little credibility in the education policy community and the implementation of policy remained largely within the remit of schools themselves, due mainly to the absence of statutory control of policy for PE. In sum, PE and sport remained marginal concerns in most schools at the time in spite of both central government policy changes and pressure from elite sports-specific interests. For example, with many budget items devolved to schools, including the costs associated with sport and PE, such as transport to swimming pools, schools had the option to make cutbacks in provision for PE and sport, and many did so.

Under pressure from the CCPR, from the late 1980s, the Sports Council gave the issue of school sport greater consideration in its strategic planning, changing its prior policy position of leaving school sport to LEAs and teachers. Consequently, the policy document, *Into the 90s* (Sports Council, 1988), identified the 13–24 age group as one of its 'target groups' for the first time. However, although educationalist's interests and values were challenged, sports interests did little to dislodge the core policy beliefs of educationalists or significantly raise the profile and resourcing of sport by schools. McPherson and Raab (1988) observe that sports interests are not well represented within the education policy community, which, by contrast with the fragmented sports policy area, is well organised and has its policy preferences and values deeply embedded in the civil service. Advocates subsequently defended PE on the basis of its instrumental value rather than its intrinsic worth, that is on its contribution to health and fitness, or its place in Britain's 'national sporting heritage'. Houlihan (1997: 2) concluded that 'the political distinction between sport and PE had the effect of legitimising the marginalisation of PE teachers in the Curriculum design process and legitimising a degree of political direction which was exceptional in comparison to most other areas of the Curriculum'.

It was from the mid-1990s, however, that the rise in the political salience of school sport and PE gathered momentum, albeit the focus was on competitive team games and elite sport-specific interests (Evans and Penney, 1995; Penney and Evans, 1999). With the arrival of John Major as prime minister, school sport moved up the political agenda, opening up a policy window for lobbyists to gain access and influence over policy. This was the result of three inter-related developments, namely the aforementioned transfer of responsibility for school sport to the Department for Education and Science (DES); the House of Commons Select Committee enquiry into school sport and the setting up of the PE National Curriculum Working Party (Houlihan, 1992, 1997). Under John Major, the Conservative government shifted its policy priorities towards traditional Conservatism and, to some extent, away from Thatcherism. One example of this policy shift is found in *Sport: Raising the Game* that emphasised a need to 'reverse [the] decline and put sport back at the heart of school life' (DNH, 1995: 7). Major stated that *Sport: Raising the Game* represented 'the most important set of proposals ever published for the encouragement and promotion of sport' (DNH, 1995: 1). In essence, the policy statement signified to restoration of PE and school sport, albeit in terms of elitism, heritage and nationalism (Penney and Evans, 1999) and in line with the core beliefs of the key policy actors, most notably the prime minister himself (Evans and Penney, 1998).

Houlihan and Green (2006) summarise the key policy changes impacting on school sport and PE during the period 1979–1997. The authors identify the emerging policy concerns in the media and among the public around the relative failure of elite athletes and the perceived decline in health of young people, combining to produce a 'moral panic' about the teaching of PE and role and remit of sport in schools. Critically, the authors also highlight the disunity of the teaching profession that impacted on its lobbying capacity to move sport and PE from its peripheral status within schools. In sum, in the latter years of Conservative administration, sport-specific interests gained legitimacy in schools, underpinned by concerns about national sporting success and the general decline in competitive sport in schools (Green, 2004a; Green and Houlihan, 2005a) although the impact of such policy change 'on the ground' appears to have been minimal, given the capacity of educational interests to resist change. Nonetheless, Kirk (1992: 2) concluded that the Major administration represented 'a watershed in physical education discourse'.

New Labour: 1997–2008

Education, at least at the time of New Labour's election in 1997, and for the first few years in office, was the central component of New Labour's political and policy agenda and had been seen as fundamental to achieving social inclusion. With the increasing focus on resourcing and re-organising the education sector (building on the *Education Act 1996*: DFEE, 1996a), the significance of school sport and PE has again changed to take account of wider concerns in the neighbouring policy area of health, for example, and those networks concerned with social and economic regeneration, in addition to the aforementioned increasing focus on elite sport policy objectives. Thus school sport is an increasingly crowded policy space (Houlihan, 2000a). In this space, Houlihan and Green (2006) note the recurring value dissonance between PE and sport in schools and the absence of an institutional focus, or embedded organisational and policy processes, within central government, that could prioritise PE interests in particular.

The period 1997–2000, in respect of school sport, can be described as 'a period of muddle and retreat' (Houlihan, 2002: 198), despite the aspiration demonstrated in Labour's *Sporting Nation* (Labour Party, 1996). The period in effect endorsed the priorities identified in *Sport: Raising the Game* (DNH, 1995). It was not until 2000, with spending commitments to the prior regime lifted, that central government could pursue its own agenda for sport. It was not until the launch of the policy statement *A Sporting Future for All* (DCMS, 2000) that the role of school sport emerged with any degree of clarity. Within this statement, SSCs, introduced under John Major, were retained and expanded although with a greater emphasis on social inclusion (Collins and Kay, 2003; DCMS, 2002), following the PAT10 report on *Sport and Social Inclusion* (DCMS, 1999). The aim of SSCs was to encourage all secondary schools to develop a distinctive subject specialism, one of which is 'sport', although a broad curriculum is maintained in schools (for an analysis of specialist sport colleges, see Penney, Houlihan and Eley, 2002).

Other initiatives followed that impacted on school sport including the establishment of School Sport Partnerships (SSPs) with PDMs at the hub, the appointment of SSCos (Sport England, 2002b) to work across schools, and the PESSCL launched through the policy document *Learning Through PE and Sport* (DfES, 2003, 2004). Partnership-working has therefore become a key theme and action at national level, but also at local level where given the ideological context of 'social inclusion' through education, a closer working relationship 'on the ground' has emerged between education and community interests where 'regeneration' is the common theme and thread. These actions are underpinned by additional resources from the

Exchequer and the National Lottery, particularly via the NOF (now known as the Big Lottery Fund).

A significant organisational change under New Labour was the emergence of cross-departmental working within central government, notably between the DCMS and DfES, and partnerships with external bodies such as the YST, via the School Sport Alliance which signalled a closer working relationship between government departments and related external organisations than in prior years (Flintoff, 2003). Whether the new School Sport Alliance will have more success in influencing policy 'on the ground' than prior attempts at finding policy consensus remains to be seen, but what is clear is that central government has shifted from an arms-length approach to implementing policy to one more pro-active in facilitating policy change.

In this regard, Green and Houlihan (2005b) argue that Sue Campbell, former director of the influential YST, has acted as the key policy broker in the space between DfES and DCMS interests. Moreover, Houlihan and Green (2006: 22) argue that the YST has become the 'pre-eminent institutional force in the sector behind the recent emphasis on school sport and PE'. Green and Houlihan (2005b) observe that the government agenda, driven through the YST, the 'insider' interest group, was supported by an expanding network of advocates, including the SSC network, The Office for Standards in Education, Children's Services and Skills (OFSTED) and the PESSCL board, and this met with very little opposition on account of ineffective interest group activity, most notably from British Association of Advisors and Lecturers in Physical Education (BAALPE), Physical Education Association of the UK (PEAUK), and also from Sport England.

In sum, New Labour has utilised sport and PE in schools to meet a diverse set of objectives through the use of policy instruments such as re-organising the structures, systems and processes that impact on relationships and patterns of interests, into partnerships aligned to key government policy priorities and the use of conditional funding mechanisms, access to which requires compliance with government policy priorities. At the local level, as a consequence of national policy, there exists a multitude of policy implementation challenges for schools, local authorities, sports bodies and partners in the health policy area and the 'regeneration sector' generally.

ANALYSIS: THE NATIONAL CONTEXT

In light of these recent changes, the school sport policy area can be viewed as a complex and crowded policy space where a number of competing interests can be identified. Houlihan (1992) identified three clusters of interests in the school sport policy area that remain today, albeit that structures and organisations have altered, indicating the strength of core beliefs held by the various interests.

The first 'cluster' of interests represents those concerned with educational interests or 'school sport through teaching' and has membership with the broader education policy community inclusive of the government department for education. The second cluster of interests represents those concerned with the organisation and administration of sport, particularly elite sport, and the third cluster is identified as 'much looser' set of interests and includes bodies concerned with sport policy but only indirectly with school sport, and those focused on youth work and play, but not specifically sport. Houlihan (1997) identified three overlapping themes that provide the context to the shaping of school sport policy. First, the politics of education, bound up with questions of teacher status, authority and autonomy, second, the administrative context being significant as several government departments have a stake in how school sport is delivered and third, the place of sport and PE within the school curriculum that has proved to be an enduring debate within the education policy sector.

From a neo-pluralist perspective, the making of school sport policy is therefore the outcome of a process of negotiation between these 'clusters' of interests, given the context of the wider debates identified within Education, although the negotiation does not take place on a 'level playing field'. These clusters of interests are bound by both a value consensus (policy core beliefs) and pragmatic concerns such as resource dependencies and organisational 'survival'. In terms of beliefs, Bergmann Drewe (1998) identifies debates around the role of competitive sport in PE; Kirk (1992) observes the redefinition of sport in schools from 'sport as skill' to 'sport as knowledge' in the pursuit of academic respectability as a subject of value; and Penney and Evans (1999) focus their analysis on the contemporary struggles between central government and educationalists in defining PE in schools, exploring how political interests define what is included as 'worthwhile knowledge'.

Houlihan (1997: 267) concluded that although school sport not only survived the uncertainty of educational reform, but enhanced its position, this cannot be claimed as evidence of effective lobbying on the part of sports bodies, as much as support from government for sport in schools, at least in respect of the protection and promotion of elite sport objectives. Houlihan (2002: 206) concludes that 'In large part the ability of successive governments to treat sport and physical education in an instrumental fashion and to promote and pursue arguably idiosyncratic policies reflects the weakness of the sport-related interest groups and their ability to establish an institutionalised presence in the policy process.' As a result, Kay (1998) argues that the distinctive purposes and practices of PE have been marginalised by political interests concerned with competitive, elite sport in recent years.

School sport policy in England, however, cannot be fully understood without taking account of non-domestic policy influences. For example, Deacon et al. (1997) identify the significant influence of neo-liberalism in economic policy that impacted on the parameters of the debate around education in England, particularly from the period of the Thatcher administrations. 'The concern with international economic competitiveness, the critique of public sector professions such as teachers, and the concern with the achievement of international sporting success were all ideas that informed neo-liberal policy' (Houlihan, 2002: 202). Thus domestic issues such as formulation of the NCPE and school sport policy are informed and mediated by international policy debates, in this case in respect of the relationship between economic and education policy.

The following section will describe and analyse school sport in Liverpool, focusing primarily on the period 1995–2005, although setting change in the last decade within a time span of 35 years since LCC Leisure Services first intervened in school sport. The author will draw on the recent work of Houlihan and Green (2006), who analyse school sport and PE policy change through the lens of four variables, namely change in beliefs, values and ideas; organisational and resource arrangements and dependencies; interests group activity; and via influential individuals, but also noting the role of serendipity and networking in policy change.

SCHOOL SPORT POLICY IN LIVERPOOL

There are 133 primary and 33 secondary schools in Liverpool across the state and independent sectors. Many of these schools work with the voluntary sector school sport, which in Liverpool has a long tradition, particularly in primary education that continues to thrive today. School sport in Liverpool has been subject to a number of national and local pressures over the last 30 years that have had differing impacts on the fortunes of individual sports (see Chapter 6). These pressures ranged from industrial disputes affecting teacher commitment to sport, re-organisations of secondary education, the sale of playing fields and the decline of competitive sport in the 1980s to the recent government investment in school sport from the late 1990s, given the introduction of the National Lottery, specialist sport colleges and the '5-hour offer'. Further, schools in the city must meet national policy targets for sport and PE, where the objective in Liverpool was to have 75% of children doing 2 hours PE/sport per week in all schools by 2006

(DfES, 2003, 2004). A subsequent audit revealed that 87% of schools meet the government target in 2008 (slightly above the national average) although the quality of provision is largely unquantified.

It was industrial action by teachers in the mid-1980s that had a fundamental impact on secondary school sport in Liverpool, given the introduction of the teacher contract that resulted in many teachers being no longer willing to undertake extra-curricular sports activities without compensation in terms of time and money. In contrast, the 1970s was characterised by non-specialist teacher support for sport in a context of schools encouraging sports activities. Sport was valued and there existed an expectation among teachers that they should contribute. Further, parental involvement in extra-curricular sport decreased in the 1980s and, to an extent, the goodwill and trust between schools and parents were affected. The decade also witnessed the introduction of large comprehensive schools, replacing many smaller schools across the city and impacting on sports such as swimming, where many school pools were disposed of. Moreover, Liverpool, up until the mid-1980s, had a tradition of inter-school sport where Trade Unions supported sport, but with the demise in the influence of the Trade Unions in the 1990s came a decline in the financial commitment to school sport. A key influence on school sport at the time was conflict between the ideology of the Militant controlled City Council (see Chapter 4) and voluntary-aided schools in Liverpool, with attempts to expand comprehensive education resisted by independent and church schools.

In respect of the relationship between LCC, state schools and the voluntary sector for sport, in the 1970s, a School Sport Liaison Committee existed that included LCC Leisure, Education and school sport representation. This body can be characterised by cooperation and a common agenda where these organisations had a similar remit within the ethos of the welfare state. Again, it was from the mid-1980s that this relationship began to fracture. The decline of competitive sport in schools had a significant immediate impact on some sports, such as cricket, and an enduring effect on local sport where, as of 2008, only a few secondary schools take part in school-club competition, and inter-school-club competition is limited. Nonetheless, in the last decade, in a policy context where competition is once again fashionable, competitive sport in schools is beginning to re-emerge.

Prior to the 1990s, the Liverpool School Sport Federation (LSSF), representing schools and the local voluntary sport sector, had a close working relationship with LCC Leisure/Sport Services. LSSF became an independent body at the suggestion of Leisure Services, who sought to devolve responsibilities and costs of school sport. However, LSSF struggled to survive and subsequently altered its remit to focus on specific sports that, to an extent, divided the organisation where some sports are closely aligned to LCC Sport priorities and receive financial support and others do not. Further, the introduction of the NCPE impacted on teacher workloads and subsequently on regular meetings between schools and the voluntary sector. However, in the last few years, the school–voluntary sector relationship has been revitalised by the introduction of SSPs with voluntary sector-led school sport 'running alongside' the National Curriculum provision. Leisure Services and some schools have re-established a positive relationship although the foundation of the relationship is underpinned by a discourse around how school sport can merge into Sport/Recreation Service programmes, which indicates the strength of local authority policy priorities and resources.

The local history of extra-curricular sport in Liverpool is an important component of the policy context. Extra-curricular sport activities have a long history in Liverpool primary schools, unlike most of England, and further, it is currently thriving, and thus the primary level has been insulated to some degree from the policy change, impacting on secondary education in the last two decades. This difference is based on the career histories and personal interests of teachers at primary level linked to a semiautonomous primary school sport network embedded into the organisations such as the Liverpool and District Catholic Schools Association, the LSSF and the Liverpool Schools Football Association that have a strong local history. Importantly, affiliation fees facilitate a degree of autonomy from local and central government, although LCC does provide minimal grant aid, for example to the LSSF. Consequently, there has always been effective resistance to national policy change even in the anti-competitive sport trend in schools most prevalent in the 1980s. The extra-curricular activity base in Liverpool now corresponds with the current government agenda on extending physical activity. However, despite a thriving primary level sporting culture in Liverpool, an 'underclass' nonetheless exists of physically inactive children, particularly in secondary education.

Although primary school sport has been largely insulated from national education and sport policy, this cannot be said of secondary school sport. The recent increasing focus on school sport in Liverpool is largely a consequence of National Lottery funding, largely via the NOF, although school sport and PE funding are essentially for developing 'physical activity' rather than sport specifically. The establishment of three specialist sport colleges in Liverpool (Cardinal Heenan boys school, Archbishop Beck and Childwall Comprehensive) and one school with 'pending' status (Parklands School) act as hubs for families of schools in the four 'quarters' of Liverpool. These schools provide a degree of organisational coherence for delivering the government agenda for school sport.

Critically, with the introduction of the SSCs, it is, as a PDM noted, 'legitimate to spend money on sport'. Further, interviewees cited the introduction of the PESSCL strategy to link schools with sports clubs and the SfSA scheme as important (government-led) developments impacting on the local level. Also of note, however, are the activities of the YST, through its TOPS programme, that has attempted to reinvigorate school sport locally, with variable outcomes in practice. As a consequence of these changes over the last decade, more head teachers have placed a value on sport and PE defined in terms of 'physical activity', from a prior position of support based on personal interest, although its value is short of being on a par with literacy and numeracy. Change was specifically the result of the introduction of the specialist sport college framework locally and the increasing impact of the health agenda in schools. The emergence of a 'target-setting culture', for example through the PESSCL strategy, has also delivered visible data on schools, giving rise to a school focus on accountability to external bodies and parents.

In respect of the city's specialist sport colleges, it is anticipated that they will have a greater but variable impact over time, given the differing lengths of time each SSC has held the status and resource-base. Cardinal Heenan School, the longest established, since 2001; Archbishop Beck School since 2003 and Childwall School became a SSC in 2004. Parklands acquired the status in 2006 but due to poor General Certificate in Secondary Education (GCSE) results, and under threat of 'special measures', it may lose the status. Critically, each school has a different history and educational focus and each is embedded to a greater or lesser extent in quite different relationships with LCC, local sports organisations and regeneration agencies. A simplified diagram of the organisational infrastructure for school sport in Liverpool is given in *Figure 7.1*.

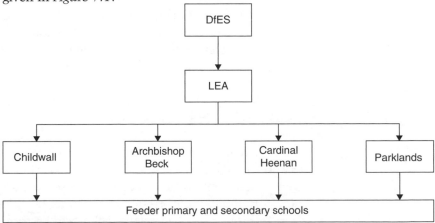

FIGURE 7.1   *The organisation of school sport in Liverpool in 2008.*

As of 2008, the SSCs are a key component of four area-based SPAAs (see Chapter 10) that incorporate key agencies from the 'regeneration sector' including health and youth justice organisations. The aim is to bring together key agencies representing sport-specific and educational interests. Links between school sport and regeneration in Liverpool are not new, however. Cardinal Heenan SSC has been at the forefront of alliance building around education and community sport since 2001. This type of relationship emerged in part from ideas embedded in the work of MSP that culminated in the *Merseyside Sports Partnership strategy 2003–08* (MSP, 2003), from where, as of 2004, an area-based 'Sports Alliance' was founded around the specialist sport college. Policy change at the national level stimulated local partnerships between schools and regeneration agencies. In particular, an alliance between sport, education and health is well supported at the local level, at least in respect of three of the four SSCs.

In practice, Cardinal Heenan SSC and others have actively promoted the benefits of sport to regeneration agencies where the influence of key policy brokers can be identified in these developments. The intertwined career histories of key advocates for this relationship, dating back to the Merseyside Youth Games in the 1990s, can be identified. Subsequently, Cardinal Heenan SSC has based its 'development model' on the SAZ model (see Chapter 10). The outcome was a successful partnership between the Eastern Link Regeneration Board and Cardinal Heenan SSC that has driven local policy and practice around sport and regeneration. The pro-active alliance based around Cardinal Heenan SSC has influenced similar alliance building in other areas of the city. Childwall SSC too delivers central government priorities locally through the SSP, SAZ, health sector bodies, regeneration agencies such as Neighbourhood Renewal Managers, and Learning Network Managers inclusive of Higher Education. Reproducing the 'model' across the city has proved problematic, however. To explain the reasons why this was the case, the relationship between alliances of school sport and regeneration agencies, and LCC Sport and Recreation Services, needs to be explored.

ANALYSIS: THE LOCAL CONTEXT

The research underpinning this book revealed the emergence of a policy network or advocacy coalition around education and community regeneration, where sport is an instrument of social policy, in opposition to the core sport-specific priorities of LCC Sport. LCC has been resistant to the 'sport in regeneration' agenda and the new Eastern Link alliance (including one SSC) was initially perceived to be a threat rather than an opportunity.

The coalition consists of a network of like-minded pro-active individuals who are bound by overlapping career histories and overlapping professional interests. It is also evident that this network shares common ideas and values in respect of sport policy rationales. The network may also act as an epistemic community (Haas, 1992), sharing a common policy enterprise and a shared set of normative, principled and causal beliefs.

Further, in the south of the city, the SAZ and Childwall SSC were components of an alliance including regeneration agencies. LCC Sport was not part of the alliance not only on account of differing policy priorities but also given concerns over the capacity of the local authority core team to deliver programmes in this area of policy. Nonetheless, there has been support for school sport from aspects of LCC sport services including some of the SDOs, indicating a fragmented strategy across components of the local authority service area. At the LSF meeting of 28 October 2004, a member stated that he 'would like to see more sharing and integration of resources between local authorities and schools' but this has not emerged to date where priorities, resources and expertise differ. Further, a lack of integration of the new school sport organisational structures with the voluntary sector sport sector is demonstrated in the minutes of the LSF of 23 November 2004, where 'turf wars', 'community use of school sites' and a 'lack of action' were cited as issues.

Within LCC, as one senior officer stated, Education are 'helping everyone to see the significance of partnerships' and the benefits of an area-based approach, but there is recognition that an increasing focus on education rather than leisure within LCC, in delivering the central government sport and PE agenda has 'caused a little bit of tension', adding that 'funding always has an influence on relationships'. Given demands on local schools, leisure/sport budgets have been cut in recent years in favour of increasing resources for education. This policy action coupled Leisure/Sport Services, retaining a focus on specific sports in contrast to Education that has a grassroots and participation focus, has demonstrated that achieving a mutuality of policy objectives across two service areas can prove to be problematic.

Interviewees agreed that it is the value placed on sport by key individuals that has, to some extent, shaped school sport policy in Liverpool. A PE and School Sport PDM stated that 'If Head Teachers believe in school sport, they'll invest in it.' More specifically, the sports interests of male head teachers, in particular, who perhaps have a personal history of active sports participation, are considered to be a key factor in 'getting sport onto the agenda' in schools. A PDM states that 'we are meeting the agendas of Heads … (and) getting support from them … we've gone with what schools want'. Further, there has been little resistance from local head teachers to government policy impacting on sport.

A school valuing and investing in sport can reap financial and status rewards. For example schools that have a history of valuing and supporting sport and PE, where the head teacher was critical, have been the key beneficiaries of funding allocations. A senior officer highlighted how the LEA controlled funding allocations from the NOF. Of note was the skewed bidding process for NOF monies where the steering committee made up of schools and the LEA had the capacity to steer funding towards local vested interests, giving priority to specific schools (usually schools in wealthier areas of the city). However, the status of the school and its attendant degree of autonomy from central government funding was also a factor critical to decision-making processes and policy outcomes. One interviewee identified an 'old boy's network' that steered decision-making towards the status quo. A school in a poorer area of the city was, nonetheless, eventually successful in a major lottery-based funding bid, despite embedded interests, as a result of the skilled brokering of a member of the SAZ, in introducing local councillors into the policy process and co-opting LCC officer support, coupled with the collapse of a rival bid that provided a window of opportunity for the broker to act (see Chapter 10).

In terms of policy implementation, there are a number of issues and challenges facing managers and teachers. First, underpinning these relationships is the funding context, underpinning the changing relationship between LCC Leisure/Sport Services and schools. In the 1980s, the costs associated with schools using LCC facilities rose with the introduction of CCT, and relationships with the education sector were damaged. More recently, government strategy promotes 3-year budgets to facilitate planning for school sport and PE, furthering the autonomy of the schools from pressure from Leisure Services, and with resources for SSPs having been mainstreamed by the DfES, this allows schools to plan for the longer term and be less susceptible to external influence from Local Authorities. Crucially, the funding arrangements within the school sport organisational restructuring under New Labour in effect bypass LCC (Sport), with a PDM stating that 'the government are giving money directly and cutting out local government ... [where there exists] too much red tape'.

A struggle related to funding between schools, the LEA and central government is at the core of tensions around school sport. As one PDM observed, 'Leisure Services always go over budget ... (whereas) schools must match funding.' It was added that the budgetary context impacts on trust between schools and LCC and raises questions of accountability and confidence in the competence in the financial management of LCC. By contrast, SSC policy actions that relate to funding mechanisms and timescales require a high level of pro-activity. Cardinal Heenan SSC has drawn down funding from the Neighbourhood Renewal Fund, Housing Associations, and City Safe amongst others, to support mainstream funding from the DfES. Importantly, this allows a significant degree of autonomy from Leisure/Sport Services. In contrast, as a School Sport Coordinator (SSCo) noted, 'the local authority moves slowly ... as (to LCC) it doesn't really matter'. Moreover, LCC Leisure Services is 'constrained by restrictive practices' and therefore focuses in 'protecting jobs ahead of improving services' as this might lead to job cuts.

Although there has been significant additional resources for school sport in recent years, such as Sporting Playgrounds (18 sites at £20K each), SfSA (£3m) and NOF PE and Sport (£9.2m), it should also be noted that clawback by central government has occurred in some cases, for example with Sporting Playgrounds and SfSA, where delays have occurred due to the problems of finding the match-funding, contractor availability and 'inflated tenders' due to *Capital of Culture* (for an overview of the funding context for sport in Liverpool, see Chapter 4).

Again, with resources come conditions and pressures in policy processes. A PDM noted that 'there is a lot of pressure to deliver a raft of agendas on School Sport Partnerships' where central government apply a 'top-down' approach to policymaking and implementation. Moreover, tensions have increased in the last decade where school sport has received increased central government support. These tensions are most evident within LCC, between Leisure/Sport Services and education, and between Leisure/Sport Services and schools. In brokering these tensions, one policy actor was identified by a PDM as 'visionary and practical enough to gel any tensions between Leisure Services, schools and the voluntary sector'.

However, LCC sport programmes sit uneasily with the school sport and PE agenda under New Labour. For example, the flagship project for Leisure Services, *Sportslinx*, has its roots in schools but is funded through Leisure/Sport Services (although not mainstreamed), created the potential for overlap and duplication of effort. According to interviewees, *Sportslinx* has evolved from a health-related initiative but 'it is not grass-roots development as claimed' by LCC. In fact *Sportslinx* is used as a brand, and it 'gets the profile' LCC seek for the council. In practice, schools are not wholly supportive of the programme as there is limited sustainability built into the initiative. Moreover, with growing autonomy from the local authority, schools can choose not to engage with local authority sport priorities.

Second, the theme of coordination and cooperation across school sport is a recurring one in Liverpool, as elsewhere. A senior officer stated that 'coordination across agendas is needed' with strategies needing to be 'merged' as there exists a lack of understanding of 'who does what' in an increasingly fragmented policy area. Interviewees noted that there are too many groups;

organisations do not always have a regional body; formal relations are lacking between some organisations and no single organisation possesses an overview of the existing structures. In sum, as one officer observed, 'Thematic working in schools ... has a long way to go.' Moreover, a school head noted that competing interests 'compromise high-quality PE and sport', identifying four clusters of interests, namely sport-specific interests, educational interests (the 'PE lobby'), health education and promotion linked to sport, and sports development.

In terms of partnerships, a relationship that is shaping local school sport policy is between primary and secondary education in Liverpool. A PDM stated that 'Engaging primary schools is the key' but there are difficulties in integration between primary and secondary school sport. A head teacher observed that 'secondary schools are not wholly supporting extra-curricular primary activities ... within the SSCo programme framework.' Secondary schools assume a lack of expertise at primary level, and a further tension is found in primary support of extra-curricular sport being voluntary, whereas secondary support is paid employment. Hence, third, retaining voluntary support for extra-curricular sport-related activities, where it exists, has been problematic in the city. For example, *Excellence in Cities* funding has recently ended in the city and that this had paid teachers to 'volunteer' for extra-curricular sport, including the running of Summer Camps, that many schools now no longer organise. A head teacher noted that 'the extra-curricular picture is varied' ... (it is a) 'mixed economy of voluntary and paid work' and this creates tensions. Fourth, cutting across the possibilities for effective coordination and cooperation is the difference between the statutory status of education including PE in the NCPE and the non-statutory status of Leisure/Sport Services within the local authority. Fifth, the culture of organisations as reflected in the working practices of local authorities and schools can serve to undermine partnership-working. Sixth, and critically, LCC has a strong tradition of localism or resistance to central government policy, and the funding directed at schools for sport-related objectives has served to amplify tensions between SSCs and LCC Sport in particular. One school representative noted that LCC Sport 'say we have to follow the same regime as theirs', citing 'demarcation' as a key issue in the local sport policy area. Further, a PDM, in respect of the recent re-structuring of school sport, stated that LCC Sport 'haven't liked this way of working'.

Finally, there are difficulties in the local school sport policy area of balancing the relationship between the requirements of the NCPE and the availability, and usage by the community and clubs of school facilities. A head teacher noted that the *Building Schools for the Future* programme (DfES, 2005b) will impact on clubs and the usage of school site facilities and this will be an issue, adding that 'clubs are not fully aware of (its) impact'. The demise of school-club competition in the city, where, as of 2005, only two schools take part, has resulted to a large extent from resistance from schools, and the revival of school-club links in extra-curricular settings, particularly in respect of competition, may take time to re-emerge. However, Cardinal Heenan SSC has been successful in forming partnerships with local clubs within walking distance of the school across a range of sports, but this 'model' may prove difficult to replicate in areas of the city with fewer clubs. A former head teacher observed that schools were not purpose-built to account for dual-use with the community and the balance of school to community use remains problematic, stating that some schools remain resistant to community usage of the site. It is anticipated that the *Building Schools for the Future* programme will result in fewer schools in the city and an increasing role for the private sector, which will introduce another dynamic into a complex, crowded and fragmented policy area.

CONCLUSIONS

In sum, the school sport policy area can be characterised by persistent historical struggles that relate to the core beliefs of policy actors and competition for recognition, autonomy and scarce resources. Despite national policy change impacting on the local re-organisation and delivery of school sport, it is not until the last decade that central government can be said to be gaining any control over local authorities, schools and interest groups, who for their own part, welcome new resources but not the conditions associated with acquiring them.

At the centre of local policy and practices are the recently established SSPs within which the SSCs have acquired significant influence over sport and PE. Subsequently, the influence of LCC Leisure/Sport Services in school sport has diminished largely as a result of the local authority's performance-related sport priorities that are in direct opposition to a local advocacy coalition including SSCs and community regeneration agencies that value and prioritise sport within a social policy framework. However, as Houlihan (1997) found, a 'coalition' may only exist at a high level of generality and, in practice, coalitions can be far less cohesive at the level of detailed policy, given tensions within the network, between teachers, coaches and health promoters.

Houlihan (1997: 269) concludes that school sport issues are often submerged by other political priorities, where 'school sport interests ... operate within policy contexts not of their own choosing and over which they had little influence'. In the case of school sport policy in Liverpool, the emergence of the 'development through sport' agenda (Houlihan and White, 2002), and the focus on talent identification and development in school sport (Green, 2004a) have both impacted on sport policy over time.

What is clear is that the role of voluntary sector sport bodies in secondary schools has diminished as public sector professionals shape the future of school sport. A former chair of the voluntary body, the Liverpool Teachers Association, states that 'with the introduction of PDMs, SSCos, LCC School Sport and PE Advisors, and others ... there are now more managers, but not enough teachers' to delivering sport and PE. Further, interviewees noted that some NGBs are pro-active in developing school sport within the new organisational framework, citing rugby union, tennis, basketball, netball and athletics locally, but interviewees agreed that LCC provides very little support at the school/community level. In practice, schools need sports advocates who can offer a continuity of service over time for voluntary sector inclusion to become entrenched in the culture of a school. Recently, schools have not taken up offers from local voluntary bodies representing badminton and sailing, as few advocates remain.

CHAPTER 8

Sport, Physical Activity and Health Policy

Contents

INTRODUCTION

This chapter will explore the evolving relationship between both sport and health policy at the national and local levels. The chapter provides an evaluation of the influences shaping policy, the funding context, relationships between key policy actors and the capacity of the local infrastructure to facilitate effective policy implementation.

Sport Policy and Governance: Local Perspectives
Copyright © 2009, Dr. Neil King. Published by Elsevier Ltd. All rights reserved.

Before assessing policy processes in Liverpool, this chapter will review, in brief, policy change in the health sector in England with a focus on pre-care intervention and health promotion (Adams, Amos and Munro 2002; Ham, 2000, 2004; Klein, 2000, 2003; Oliver and Exworthy, 2003; Tones and Tilford, 2001) in the period 1997–2008. However, contemporary policy is located in a historical context by examining the Conservative admin-istrations of 1979–1997 and a period in the early–mid 1970s when both health and sport were treated as components of the welfare state. Parallels are drawn with sport policy priorities during these periods (Green, 2004a; Green and Houlihan, 2005a; Henry, 2001; Houlihan, 1997; Houlihan and White, 2002), highlighting the policy spaces where health and sport inter-ests overlap, as briefly outlined by Robson (2001) and Robson and McKenna (2008). Further, an account is constructed of the emerging relationship between the sport and health policy areas from a review of central and local government policy statements and strategy documents, due to the paucity of published research that accounts for the overlap between these policy areas. This chapter also draws on interviews conducted with senior person-nel in both the sport and health policy areas and those working across the policy areas.

THE EVOLUTION OF THE RELATIONSHIP BETWEEN SPORT AND HEALTH POLICY

Although a contested concept, health policy can be viewed as a philosophy of intervention intended to protect and promote the health of the general population (Webster and French, 2002). Participation in physical activity including sport has long been associated with health and fitness improve-ments, and health policy closely linked with leisure and recreation. The Wolfenden Report (1960), for example, cites legislation for public health that encourages local authorities to provide spaces and facilities for sport and recreation. Subsequent sport policy statements refer to health-related objec-tives (DoE, 1975; DCMS, 2000; DNH, 1995); however, it is only recently that the policy processes for health and sport have been intertwined as a result of the current central government focus on policy objectives around young people and obesity in the context of the rising costs associated with ser-vicing the National Health Service (NHS). In this respect, *Game Plan* (DCMS, 2002) was the first sport policy document to explicitly highlight how sport and physical activity contribute to public health policy.

A review of health policy processes and change (as undertaken, for example, by Ham, 2004) reveals striking parallels with sport policy as a component of the welfare state. The two sectors share common characteristics and common problems, such as ideological divides, fragmented organisation and increasing government intervention. Ham (2000, 2004) highlights how bargaining and negotiation between interests have characterised the sector and provides a neo-pluralist account of the policy process, a perspective shared by authors in the sport policy field (e.g. Houlihan, 1997; Houlihan and White, 2002). Nonetheless, there are some key differences between the sectors that may both facilitate and constrain policymaking and implementation. For example, it can be argued that a distinct policy area characterised by relatively coherent and embedded structures and processes has evolved around health interests. By contrast, 'sport' has been at best a series of overlapping interests in an ill-defined policy area apart from an emerging policy community around elite sport (Houlihan and White, 2002). The two policy sectors have recently engaged where (community) sport development relates to health promotion (Robson, 2001, provides examples).

However, both sets of interests have been relatively marginal within wider sectoral interests, where elite sport development has dominated the sport sector, and post-care focused interventions, institutions and professionals have dominated the health sector as opposed to pre-care interests such as health promotion. The two sectors have experienced intervention by successive governments that have utilised similar policy instruments to effect the desired policy change, most notably combining the use of conditional funding arrangements and organisational re-structuring. More specifically, in the last decade, key government actions in both sectors have included the introduction of cross-sector partnerships incentivised by new funding streams. The establishment of area-based initiatives such as HAZs and SAZs has been an aspect of this approach to governance.

This chapter will now outline the evolution of public health policy where it intersects with policy for sport and physical activity across three time periods: the early to mid-1970s, 1979–1997 and 1997–2008.

Sport and health policy: pre-1979

The dominance of specific political ideologies at particular times can be seen to have impact on both sport and health policy. For example, the *Health for All* (HfA) policy initiative that originated in the 1970s via the World Health Organization (WHO) is replicated in the SfA emphasis in the European Charter for Sport [Council of Europe (COE), 1976] and reflected in much of the work of the Sports Council in England at that time. These movements, arguably one and the same, are founded on progressive values of social justice, equity and participation for all.

However, there has arguably only been moderate engagement in practice with HfA by successive governments and the same claim can be made for *Sport for All* policy (Lentell, 1993; McDonald, 1995). In part, major funding pressures led central government to seek radical alternatives to the growing cost of funding the welfare state where the ever-expanding NHS was a key component (Ham, 2004). The economic crisis of 1973 is viewed as a watershed event for the welfare state and, in the era of 'retrenchment' that followed, this impacted severely on policy aspirations in the leisure and sport sectors (Henry and Bramham, 1993). With the end of the expansion of public services and expenditure came the end of the corporatist style of politics that characterised the post-war consensus (Greenleaf, 1983), where the subsequent controls of public spending resulted in the overt conflict between central and local governments (Stoker, 1991; Wilson and Game, 2006), most notably in Liverpool in the mid-1980s (see Chapter 4).

It was not until the late 1970s, however, that government first issued policy statements that stressed health prevention rather than focusing on curative health, such as *Prevention and Health: Everybody's Business* (DHSS, 1976). Despite government intervention, this shift in policy emphasis did not impact on health practice due in part to embedded interests resisting change (see Webster, 1996: 660–686). However, policy style and ideology changed significantly with the election of a 'New Right' Conservative administration in 1979, where egalitarian and re-distributive principles began to be challenged as the economic costs of universal provision have grown (Webster and French, 2002). The health promotion movement is less about equity of provision and more concerned with empowering citizens so that they can 'take control' of their health. In other words, the focus in health promotion is on the individual, not on 'society'. Moreover, as Bunton (1992: 6) states, health promotion 'deliberately tried to address issues of power, political, economic and social structures and processes'.

Another key policy tension that surfaced in the 1970s relates to the conflict between medically dominated conceptions of health, defined as the biomedical model, and the social model preferred by those seeking to reduce health inequalities (Pascal, 2003). The economic crisis of the late 1970s prompted concerns about poverty and public health, leading to a policy focus on 'social medicine' with its priority of tackling poverty and health inequalities. The social model eventually found expression in the *Black Report* (DHSS, 1980). However, the report was sidelined by the incoming Conservative administration in 1979 because of the report's emphasis on reducing health inequalities through increasing government expenditure on health. An unintended consequence of its 'suppression' was an enormous growth of research into health inequalities which later re-surfaced as policy under New Labour (Berridge, 2003).

Conservative administrations: 1979–1997

The political values of successive Conservative governments (1979–1997) were explicitly opposed to the values underpinning HfA and SfA. Subsequently, HfA gained little ground within statutory, professional and voluntary sectors of health care during this era. Nonetheless, grass-roots support for HfA in England remained, invigorated at the international level by the *Ottawa Charter* and by the formation of the UK Health for All Network (UKHFAN) in 1988. This followed the founding of the UK Public Health Association (UKPHA) in 1987 which is informed by HfA values. In practice, however, as Ham (2004) notes, the HfA initiatives struggled to influence health policy and practice. He cites Glasgow and Sheffield as examples of cities where 'hostile national policy environment' cut across project objectives and implementation at the local level. In contrast to the HfA focus, the 'New Right' Conservative governments placed an increasing policy emphasis on individual lifestyle, where physical activity featured as an element of preventative health programmes rather than attempting to reduce health inequalities specifically.

In terms of the organisation of health, the Conservative government placed little faith in local authorities to deliver its policy priorities and therefore created quangos to address public health problems. Further, the 'New Right' introduced market principles into health with the creation of the internal market in the NHS in 1991, as reflected in the White Paper *Working for Patients, and the NHS* (DH, 1989) and the *Community Care Act* (DH, 1990), producing a radical change in the management of health services. Within this context, in respect of the focus of this study, the key health policy in this era was *The Health of the Nation* (DH, 1992) that represented the first national public health strategy. This White Paper made connections between physical activity, preventative health and individual lifestyle, although it has been critiqued as neglecting social understandings of health (Adams, Amos and Munro 2002). Parallel to these developments, under John Major's leadership, *Sport: Raising the Game* (DNH, 1995) makes reference to the connections between sport and health in stating that schools should encourage young people to 'appreciate the long-term benefits of regular exercise and (be) able to make informed decisions about adopting a healthy and active lifestyle in future years' (DNH, 1995: 6). Further, the NCPE encourages PE teachers to develop health-related exercise at Key Stage 4, and it encourages young people to adopt 'active lifestyles'.

According to Robson (2001), partnerships between 'exercise' promotion and sport emerged in the early 1990s, when the benefits of a syndicate approach to health promotion was first recognised in government policy following the Allied Dunbar National Fitness Survey (Sports Council and the Health Education Authority, 1992), that highlighted the need for greater cooperation between agencies with a remit for public health. Thereafter, a Physical Activity Task Force (PATF) was created in 1993, consisting of representatives from the medical profession, Health Education Authority (HEA) and Higher Education, with a remit to 'develop a strategy for the wider promotion of physical activity, and to design a "prescription" for health gain for the whole community through increased participation' (Robson, 2001: 137). The PATF recommended moderate level physical activity, relative to the individual, five times per week; a change from its original recommendation of the traditional health prescription of 20 minutes vigorous aerobic exercise three times per week. The original emphasis on sport-based activity is by implication replaced by a greater emphasis on 'physical activity' in which sport is the only component. The 'active lifestyles'' focus took further shape in the form of the *Active for Life* campaign (HEA, 1998) that ran from 1996 to 1999 with the aim of raising awareness and highlighting the benefits of physical activity, including sport. In achieving this end, the HEA sought to work directly with practitioners 'on the front line' of service delivery, including the health care professions, leis-ure management within local government provision and voluntary sector organisations.

The latter years of the Conservative period in office can therefore be viewed as important in raising the profile of the relationship between health policy and sport policy, although 'sport' is primarily treated as a component of generic physical activity.

New Labour: 1997–2008

New Labour's approach to health policy and practice is underpinned by the politics of the 'third way' (see Giddens, 1998). An example of the 'third way' is found in the White Paper *A New NHS* (DH, 1997), the aims of which were to improve simultaneously the health of the population as a whole *and* improve the health of the most disadvantaged sections of society, in order to narrow the 'health gap' perceived to have resulted from market forces under the prior 'centre-right' administrations. The focus on creating healthy individual lifestyles including exercise promotion was therefore retained, but the 'old' Labour focus on health inequalities returned to the policy agenda. This mirrored the 'third way' approach utilised in sport policy, where sport is a component of social policy, on the one hand (Collins and Kay, 2003), but also is a tool for elite sporting success, on the other hand (Green and Houlihan, 2005a). DH (1998) (cited in Naidoo and Wills, 2000: 191) identify the central principles and strategies of New Labour-led public health policy as: the rationalisation of services; the importance of education and evidence-based research; partnership-working; and public consultation. In sum, 'Action to improve health and to reduce health inequalities requires joined up working across Government and across sectors at national, regional and local levels' (DH, 2001: 17). These developments mirror the key themes underpinning New Labour's recent approach to sport policy and governance (see Chapter 3).

In practice, New Labour became the first government to assert that 'health' was a cross-cutting issue rather than the concern of a single department within central or local government, or wholly the concern of the NHS. The way ahead was set out in *The New NHS* (DH, 1997) where, in terms of organisation and delivery, PCTs would take greater responsibility for public health including health promotion. PCTs are intended to provide a 'third way' between 'old' Labour's top-down management style and the 'New Right's' fragmentation of the internal market, to produce 'integrated care, based on partnership' (DH, 1997: 5). Arguably, this organisational re-structuring acted as a catalyst for sport and leisure services in local government to engage with health policy as it facilitated access to health sector funding streams that could be used to strengthen the infrastructure for sport, which is seen by Sport England North-West (SENW, 2004) and other key organisations with an influence on sport and health in Liverpool, such as the MSP (2006), as a pre-condition for delivering health outcomes through sport and physical activity.

Further, the *Health Act 1999* placed a duty on health authorities to work in partnership with local authorities in producing local health improvement plans and programmes, re-invigorating the corporate approach to health (as has occurred in Liverpool). However, the 'location' of physical activity and its advocates within the policy process for health took time to evolve, as new decision-making processes developed within local government services and in multi-agency partnerships. More specifically, emerging links between sport and health followed a series of progress reports based on *The Health of the Nation* objectives that focused on 27 target areas across the UK, the 17th of which was published after the election of New Labour in May 1997, in which concern is expressed over rising public health problems such as coronary heart disease (CHD), where the links between CHD and physical activity are well documented (BHF, 2000; DH, 2000).

The theme of cross-sector partnership-working also evolved out of the *Health Survey for England* (DH, 1998) that subsequently informed the Government's Green Paper *Saving Lives: Our Healthier Nation* (DH, 1999a). The document sets out an agenda to tackle health inequalities based on the *Acheson Report* (Acheson, 1998) that recognises that health is influenced by factors exogenous to the individual. Specifically, the report examined the determinants of health using the 'layers of influence' model, first proposed by Dahlgren and Whitehead (1991). The three layers are 'individual lifestyle factors', emphasised by the 'New Right'; 'social and community relations', a focus of New Labour; and 'general socio-economic, cultural and environmental conditions', a traditional focus of 'the left'. It can be noted that, in contrast to the *Black Report* (DHSS, 1980), the Acheson Report was published in a favourable policy climate (Exworthy, 2003). The Acheson Report (1998) also recommended the further development of 'health promoting schools' with a particular focus on schools in areas of socio-economic disadvantage.

Although these key health policy documents make scant reference to the potential contribution of physical activity and sport within health promotion, these structural changes arguably facilitated the opportunity for sport interests to engage with the health sector. Robson (2001) observed that the relative absence of physical activity, and less so sport, in the emerging health agenda, in the period prior to 1999, needs to be understood in the context of 'sport' itself emerging as a distinct policy area with the establishment of the DCMS, the re-organisation of Sport England and the representation of 'sport' as a 'good cause' in National Lottery funding priorities (for a summary of these changes, see Green, 2004a).

Critically, it was the White Paper *Saving Lives: Our Healthier Nation* (DH, 1999a) that shifted the emphasis from post-care to pre-care health interventions based on prevention and the early detection of ill health and thus potentially strengthened the influence of the 'sports lobby'. Further, with a growing focus on young people, PE and school sport moved towards the centre stage. In addition, the growing focus on 'disadvantaged communities' which led to area-based initiatives such as HAZs was borrowed by the DCMS in creating SAZs with their priorities of 'development through sport' rather than 'development of sport' (Houlihan and White, 2002). HAZs were established to act as a framework for the NHS, local authorities and other partners to work together to achieve progress in addressing the causes of ill health and reducing health inequalities (DH, 1998). One such zone covered the whole of Merseyside on account of the county's poor health profile (see case study to follow). Within the same set of principles, a SAZ was subsequently designated for an area of Liverpool (see Chapter 10).

A focus of HAZs has been on health promotion in schools, hence the introduction, also in 1998, of the *Healthy Schools* initiative. *Healthy Schools* is characterised by the familiar New Labour themes of governance, including a preference for multi-agency working, the identification and dissemination of good practice or 'what works', with government agencies acting as facilitators, and funding providers and local partnerships given flexibility in policy implementation based on 'local factors'. A Healthy Schools Conference followed in 1999, in which a joint DH/DfEE (now DfES) national *Healthy School Standard* was launched, with schools defined as 'springboards to future long-term health' (see DH, 1999a). Specifically, in terms of the physical activity component of the initiative, the standard includes meeting the NCPE minimum hours recommendation (2 hours per week at the time), promotion of extra-curricular sports activities, liaison with external agencies in the health sector, and work towards nationally recognised awards for health-related physical activity. By 2000, with a relationship between sport and health emerging, 50 primary school/primary care *Health Links* projects had been established in England as part of the *Healthy Schools* programme, with the aim of educating teachers on health issues including the role of exercise/physical activity (cf. Cale, 2000).

Parallel to these developments, a report on physical activity and health was produced entitled *Young and Active?* (HEA, 1998). The report recommended 1 hour of physical activity per day per child and allocates specific roles for schools, youth groups and health services. Reference too can be made to the emerging *Specialist Sports College* network, where out-of-hours activities link sport and physical activity with health objectives (see Chapter 7). Further, the emerging focus on the role of physical activity in health promotion features as an element of building social inclusion, most apparent in the PAT10 report on *Sport, the Arts and Social Inclusion* (DCMS, 1999) where health promotion is viewed as an area that can contribute to neighbourhood renewal (for an analysis of sport's role in tackling social exclusion, see Coalter, 2007, and Collins and Kay, 2003).

By 2001, the increasing willingness of the DH to engage with sport/physical activity agencies in preventative health programmes developed new impetus due to the highly publicised issue of obesity, particularly among children and young people. This followed on in part from *The Health Survey for England* (DH, 1999b) that indicated dramatic increases in obesity in the period 1993–1997. Further, the *Health Survey for England* identified a steadily increasing level of obesity over the decade 1991–2001, with a significant 50% rise in levels over the time span. In 2000, the British Heart Foundation report *Couch Kids – the Growing Epidemic* (BHF, 2000) further re-enforced central government thinking on poor diet and obesity among young people, and reiterated the findings of the DH and Food Standards Agency survey of 4–18 year olds, which identified high levels of inactivity (DH, 2000).

Rowe, Adams and Beasley (2004) note that without significant public policy intervention to counteract these trends, and without policy learning from 'the American experience', obesity levels will exceed those of the USA by 2020 (cf. Dietz, 2001). Research findings on obesity were subsequently included in *The NHS Plan* that sets a key target to reduce health inequalities, particularly in terms of life expectancy, which is determined to some extent by CHD, cancer and obesity. Again, a role for sport within the framework of 'physical activity' gains momentum as a partial solution to a policy concern. Moreover, in 2000, government planned to extend *exercise on prescription* or 'exercise referral' initiatives across England. New guidelines encouraged GPs, local authorities and health professionals to establish schemes working with local authorities to increase physical activity and reduce obesity (DH, 2000). Chris Smith, DCMS Secretary of State at the time, stated, 'This guidance will help to make sure that exercise referral programmes are focused on people who do not normally take part in sport or (physical) activity' (DH, 2001: 2).

However, policy implementation has been slow, where by the year 2000, only 200 medical practices in England offered exercise on prescription. Moreover, as of March 2001, the Health Select Committee on Public Health reported that only 11% of GPs recognised physical activity recommendations. Also, during 2001, the CCPR surveyed all 104 Health Authorities in England and Wales on the physical activity content of their Health Improvement strategies. The findings demonstrate that few authorities cited how sport and recreation is utilised to increase physical activity levels and health. However, approximately half of the strategies did include an exercise referral element of health care (CCPR, 2003).

Nonetheless, new partnerships were emerging that added impetus to the sport–health policy relationship, such as with the Fitness Industry Association (FIA) whose chair stated, 'Exercise Referral schemes provide great opportunities for fitness professionals to work in partnership with health professionals on schemes that target people who do not normally take exercise. These can make a real contribution to public health' (DH, 2001: 2). Further, by April 2001, Health Authorities were required to create plans for physical activity promotion within *Health Improvement Plans* (HIPs) in line with National Service Framework (NSVF) objectives for CHD. However, these plans were delayed following the abolition of the majority of the Health Authorities and the transfer of work of health promotion teams to PCTs, as was the case in Liverpool in 2002.

Perhaps the key structural change, however, in shaping the role of physical activity and sport in health promotion was central government's cross-cutting spending review that introduced thematic working practices between central government departments. A cross-government delivery plan was followed in late 2002 (see Nutbeam, 2003, for further details). This review followed the paper *Tackling Health Inequalities: Consultation on a Plan for*

Delivery (DH, 2002) that recommended the cross-cutting approach and an overhaul of the spending mechanisms that tended to produce departmentalism and inhibit longer-term strategic thinking. These recommendations were in line with the Wanless review of long-term resource requirements for the NHS (Wanless, 2002) in which the cost implications of not adopting a preventative health care strategy were highlighted and the potential contribution of physical activity noted. The report stated that 'lifestyle changes such as ... increased physical activity ... could have a major impact on the required level of health care resources' (Wanless, 2002: 23). Moreover, at the same time, *Game Plan* (DCMS, 2002) argues that cross-cutting funding reviews present an opportunity to extend inclusion of sport/physical activity in the public health agenda. The *Game Plan* (DCMS, 2002: 48) concludes, 'The implication for government is that health policy objectives can be met by interventions aimed at increasing physical activity.'

Also in respect of re-structuring, horizontal coordination between government departments was improved with a partnership of the DH, DCMS and DfES, established in 2002, that underpins a £2.5m programme of community-based pilot schemes to provide free swimming in 'low-income areas'. This scheme forms part of the Local Exercise Action Pilots (LEAPs), locally run programmes that aim to evaluate new methods for increasing physical activity led by PCTs, which integrate LEAPs with existing initiatives including Sure Start, Exercise Referral schemes, Healthy Schools, SAZs, School Sports Co-ordinator Partnerships and Walking the way to Health.

To further coordinate health and sport policy and practice, where sport is an aspect of social policy, an Activity Coordination Team (ACT) was founded in 2003 to lead the development of a national Delivery Plan for physical activity and sport. ACT includes representation from 11 government bodies including DCMS, DH, DfES, Sport England, the LGA, Health Development Agency (HDA) and the Treasury. ACT committee members also included the Minister for Sport, Chief Executive of Sport England and Director of Sport within the DCMS, indicating the increasing political salience of sport's role in the 'health crisis'. Notably, the Minister for Sport co-chaired the ACT with the parliamentary under-secretary of state for Health. The significance of this structural change is in the fact that ACT both deploys existing funding through the LEAPs, SAZs and NOF board for PE and sport, and steers delivery. In effect, central government has become directly involved at all levels of the policy process from funding deployment to coordinating a network of programmes, to evaluating strategy and disseminating results of national, regional and local projects.

Although 'joined-up thinking' has therefore gathered momentum in recent years, departmentalism has arguably proven difficult to move in practice.

For example, the ACT members must report to ministers within separate government departments where policy is formulated, not within the ACT framework. Minutes from ACT meetings in 2003 reveal a number of difficulties in allocating lead and joint roles and responsibilities, extending membership to other departments believed to have a role in tackling health through physical activity (e.g. the former ODPM), including the voice of the LGA to represent local authority interests, delays, inconsistent member attendance, absence of research evidence on which to make decisions, and related problems of central–central partnership-working (ACT, 2003a, b). These tensions within the ACT have arguably constrained the full engagement of the sport sector with the health sector and with consequences for policymaking and implementation where the two sectors relate.

Following these efforts at policy harmonisation, in February 2004, the *Wanless Report* entitled *Securing Good Health for the Whole Population* (Wanless, 2004) identified the key challenges facing public health up to the year 2020. The findings were fed into the *White Paper on Public Health* (DH, 2004c). Of significance for sport policy is an increasing emphasis on prevention, particularly as related to obesity and developing 'healthy lifestyles'. The White Paper provided the overarching framework to link the many initiatives in the area and to allocate responsibilities to specific organisations in health and sport. Also in 2004, the Health Secretary launched a national consultation on public health, resulting in the two documents, one of which is entitled *Choosing Health? Choosing Activity* (DH, 2005a), where encouraging more physical activity in schools is seen as central to successful policy implementation, and in this regard the *PESSCL* strategy (DfES, 2003, 2004) is identified as being at the heart of the sport/health agenda, where a 'culture of participation' in physical activity is sought. *Choosing Health* was followed by *Choosing Activity: A Physical Activity Action Plan* (DH, 2005b), defined by the MSP (2006: 6) as 'the first truly cross government plan to coordinate action aimed at increasing levels of physical activity across the whole population'. Further, the increasing focus on young people's health and physical activity including sport, particularly in schools, is also found in the key education policy statement *Every Child Matters* (DfES, 2005a).

In the light of these recent developments, a consensus appears to be emerging between the health and sport sectors with statements made in the *Game Plan* (DCMS, 2002), mirroring that in the Chief Medical Officer's report on physical activity and health *At Least Five a Week* (DH, 2004d), that emphasised building 'moderate physical activity' into daily life, or 30 minutes per day of exercise of 'moderate intensity' on 5 or more days per week (reminiscent of the PATF recommendations in the Conservative era). However, young people are expected to achieve double this recommendation.

Importantly, the report is aimed at those formulating and implementing policies and programmes to utilise physical activity, sport and exercise to achieve a health gain including public health organisations such as PCTs.

ANALYSIS: THE NATIONAL CONTEXT

In sum, with the election of New Labour in 1997 came policy change that has led to a more substantive relationship being established between sport and health. *Saving Lives: Our Healthier Nation* (DH, 1999a) represents, in part, a shift from New Right policy priorities to a social reformist agenda to tackle health inequalities, where poor health is viewed as an outcome of a combination of structural inequalities including social, economic and environmental factors, or social exclusion. Importantly, as Robson (2001: 139) states, 'Health was no longer seen as a private domain where individuals were free to make lifestyle choices, but rather as a collective issue where citizens had rights to health care, guaranteed by strong government action and funding.'

Current government policy therefore attempts to strike 'a new balance ... a third way ... linking individual and wider action (DH, 1999a). As Pascall (2003: 397) concludes, 'The emphasis on individuals improving their own health remains, but governments now acknowledge the difficulties arising from poverty ... as well as the link between health inequality and social inequality.' The HfA ethos is therefore retained in New Labour policy, with *Health 21*, an aspect of *Agenda 21*, the latest incarnation of HfA, sharing its core values and beliefs, but with a greater emphasis on policy implementation founded on evidence-based research data or 'what works'. However, implementing policies to tackle poor health at the local level has proved problematic (Evans, 2003; Hunter, 1983).

Rowe, Adams and Beasley (2004: 26) argue that the achievement of social and behavioural change required for health gains to materialise 'requires a step change in the attitude of the Department of Health and public health providers at regional and local level'. The authors state that Sport cannot achieve these outcomes on its own, and it is 'Health' that must place physical activity (including sport) higher on its list of priorities and back up its commitment with 'real resources'. The new ACT is viewed as critical in raising the profile of physical activity and sport across government and particularly within the DH. Notably, Rowe, Adams and Beasley (2004: 19) state, 'It is important for Sport England to keep its unique identity as the leading sports development agency whilst still being seen to be a key player in the physical activity and health agenda.' The authors add that 'Sport must grasp this opportunity by having its case well prepared and by being able to demonstrate with evidence that it is ready to respond to the challenge and that it is capable of delivering the required outcomes' (Rowe, Adams and Beasley 2004: 26).

The difficulty, however, appears to be in convincing sport/recreation departments within local authorities and the voluntary sector to take up this challenge, given their own embedded set of interests. The DCMS recognises that 'it is increased physical activity ... as much as participation in competitive team sports alone, which delivers improved health benefits to a wider range of individuals' (DCMS, 2002: 52) and therefore sport-based interests are to an extent excluded from policy discourse. Nonetheless, at the national level, the CCPR, representing the voluntary sector, produced a policy statement *Saving Lives, Saving Money: Physical Activity – the Best Buy in Public Health* (CCPR, 2003). Its recommendations included a cross-departmental strategy for joined-up funding and action; a promotional campaign for GPs highlighting the health benefits of physical activity; and guidelines for partnership-working between PCTs and sports providers. In sum, the CCPR asserts that government should increase investment in sport and recreation, arguing that a small shift in the health budget would 'create a step change in sports provision and health promotion', and further, 'The Government needs to ensure that sport is funded through the budgets for health, education, social inclusion and crime reduction – a simplified cross departmental funding source' to replace the fragmented system of financing as currently exists (CCPR, 2000: 7).

In these respects, the CCPR is very much 'on message' with central government objectives, indicating a willingness of 'sport' (or at least the CCPR) to engage with the health agenda, perhaps for instrumental reasons of its own, such as recognition, legitimacy, funding acquisition and organisational survival. In contrast, other sports bodies may view these changes as counterproductive for sport-specific interests and perceive a reduction in autonomy from government interests and interventions. Robson (2001) notes that many organisations used the *Active for Life* campaign to promote their own specific activities including sport, although the campaign was far from sport specific.

In regard to local authorities, *Game Plan* (DCMS, 2002) argues that sport/recreation departments should offer a wide variety of accessible opportunities and active recreation for health purposes. Given the potential for non-cooperation, Robson (2001: 133–134) stated that there has been an emergence of 'healthy alliances' in some areas of the UK, observing, 'From a position of suspicion several years ago, healthcare professionals have developed an appreciation of the advantages of working with partners outside the health service, often including local authority sports development officers.' Robson (2001: 137) argues that 'For perhaps the first time, operational (sport-based) staff would have the political tool with which to persuade senior managers less sympathetic to the cause.' He also observes how sports development professionals seized the opportunity to draw the attention of those working at a strategic level in the health care services and who had access to financial power and responsibility for purchasing services to their work.

The next section of this chapter focuses on policy and practice where sport and health policy co-exist in Liverpool. First, a health profile of the city is documented; second, the evolution of the emerging relationship between sport and health is outlined and third, an analysis of the policy process is undertaken to underpin an explanation of policy in Chapter 12. The analysis was founded on document analysis and interviews were undertaken in the period 2005–2008 with personnel across both policy areas.

SPORT, PHYSICAL ACTIVITY AND HEALTH POLICY IN LIVERPOOL

Introduction

In the NW region, 45% of the population live in wards that fall within the top 20% of the most-deprived wards in the country, and six of the top ten most-deprived wards in the country are also in the NW region (National Statistics Online: Census data, 2001). One key element of social deprivation is poor health, in regard to which the North-West NHS region has the lowest life expectancy for both men and women of any region of England; 21% of the population experience long-term illness; and the region has the highest standard mortality ratio for CHD (Cavill 2005; Stratton, Dugdill and Porcellato 2005). SENW add that 70% of the population do not take enough exercise to benefit their health, and only 32.8% of the adult population in the NW undertakes 30 minutes of 'moderate physical activity' on five occasions per week, and this may not include 'sport' at all (SENW, 2004). Further, research in Liverpool found that 50% of boys and 40% of girls at 11 years of age are overweight, with 5% of all children surveyed classified as clinically obese (*Sportslinx* survey; LCC, 2000a). The LCC sport policy statement *On the Right Track* (LCC, 1997) cites research by Liverpool JMU that reveals relatively low levels of physical activity in Liverpool's primary schools, claiming a likely 'health time bomb'. A decade later, this statement has not proved to be an exaggeration.

In this context, sports and health bodies in the NW region, the Merseyside area and Liverpool specifically, face difficult challenges if the

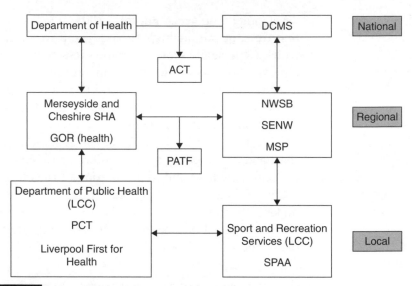

FIGURE 8.1 *Sport and health: the organisational infrastructure.*

health targets set out in *Game Plan* (DCMS, 2002) and those for the NHS (Audit Commission, 2003) are to be realised. The targets also need to be placed in the context that by 2020, 50% of the NW population will be aged 50 or over (SENW, 2004). Of note is that SENW accept that the *Game Plan* targets are 'unrealistic', and the *Regional Plan for Sport* (SENW, 2004) therefore sets a more modest target of 50% participation in 'moderate physical activity' in the region by 2020. The organisational and funding structures for sport and health in the NW and Liverpool are complex where policy areas overlap. However, a basic representation of the policy area can be constructed (*Figure 8.1*).

As this diagram indicates, a synergy exists between the national, regional and local levels of policymaking. The key bodies that create a partnership between the sectors are therefore the ACT in central government; the North-West PATF at the regional and county levels; and at the local level, a strategic document, *Active City* (LCC, 2005), is intended to bring together the various existing physical activity-based health programmes such as Healthy Schools, Sportslinx and GP Referral schemes under one umbrella. The recently established SPAAs coordinate policy implementation.

THE EVOLUTION OF SPORT AND HEALTH POLICY

Links between sport and health bodies in Liverpool are not new. In fact, a *Health and Recreation Team* was set up in 1984 that attempted to forge links with health and exercise promotion through the Regional Health Authority at the time in one of the national demonstration projects (Sports Council and the Health Education Authority, 1992). However, this and subsequent experimental initiatives failed to acquire systemic embeddedness in Liverpool. Interviewees consulted in undertaking this study stated that many initiatives around low physical activity and poor health generated a temporary interest among health professionals, particularly during periods of 'crisis' during the 1980s and 1990s, but programmes proved to be unsustainable.

As of 2006, the newly formed North-West Sports Board (NWSB) was set to lead on cross-cutting issues including sport's contribution to health, in line with DCMS priorities. The NWSB had significant representation from the health sector, including the Regional Director of Public Health in the Government Office for the North-West (GONW), and the Director of Public Health for Cumbria and Lancashire Strategic Health Authority. The NWSB produced a *Regional Delivery Plan for Sport* (NWSB, 2004) with seven overarching 'themes' including 'Sport and Health', with key targets in the plan matching those established in *Game Plan* (DCMS, 2002). Further, the plan for sport was closely linked through a new delivery structure to the regional health strategy. At the sub-regional level, five County Sports Partnerships are established in the North-West, including the MSP that was chaired by a senior NWSB representative. Also, Sport England's latest strategy (SENW, 2004) has a significant focus on health in line with *Game Plan* (DCMS, 2002). Sport England (NW) (regional communication, December, 2003: 5) stated that 'Sport England has agreed a considerable role for sport (in) the prevention of ill-health. Sport will take the lead on a range of key actions that will place us higher on the health agenda and bring a range of agencies closer to sport.'

Further, Sport England (NW) in *The North West Plan for Sport 2004–2008* (SENW, 2004: 2) stated that 'The need to develop the sporting infrastructure is now being recognised by other significant sectors', including health, without which it is argued meeting health targets is unrealistic. The plan includes a section on 'Improving Health and Well-Being', where the focus is on targeting areas of 'greatest health needs' and largest health inequalities, underpinned by the shared belief that encouraging sedentary people to do a modest amount of exercise will reap the greatest health benefit. The plan therefore follows national policy core direction, and in terms of regional policy, makes particular reference to, and takes its lead from, the 'physical activity, exercise and sport' section of the *Investment for Health: A Plan for North West England* (GONW, 2003). At local authority level, sport/recreation services are also expected to deliver health goals through sport and physical activity programmes, working in partnership with PCTs and other agencies.

Alongside sport, the organisational framework for health in the NW includes direct government representation at the regional level in the form of the NW Public Health Team, part of the DH and based in the GONW. *Investment for Health: A Plan for North West England* (GONW, 2003) focuses on how the DH and NHS can work in partnership with other agencies across the region to improve health and reduce health inequalities. It closely complements the national strategy, *Tackling Health Inequalities: A Programme for Action* (DH, 2003). In a multi-agency policy environment, a regional HDA and three Strategic Health Authorities (SHAs) span the NW region known as Public Health Networks (PHNs). Further, there are nine PCTs in Merseyside, with three in Liverpool (formerly part of the HAZ).

Importantly, policies must 'fit' the overarching policy rationale and political and economic objectives of the NW Regional Assembly and NW Regional Development Agency. Further replicating central government cross-cutting working practices via ACT, the two policy areas of sport and health in the NW, formed the Health and Physical Activity Forum (NWHPAF) in 2000, from an existing issue network that had acted informally since 1992. The 2003 conference *Towards 2020: meeting the physical activity challenge* focused on delivery of health/physical activity targets as stated in *Game Plan* (DCMS, 2002). In Liverpool, interviewees recognised *Liverpool First for Health* as the key agency overseeing public health policy and cross-cutting strategies led by the local authority, PCT and partners working across the sectors in area-based initiatives.

The most notable change locally in the last decade has been the disbanding of the HAZ. Merseyside was awarded HAZ status in 1999, the largest of the area-based initiatives, with the most complex partnership arrangements, including four health and five (latterly six) local authorities. In Liverpool, the MHAZ acted within the city-wide Neighbourhood Renewal Strategy with programmes delivered through local health partnerships via an HIP. MHAZ funded approximately 130 interventions, the majority of which were CHD programmes. MHAZ was managed by *Liverpool First*, who acted as the 'strategic issue partnership', itself reporting to the Liverpool Partnership Group, in charge of city-wide strategy. Membership of the MHAZ consisted of the PCTs, LCC and voluntary sector representation.

As of May 2003, the HAZs were disbanded, with the responsibilities for strategic planning transferred to Cheshire and Merseyside strategic partnership, and responsibilities for health promotion, including physical activity-based programmes, transferred to the newly established PCTs. The remaining MHAZ funding, agreed until March 2006, was administered through the nine area PCTs. Policy delivery across Merseyside now consisted of nine

PCTs, sixteen NHS Trusts, six local authorities, the Strategic Healthy Authority, two Community Health Councils, three Universities and numerous voluntary sector agencies. SENW (2004: 10) have attempted to clarify the role of sport and health agencies subsequent to the demise of the HAZ, by making a distinction between 'Sport' and 'Active living' (such as walking to school or work, or activities such as gardening), and within the category 'Sport', between 'Organised Sport' defined in terms of structured competitive activity; 'Informal Sport' defined as unstructured sport-related activities such as street games; and 'Active Recreation' identified as general exercise such as recreational cycling, dance or play. Clearly, health agencies would be more predisposed to invest in programmes that promote active living and sport-related activities outside of 'Organised Sport'.

The health sector in Liverpool is hierarchical, with strong elements of top-down governance via Liverpool First for Health, itself steered by the DH through layers of administration at the county and regional levels. Within this structural context, primary care is the 'poor relation' in Liverpool, but of late, secondary care organisations and actors are beginning to appreciate the value of PCT work if only in terms of 'reducing their workload'. The 'top-down' style of governance had been briefly challenged by the 'bottom-up' HAZs. However, as noted by Armitage and Povall (2003: 30), 'with a change of minister, the focus became more on NHS priorities and health services', highlighting the significance of 'ministerial activism' in the policy process (Taylor, 1997). The growing centralisation of health policy compromised the capacity of the MHAZ to deliver health objectives. Armitage and Povall (2003) argue that institutional re-organisation, with the formation of Local Strategic Partnerships and the demise of Health Authorities, compromised the work of the HAZ, with long-term planning problematic.

Further, given that there was limited scope for innovation within existing structures prior to the introduction of the HAZ, one of the idea of the HAZ was increasing the capacity for innovation at a local level, particularly in regard to tackling health inequalities. In part, the MHAZ was disbanded as resistance to innovation was high in the health sector, where post-care priorities and their vested interests dominate. Armitage and Povall (2003) also note the difficulties of translating policy into practice within a 'turbulent institutional and policy environment' (Bauld and Judge, 2002) steered by central government. The 'double whammy' of steering from central and local sources has also had an impact on the role and delivery of sport/exercise-based programmes locally. In particular, innovation was resisted by the embedded Liverpool Health Authority who perceived the MHAZ as a threat. As one senior policy officer stated, 'The view was that the Health Authority was too big ... and a conservative force' as regards policy and practice. Concerns over 'who pays for services' and duplication of effort eventually resulted in the joint commissioning of services. Further, few projects that emerged out of the MHAZ were mainstreamed within LCC service structures.

Subsequently, in 2002, three PCTs were established in Liverpool that had differing responsibilities with funding allocations relating to local population and demographic factors. Locally, some PCTs found it difficult to innovate and the costs of running three separate PCTs with three chief executives and three boards were high. In 2004, the PCTs were re-organised into a single entity for the city with one chief executive and board overseeing the processes. The significance of these structural changes is in the impact on relationships with sport and education and other sectors, and on the fledgling thematic networks that cut across policy sectors. The PCT and LCC now have joint-funded posts working to agreed goals with thematic working, the outcome via the *Active City* Strategy (LCC, 2005) that aims to meet a target of a 1% increase in participation in physical activity per annum, but it is recognised by interviewees that thematic working practices will take a long time to get into place. In 2006, the fact that funding for *Active City* was not guaranteed beyond 2008 allowed little opportunity to entrench new working practices across policy areas, particularly as the strategy itself is for the period 2006–2010. The main difficulty, interviewees acknowledge, is around mainstream funding and avoiding producing documents that 'sit on the shelf'.

Active City (LCC, 2005) incorporates existing programmes that link 'sport' and health including *Lifestyle gyms*, based in existing LCC-run leisure centres. *On the Right Track* (LCC, 1997: 45–47) and a draft of the latest LCC sport strategy (LCC, 2008a: 21–23) identify a significant role for 'sport' in health policy. The earlier document states that the single biggest growth area has been the demand for structured exercise-related activities, such as aerobics. This led to the conversion of leisure centre spaces to *Lifestyle gyms* that have focused more on women, health and changing lifestyles, with a shift to cardiovascular exercise and away from a 'body building and weights culture'. In 1993, the leisure centre in Fazakerly became the first *Lifestyle gym*, and by 2006, there were 13 lifestyle centres across the city. Within *Lifestyle gyms*, programmes are coordinated by Liverpool Health Authority and funded via NRF monies. However, it is assumed that the greatest impact on health can be achieved in the school setting (Wold and Henry, 1998). Hence, the latest developments include links between health bodies and SSCs in establishing after-school multi-activity clubs, as thematic working between Education, Health and sport/recreation gathers momentum within LCC.

In terms of policy implementation, LCC Sport has accessed NRF monies to support this city-wide strategy that links a number of initiatives through a partnership with the PCTs. Funding for health is generally organised on a 3-year cycle, and health funding cycles do not necessarily link to sport policy funding cycles which can cause difficulties. Projects that have been mainstreamed include Exercise for Health (PCT/LCC), Cardiac Rehab (PCT/LCC/Secondary Care organisations), Walking for Health (PCT) and REACT (PCT). However, many initiatives are funded on a short-term basis, subject to re-applications. For physical activity initiatives, short-term funding militates against any possibility of sustained action to address poor health, and the aim of reducing health inequalities is, in this context, unrealistic. Moreover, in practice, projects can take up to 6 months to establish.

A partial solution to implementation issues is to adopt a strategy used by LCC Sport, namely to attract 'magnet funding' based on small-scale successes that can be demonstrated, then rolling-out initiatives, for example walking and cycling schemes. Skilled fund-raisers are therefore at a premium in a sector that demands expertise in accessing the multitude of funding streams that exist for health. Funding acquisition is a process of ongoing negotiation around targets and outcomes. In this respect, the PCT has established a marketing team to help 'sell' its services and access funding. In 2007, Sport and Recreation Services adopted a similar approach in establishing a marketing team and one of the SPAAs is actively engaged in highlighting the success of programmes in order to retain and increase funding and acquire political support.

The most notable local authority 'health through sport' project in Liverpool, however, is the *Sportslinx* programme. This programme dates back to 1996, post the Olympics, where the Great Britain team performed poorly. The programme originally had a sport-specific focus following consultation with the local authority SDOs, and concentrated on talent identification and development. However, *Sportslinx* has since evolved into a health promotion tool in response to a changing national policy context and the related spending priorities. In brief, the programme monitors health-related fitness in young people, in addition to providing guidance on health, fitness and nutrition with the overall emphasis on developing the concept and practice of long-term participant development (LCC, 2003a). The scheme is primarily funded through the NOF, NRF and Sure Start, all non-sport specific 'funding pots' and includes almost 100 schools in Liverpool.

Critically, *Sportslinx* was the first example of thematic working involving sport/recreation within the local authority, and it helped to raise the profile of sport within LCC. The shift to a health promotion emphasis raised questions of capacity in meeting health and sport objectives, noting that in 1996 the structures were not in place to deliver this type of initiative. More than a decade later, partly as a result of central government intervention, the organisational infrastructure for delivering sport-based health initiatives, or health-based sport initiatives, is beginning to materialise. However, it can be noted that the *Sportslinx* programme is still not mainstream-funded after a decade of operation, and given the emphasis on sport-specific development within LCC Sport, a tension exists around defining the parameters of the programme.

Although health promotion has gradually gained momentum within the sport/recreation service area, it was the GP (Exercise) Referral scheme which acted as the catalyst that brought the health and sport sectors together in Liverpool. LCC was one of the first local authorities to develop GP Referral schemes that have now been rolled out across the city. Through 'freeing-up' doctor's time, the scheme acquired a positive status among health professionals, although there were difficulties at first in the medical professionals understanding the perspectives of sport science professionals. The scheme became a working partnership based between LCC Leisure Services (including sport/recreation), Liverpool Health Promotion Service and the PCT in the city. The programme targeted the most sedentary element of the population where consultation with a GP leads to referral to the scheme that is implemented via a network of fitness professionals working in leisure centres or gyms.

In terms of programmes that in part consist of physical activity and sport in schools, for health-related purposes, another programme of note that now sits within the *Active City* framework is *Healthy Schools*, where Liverpool was one of the first cities to become nationally accredited in the year 2000. Penney and Evans (1999) trace the evolution of health education in schools. 'Health promoting schools', an idea that emerged from World Health Organization (WHO, 1986), leading to the establishment of the European Network of Health Promoting Schools in 1992, and to aspirational policy statements by the European Parliament such as to 'encourage the establishment throughout the community of pilot projects which adopt a comprehensive approach to health education by involving not only schools but also … local communities, sports clubs, voluntary services etc' (European Parliament, cited in St Leger, 1998). However, the programme was re-developed in Liverpool following an audit in 2006 that reviewed effectiveness, given that the programme to some extent duplicated health promotion work organised through other service areas. This highlights the difficulties of avoiding duplication where two or more policy areas oversee similar policy remits.

At the core of these new alliances is a policy concern with promoting health, particularly in schools. However, as Penney and Evans (1999: 131) conclude, 'There remain tensions and contradictions between the discourses of sport and health in relation to physical education and neither politicians nor members of physical education professional associations seem particularly eager or able to resolve them.' Fox (1986: 10) states that 'Although health-related concepts should always be reinforced through other activities, they will always remain incidental and superficial unless at some point they provide the central focus in a distinct programme of study.' The SPAAs in Liverpool may be able to offer this distinct focus.

Although 'health' was not a policy concern within LCC Sport, this has begun to change. Prior to *Active City*, a series of improvised short-term arrangements to draw down government funding existed where health priorities were fitted into existing structures and priorities. More recently, the service area has raised awareness of health issues through a programme of running events, utilising Liverpool's 'strong culture of jogging and road running' (LCC, 1997: 46), and links between boxing development and obesity are evidenced in the 'Make the Weight' scheme. Swimming, perhaps, offers the greatest opportunities to meet health objectives with the policy of 'free swimming to under 16s' introduced by LCC in recent years. However, sustaining programmes dependent on subsidy remains problematic. The local voluntary sports sector, by contrast, is not equipped to access non-sport funding sources, and there exists little interest in this sector to consider and quantify health gains through sport.

ANALYSIS: THE LOCAL CONTEXT

The key issue to emerge from the empirical research is the significant impact of changes to the organisational and funding context on (1) relationships between interests that span the sport and health policy areas, (2) the capacity for innovation and change and (3) the strategic response of policy actors seeking to build capacity to further influence the policy processes. Thus policy can be defined as a strategic response to a set of structural conditions that mediate action where changes to that structure both facilitate and constrain policy change. This appears to be the case in Liverpool in respect of contemporary policy concerns in and around sport, physical activity and public health.

Policy change can be viewed as incremental where, for example, the GP Referral scheme has grown through a series of 'big pushes' where depending on the 'flavour of the month' that reflect shifting central government policy priorities and media concerns such as obesity. Given that the health sector is dominated by post-care interests, there has existed a limited will to engage with 'sport'. New initiatives bring new funding to the sport and health sectors, and with it, a scramble to acquire it. Initiatives then peter out as the issue matures in the issue attention life cycle (Downs, 1972), and as the funding streams dry up, the legacy is negligible.

Although embedding the health/sport partnerships in an existing network of power relations has proved to be an incremental process, Armitage and Povall (2003) take an optimistic view that a 'coalition' has emerged from the MHAZ based on the shared goal of reducing health inequalities, including sympathetic individuals within statutory organisations, which is considered important to policy development (Adams and Cunning, 2002). These individuals and their core policy concerns are therefore anticipated to move their agendas forward in and through PCTs. However, it was the disbanding of the MHAZ and creation of the area-based PCTs that was the catalyst for the development of a more sustainable cross-sector relationship between sport and health. In other words, 'top-down' governance may have been more effective than the 'bottom-up' approach for meeting policy goals that utilise sport in health policy. However, questions are outstanding as to the genuine commitment of government to improving health where the funding infrastructure is short term and adversarial in the pursuit of 'quick wins' that is a reflection of the political context. It could be argued that the embedded interests within both the national and local health sectors and sport policy area serve to undermine central government policy, although government policy is itself ambiguous and a reflection of internal disputes between departments.

Moreover, emerging macro-level agreement on policy aspirations does not necessarily result in effective policy implementation, where embedded interests and priorities within both the Sport and Health sectors have the capacity to resist proposed change. The areas for disagreement in this type of partnership include who is responsible for funding initiatives; who has authority in the policy process; who gains the status, recognition and rewards associated with the initiative (or 'who takes the blame' for policy failure); and what should be measured as proof of policy success. The findings of this study mirror research by Coalter et al. (2000), who found that professional groups tend to differ in their understanding of community/individual 'needs' that present difficulties for partnership-working. Professional disagreement exists between proponents of the 'education' and 'medical' models, particularly in regard to the nature of the evaluation process and relevant outcome measures. A particular problem for the former

MHAZ was in the representation of their work through research and evaluation, especially as central government preferred an 'evidence-based' (investigative) research paradigm which measures outcomes quantitatively, whereas health promotion programmes tend to focus on processes as much as outcomes, and therefore use qualitative methods to evaluate their work within the interactive research paradigm (Raphael, 2000).

Further, working within the 'medical model', GPs were focused on ensuring freedom from major illnesses, whereas health promotion and community development workers preferred an 'education model' with the focus on behavioural change, and sports development professionals adopted a 'marketing model' in which sports/activities were utilised to increase participation rates and also, where traditional sports development and leisure service provision offers a 'product.' By contrast, heath promotion professionals focused on a 'process' where 'healthy lifestyles' replace inactivity over time. The absence of a shared professional paradigm within and between the health and sport policy areas lies at the heart of competing agendas, in conjunction with familiar disagreement concerning resource allocation, authority, responsibilities and recognition.

Finally, it is worth returning to the LCC Sport policy statement *On the Right Track* (LCC, 1997) that identified key issues, priority tasks and the key players in a 'framework for action' in utilising sport for health gains. A growing number of partnerships for sport/health are noted in the document too, including the establishment of the Physical Activity Promotion Group (PAPG) that mirrors the NWHPAF at the regional level. Defining the role of PAPG is seen as a 'priority task', where Liverpool Health Authority and Sport and Recreation Services are 'key players', alongside the Leisure DSO, Education Directorate, Social Services Directorate, Healthy Cities Unit, Health Start Ltd, a city university and representation from the voluntary sector (*On the Right Track*, LCC, 1997).

However, despite these insights and recommendations, it has taken nearly a decade for thematic working to gather momentum. This timescale raises questions concerning the relative value placed on sport and physical activity by those in positions of influence within the Health sector, for example. Further, all of the 'key players' identified as partner agencies have undergone significant organisational change over the last decade, and some bodies no longer exist. As a result of endless re-structuring and changes to resourcing, in the context of shifting central government political priorities and wider economic change, and recognising that existing interests tend to resist change, it is perhaps surprising that *Active City* surfaced as an idea or in practice.

Key factors in its materialisation have been a 'health crisis', central government pressure, the influence of 'policy entrepreneurs' seizing an opportunity for career progression, and organisations (including local authority departments) pursuing and acquiring influence and resources. Instrumental in developing the sport/health agenda locally, have been a network of policy actors with career histories that to some extent have spanned the two policy areas. For example, relationships between personnel who have worked for the MSP, the SAZ, PCT, the former HAZ, the LEA and components of the local authority have in effect brokered the emerging relationship of sport and health. However, their actions must be located in a policy environment that has at various times been favourable and unfavourable to progressing policy values, beliefs and ideas. For example, support for the agenda at Liverpool Partnership Group (LPG) level locally and via central government has been critical. It should also be noted that central government departments do not exist in isolation and are subject to influence from local and regional policy actors. A neo-pluralist explanation of this case may therefore be applicable (see Chapter 12).

CONCLUSIONS

In sum, policy where the health and sport sectors overlap appears to be made in a fog of disagreement about goals, causes and means (Klein, 2003). Disagreement about goals can rest on values such as *health for all* and *sport for all*; objectives that often sit uneasily with programmes that target and prioritise specific socio-economic groups or areas. In Liverpool, it does not appear that for the health or sport policy areas, or in the spaces shared, that agreed policy objectives, feasible mechanisms and processes to meet objectives or adequate resources have existed historically, although a nascent policy community based on shared health promotion through physical activity goals may be slowly emerging. A senior officer within LCC noted that 'the arguments have changed ... health is now supportive of the sports infrastructure' and 'huge strides have been made in recent years' in bringing the two sectors together. However, another senior officer observed that the 'Health sector (is) not fully on board', adding that 'prevention is not a key focus in practice ... despite White Paper rhetoric and resources don't follow.'

The importance of sport and physical activity in health promotion has gained ground as issues such as obesity in young people have passed the three tests to survive the policy process, namely commanding attention, claiming legitimacy and invoking action (Solesbury, 1976). However, acquiring systemic embeddedness (Granovetter, 1985) has not to date been achieved.

In a complex policy area that spans many interests, the role of physical activity in health policy remains contested and 'sport' stands at the margins of the debate in practice. Conversely, in combination with *Active City* (LCC, 2005), the establishment of SPAAs in Liverpool, a core strategic and delivery component of the local authority's most recent Sport and Recreation Strategy (LCC, 2008a), may serve to strengthen the influence of interests central to the policy area spanning sport and health, particularly with sustainable support from key partners and funding agencies.

On the contrary, without erecting an robust infrastructure to seriously challenge dominant interests in both the health and sport policy areas, it can be argued that the necessary changes 'won't happen through the existing infrastructure; there is too much baggage and too much vested interest in maintaining the status quo!' (Riley, 2004: 55). Moreover, where sport interests have engaged with this policy concern, it can be argued that it has largely been for instrumental purposes and this is a strategy that is likely to militate against policy goals, particularly when funding for pre-care health interventions begins to recede.

Note: The COE definition of 'sport' as expressed in the European Sports Charter (COE, 1993) is, 'all forms of *physical activity* which, through casual or organised participation, aim at expressing or improving physical fitness and mental well-being, forming social relationships or obtaining results in competition at all levels' (*italics added*).

CHAPTER 9

Sport, Land-Use Planning and Playing Fields Policy

INTRODUCTION

The issue of the protection and usage of playing fields including pitches for sport is a persistent one that has attracted public, media and political interest. Of particular political significance is the use and protection of school playing fields, where the planning and management of playing fields and pitches is one element of a wider set of issues based around how best to conserve a scarce resource for a range of sport and recreational interests. This chapter seeks to understand the influence of sport interests in policy for playing fields and pitches. First, an analysis of the evolution of national playing fields policy is undertaken. Second, an explanation of playing fields policy is attempted that highlights how competing interests seek to influence policy. Third, playing fields policy in Liverpool is documented, and fourth, an analysis is provided of how and why playing fields policy has been made and how and why policy has changed.

THE EVOLUTION OF NATIONAL PLAYING FIELDS POLICY

1970–1979

In the 1970s, local authorities included playing fields as a core element of sport and recreation within a welfare services remit, alongside parks, swimming pools and sports halls. Research by the London Council for Sport and Recreation (LCSR) (1990) highlighted the changing patterns of provision from 1972 to 1987 and identified a number of overlapping issues that continue to shape debates around playing fields. First, there are debates about protection, conservation and sale or disposal of sites, where the LCSR (1990: 9) stated, 'We are not primarily concerned with preventing the loss of recreational land, but with encouraging and enabling participation.' In contrast, the NPFA and other organisations such as the CCPR sought to conserve sites and have historically resisted the loss or change of use of any playing field site, and the tensions between these interests have been a constant issue in the last three decades.

Second, the LCSR noted the scant attention paid to recreation and sport compared with other land uses in local authority policy and planning processes where arguably a relatively low value has been placed on sport. For example, the LCSR found that many local authorities had no systematic record of recreational space; few had undertaken audits of quantity and quality, supply and demand, availability and access, on which to base decisions. In addition, the LCSR reported that space to play sport was often the responsibility of several council departments who had no mechanism for the exchange of information or a coordinated strategy. Third, the LCSR research highlighted the variety in ownership of playing pitches, namely local authorities, Health Authorities and Education Authorities, highlighting the policy differences between them. For example, community use of school playing fields was highlighted as a source of conflict in the LCSR research. In sum, the core policy concerns shaping these inter-related issues revolved around conservation and participation. Arguably, little has changed in the last 30 years where the issues cited continue to cut across attempts to conserve and utilise playing fields.

Conservative administrations: 1979–1991

Under the Conservative administrations of the 1980s, the introduction of market principles and competition into the management of public sector leisure services and the sale of public assets were key features (Henry, 1993, 2001). An aspect of privatisation was the sale of recreational land, including school playing fields. The *Local Government Planning and Land Act 1980*, coupled with the Department of Education and Science *Circular 909*, effectively encouraged local authorities and LEAs to rationalise their assets in order to raise finances (cf. Stoker, 1991). One of the results of this policy was that many local authorities sold playing fields to developers for housing and business development. Further, this legislation impacted on the community use of school playing fields that remains an issue even today, where 'A major concern has been to find ways of offsetting the adverse effects of recent education legislation upon the future development of joint provision on school sites. Section 42 of the *Education Act 1986* has had the unintended effect of discouraging investment by local authorities in sporting facilities located within schools' (ESC, 1991: 15).

In the 1980s, as noted in *The Playing Pitch Strategy* (ESC, 1991), there existed a wide variation in provision by locality, ownership and sport, and therefore there were difficulties in developing defensible planning strategies in the absence of robust data. The playing pitch strategy explains the loss of sites at the time in terms of pressures on local authority finances, legislative change and increasing pressure on scarce land resources. In sum, the policy and planning context at the time clearly militated against field and pitch retention.

Conservative administration: 1991–1997

With the replacement of Margaret Thatcher as Prime Minister and the re-introduction of more traditional Conservatism under John Major, policy impacting on playing fields, in effect, sought to redress former legislation. Government guidance on planning for recreation and sport emerged in the early 1990s expressed in a series of Planning Policy Guidance Notes (PPGs) designed to shape local authority policy and decisions. Importantly, PPG1 was revised in 1992, following legislative change introduced via the *Planning and Compensation Act* that had previously made a presumption in favour of land development rather than conservation (NPFA, 1989: 56). PPG12 aimed to align central, regional and local government planning policy in respect of potential and actual conflict over development and protection, and the general position of PPG3 on housing can be summarised as one of finding a balance between development and conservation needs, stating that 'development of vacant urban land should not involve the loss of valuable open space' (cited in NPFA, 1989: 59). Further, the White Paper *This Common*

Inheritance (DoE, 1990) acknowledged the need to establish a register of recreational land in order to determine which sites should be conserved.

However, it was the introduction of the *Planning Policy Guidance for Sport and Recreation* or PPG17 (DoE, 1991) that set a precedent in placing a value on sport and recreation as an aspect of local authority policy, planning and provision. The Sports Council stated that the publication of PPG17 represented a 'significant watershed in planning for sport and recreation' (ESC, 1998a: 4) as it places a statutory duty on local authorities to implement a local plan that makes 'appropriate' recreational provision for local communities. Further, PPG17 states that playing fields should normally be protected, except where sports and recreation facilities can best be retained and enhanced through the re-development of a small part of the site or alternative provision of equivalent community benefit is made available or the local plan shows an excess of sports pitch provision.

Moreover, PPG17 recognises the need for longer-term strategic planning that takes account of demographic change such as increase and decrease in school age populations. Of particular note is that PPG17 draws on the NPFA *The Six Acre Standard* in its planning guidance to local authorities, indicating a close working relationship between the Conservative government at the time and the NPFA (Gyles Brandreth, Conservative Party MP, chaired the NPFA). Despite the intent of PPG17, however, identifying 'appropriate recreational provision' or 'community need' has proved problematic for local authorities in practice. As the ESC (1995: 2) noted, 'Analyses of planning appeal decisions involving the re-development of playing fields have shown that the ability of the local planning authority and other interested parties to identify ... sporting need ... has been a crucial factor.'

In 1991, the Sports Council, NPFA and CCPR collaborated to develop *The Playing Pitch Strategy*. This strategy can be viewed as a compromise between those interests who advocated a complete embargo on any loss of playing pitches and those who believed the existing legislation at the time was adequate. The strategy 'aims to make any loss of land subject to far more stringent safeguards, but recognises that in some circumstances the modest loss of land will be in the best interests of sport' (ESC, 1991: 4) and in line with PPG17 recommends a register of recreational land. The strategy proposes giving a key role to local authority sport and recreation services and also recommends the involvement of key stakeholders in policy processes such as National Governing Bodies for sport, regional sports bodies, school sport representatives and voluntary bodies, in a partnership approach to addressing the concern.

Importantly too, the Sports Council noted that within *The Playing Pitch Strategy* terms such as 'playing field' and 'playing pitch' as well as 'catchment', 'suitable location' and 'equivalent quality' were defined for the first time, enabling greater safeguarding of playing pitches. A playing pitch was defined as 'a delineated area which, together with any run-off area, is 0.4ha or more, and which is used for association football, American football, rugby, cricket, hockey, lacrosse, rounders, baseball, softball, Australian football, Gaelic football, shinty, hurling, polo or cycle polo' (cited in Sport England, 2000a: 2).

PMP Consultancy (PMP, 2001) conducted research into the relative utility of the 1991 *Playing Pitch Strategy*, where organisations were asked to comment on the value of the strategy and, where relevant, the extent of which they had achieved the recommendations of the strategy. Responses indicate that between 1991 and 2001, despite the majority of general recommendations being realised, a number of specific recommendations affecting playing pitches remained largely unachieved. These included a failure to promote the recommendations of the strategy among the planning profession, develop appropriate partnerships, facilitate relevant funding arrangements, develop latent demand for playing pitches or develop their quality. Arguably, these are serious omissions that indicate a less than pro-active approach to safeguarding playing pitches, and further, respondents indicated that issues of *quality* were largely ignored.

Other overlapping concerns with the 1991 strategy included school pitches not being fully included in audits; some sports and trends in sports are ignored as are training and informal games; cross-boundary issues are ignored (e.g. local authority ward areas); the methodology proposed to audit provision was seen as overly complex and potentially costly; and the overall strategy was too detailed, complicated and lacks the support of a statutory requirement. Moreover, of the local authority leisure departments who replied, less than half had a playing pitch strategy in place and only half had undertaken local assessments of playing pitch requirements. The CCPR concluded that 'Since the publication of the [Playing Pitch] Strategy in 1991, local authorities continue to show a resistance to carrying out voluntary audits. In particular, it could be suggested that those authorities with the most need of audits are those least likely to participate' (PMP, 2001: 13). In practice, the interests of developers have been served by inaction, where if the local authority has not done a PPG17 needs assessment, the Public Enquiry may accept the developers' proposition that the open space is not valued.

Although local authorities claim to view existing playing fields as 'an essential component of the environment' and not 'cheap land for their own developments nor a potential source of capital receipts' (PMP, 2001: 48), this claim is not mirrored in practice, with little action taken to protect sites by local authorities' own admission. Further, little or no financial or other support was provided to governing bodies of pitch sports and in almost all cases, transferring the ownership of pitches to the NPFA was not considered, implying that local authorities sought to retain control of playing fields and pitches, even if they were reluctant to develop a policy for the resource.

In respect of school playing fields and pitches, it is notable from the PMP research findings that the majority of LEAs had not placed a high value of retaining playing fields and pitches by comparison with the conservation coalition. The PMP research found that approximately 40% of LEAs had not collated data on school playing fields and pitches in order to develop a register of recreational land, and that only 50% had worked with local authority leisure departments in auditing pitch requirements. Further, most LEAs had not offered guidance or financial support to school governors in order to develop the community use of school pitches as recommended in the Strategy. Moreover, only approximately half of LEAs had offered financial or practical support to governing bodies of sport planning to develop pitch sport opportunities for young people, and few LEAs took opportunities to gain funding for new playing fields and pitches, indicating a lack of pro-action to protect sites.

The key issues that emerge from this research revolve around first, definitions, of quality, capacity and adequacy of provision; second, adaptability to changes in supply and demand, and exogenous change shaping provision; and third, differences in the understanding of policy processes, requirements and obligations involved in the issue. Tensions underpinning the differing core priorities of those central to the policy process are evident in this survey, indicating an uneasy relationship between government and non-government bodies. Areas of disagreement include the accuracy and validity of both quantitative and qualitative data collected on playing pitches; the robustness of legislation and stringency of planning processes required to conserve existing pitches; and the ownership and usage of pitches.

The NPFA, in response to these issues at the time, produced an updated version of *The Six Acre Standard* (NPFA, 1991) that superseded the publication *Space Requirements for the More Popular Outdoor Games* (NPFA, 1986) and recognised the need for more detailed recommendations than previously given, to take account of location, size and proximity of playing spaces to other aspects of the environment, whilst nonetheless retaining the minimum standard recommendation of 6 acres (2.4 hectares) per 1000 population. In respect of playing pitches, the NPFA specifically recommended 3 acres (1.2 hectares) in line with a recommendation of the *Playing Pitch Strategy*. The guidance recommended that all planning authorities adopt the standard or, where land scarcity exists, aspire to meet the standard in future plans, although the NPFA (1991: 52) acknowledged the difficulties of achieving a consensus between the range of interests seeking to access and utilise playing space.

In understanding playing fields policy, one dimension to explore is arguably the evolving relationship between the protectionist lobby, central government and local authorities. In respect of this relationship, one tension to emerge was around the differing methods and models used to determine 'adequate space' for sport and recreation, with the NPFA wedded to *The Six Acre Standard* but the ESC (1995: 3), and local authorities, in practice, taking a more 'flexible approach' to 'adequate space'. In regard to 'excess provision', this is defined by the ESC (1995: 3) as when the number of pitches available exceeds the current demand.

Latent and future demand, the ESC propose, should be taken into account when auditing local provision, as should issues of quality, use and capacity (ESC, 1995: 16). Further, 'excess provision' does not equate with pitch disposal, which 'should not be contemplated or permitted except in very limited, qualified circumstances' (ESC, 1995: 17) and if 'genuine space capacity' exists, the policy options suggested include generating demand, change of sporting use, creation of an informal recreational space and taking account of long-term demographic change. However, as the PMP (2001) research found, few local authorities have been pro-active in ascertaining latent demand or generating demand.

In respect of the relationship between the Sports Council and local authorities, a significant change occurred in 1996 when the ESC were given Statutory Consultee Status on all playing fields over 1 acre, via statutory instrument 1817, known as the Town and Country Planning [General Development Procedure (Amendment) Order (DoE, 1996)]. This strengthened the position of the ESC whose earlier attempts at influencing the planning process via *Planning Obligations for Sport and Recreation – A Guide to Negotiation and Action* (ESC, 1993) had limited impact on local authority policies and practices in regard to protecting playing fields (as noted in Sport England, 1999d: 5).

Despite statutory consultee status, however, planning authorities remained under no obligation to accept Sport England's advice or to inform Sport England of the final decision, thus limiting the extent of the Sport England's actual influence. In fact, *The Effectiveness of Planning Policy Guidance on Sport and Recreation* (Department of Environment, Transport and the Regions, 1998a) that found local authorities had not fully capitalised on the existing legislation in ensuring developer contribution to sport and recreation provision. Despite statutory consultee status, Sport England

(1999c) admitted that negotiations to secure playing fields had been hampered by deficiencies in local authority capacity to secure provision for sport and recreation. Sport England (1999c: 5) concluded that 'Relatively few local planning authorities appear to have all the elements in place. As a result the opportunities offered by planning obligations are not being fully exploited.'

In sum, policy in the period 1991–1997 can be characterised as a response to a perceived crisis resulting from prior legislation. Pressure from the NPFA, although operating in a favourable policy climate, resulted in a loose coalition of support in some quarters of central government. The influence of the protectionist lobby can be found in *Assessing Playing Pitch Requirements at the Local Level* (ESC, 1995: 1) where it is acknowledged that 'The protection and provision of recreational open space are now firmly on both the local and national political agenda following mounting concern over many years about the loss of playing fields to development.'

Arguably, the core beliefs and values of central government, most notably the Prime Minister, mirrored those lobbying to protect sites, where shared values existed around heritage, nationalism and elitism, made explicit through a focus on traditional pitch sports as reflected in the policy statement *Sport: Raising the Game* (DNH, 1995).

New Labour: 1997–2008

In some respects, New Labour policy towards playing fields was a continuation of the period 1991–1997 in which government sought to reverse the impact of earlier legislation and planning priorities. However, more recently, New Labour has sought a 'third way' between interests representing conservation and those representing development. How this policy shift has impacted on relationships between bodies with a remit for the issue is explored in this section, where a gradual marginalisation of the protectionist lobby has occurred.

In the period 1997–2000, the Sports Council produced a series of planning bulletins claiming these were 'launched to a receptive planning and leisure audience' (ESC, 1998a: 1). *Strategic Planning for Sport* re-emphasised the need for local authorities to audit provision and produce plans in respect of playing fields, include planning for sport and recreation in Unitary Development Plans (UDPs) and, from late 1998, ideally use models other than *The Six Acre Standard* to assess community requirements for sport and recreation. These bulletins followed on from the launch of the key planning policy document *A Sporting Future for the Playing Fields of England* (ESC, 1997a) which, as a policy statement, distances itself from the NPFA core policy position. In taking account of trends in sports participation, the statement acknowledges that indoor sports facilities 'may be more relevant to contemporary needs than the continuing use of grass playing fields' (cited in ESC, 1998a: 7). Further, the debate is re-framed from one centred on site-specific 'conservation versus development' to an area-based evaluation of public benefits and community needs.

A Sporting Future for the Playing Fields of England recognised the limited influence of the Sports Council and acknowledged that local authorities can ignore guidance, stating that 'Although we expect that local planning authorities will attach great importance to the views we express, we do not have the power to prevent development' (ESC, 1997a: 1). Nonetheless, ESC claimed that 'The majority of local planning authorities now appreciate that the ESC's regional offices should be consulted on planning applications for development that would lead to the loss of, or prejudice the use of, playing fields for sport' (ESC, 1998a: 1).

Nonetheless, in order to address disputes between local authorities and the ESC, and to effectively over-rule local authority decisions that may result in the loss of playing fields, the New Labour government introduced Circular 09/98 (Department of Environment, Transport and the Regions, 1998b), known as the *Town and Country Planning (Playing Fields) Directive*, for the Secretary of State to 'call in' planning applications where a local authority decided to dispose of playing fields. In practice, however, the directive resulted in the ESC only being able to object to disposal where the proposed development would result in a deficiency in the playing fields in a local authority area, or where there already existed a deficiency, or where any replacement playing field proposed by developers did not equate with the quality, quantity and accessibility of the existing site. In other words, local authorities could still dispose of sites where an 'excess' of provision could be argued or where it was accepted that developers had compensated for losses.

Also of note in this period are rulings on the development of school playing fields that for the first time viewed the sale or preservation of playing fields in terms of the 'wider public benefit' (see ESC, 1998a, for case study examples). The New Labour government repealed Circular 909 and replaced it with the *School Standards and Framework Act* (DfEE, 1998c) that gave greater presumption towards the protection for school playing fields by requiring the Secretary of State for Education to give consent to sales. Under this act, playing fields are to be retained which are at least equivalent in size to the minimum areas recommended in the Department's guidance for new schools, *Area Guidelines for Schools* (DfEE, 1996b).

Moreover, the Act tightened statutory protection for that part of school playing fields exceeding a minimum for team games and closed the loophole regarding the absence of a requirement to provide playing fields for schools with children 8 years of age or younger. However, the Act still permitted schools to sell land to provide funds for educational facilities and has difficulty in protecting playing fields used by the wider community. *The Protection of School Playing Fields* (DfEE, 1999d) provided further guidance in stating, for example, that if disposal or change of use is agreed, the revenues raised must be allocated to sporting and educational provision, and the remaining fields or pitches must cater for existing and future needs of both the school and local community. However, in practice, grass surface playing pitches can be replaced by artificial surfaces or an indoor facility where the grass pitch is not currently in use, raising concerns around the impact on traditional grass-based sports. Further, the sale of whole school playing fields can only occur at closed schools or those moving to a new site with replacement fields. Thus 'adequate' provision for pitch sports may be retained in some cases.

The ESC was re-structured in 1999 and re-named Sport England, who were active in publishing a further series of planning bulletins, including *Planning Obligations for Sport* (Sport England, 1999d), the new *Land Use Planning Policy Statement* (Sport England, 1999e), *Playing Fields for Sport Revisited* (Sport England, 2000a), *Planning for Open Space* (Sport England, 2002a) and *Sport in the Green Belt* (Sport England, 2003). *Planning Obligations for Sport* explains the use of planning obligations to secure sport and recreation provision, the concept introduced in the *Planning and Compensation Act* with the principle being to use agreements between local authorities and developers to regulate or restrict land use. As stated in the DoE Circular 1/97 (cited in Sport England, 1999c: 2), 'Properly used, planning obligations may enhance the quality of development and enable proposals to go ahead which might otherwise be refused.' More specifically, local authorities and developers can arrive at an agreement whereby sport and recreational provision was included as an element of, for example, a new housing development, assuming playing fields or other recreational space is lost through the development taking place.

Playing Fields for Sport Revisited (Sport England, 2000a) updates planning procedures and intends to facilitate greater scrutiny of planning applications involving playing fields, given that 'playing fields have continued to be threatened by, and lost to, other forms of development' (Sport England, 2000a: 1), where it is noted that in some cases, notification of planning applications affecting playing fields has not been received from local authorities, and this is not considered by Sport England to be a 'lack of awareness' of Sport England's statutory consultee status. Further, Sport England (2000a) noted that sites can be deliberately left vacant for more than 5 years so that disposal can legally be attained. It could therefore be argued that during this period, many local authorities continued to ignore Sport England. Moreover, as research highlighted, inconsistencies existed in the interpretation of exemptions from protection, with the terms 'excess', 'equivalent' and 'small' being specific examples (Sport England, 2000a: 5–6).

In respect of school playing fields, the DfES launched the updated *Guidance for the Protection of School Playing Fields* (DfES, 2001). In brief, the new guidance gives greater emphasis to community use of school sites and an increased expectation that the proceeds from sales of sports pitches should return first and foremost to school sport (although other capital projects are still permitted). Additionally, Circular 3/99 was subsequently tightened in 2001 in a revised circular entitled *The Protection of School Playing Fields and Land for City Academies* (DfEE, 2000) that proposed that all applications be referred to a *School Playing Fields Advisory Panel* that has now considered applications since mid-2001, and includes representatives from the NPFA, the National Association of Head Teachers, the LGA and the CCPR.

The DCMS too pledged in *A Sporting Future for All* (DCMS, 2000) to close the remaining loopholes in a revised PPG17 and establish a monitoring unit, *The Playing Field Monitoring Group* including representation from government departments, Sport England, NPFA and CCPR. However, the NPFA criticised the DCMS Playing Fields Monitoring Group as 'beset by inertia', particularly in respect of producing statistics on field 'losses' (NPFA, June 2003: press release), adding, 'Our hope in gathering figures is that they would help shape policy to stem the loss of playing fields. We haven't even reached the starting gate on policy yet.'

The revised PPG17 was finally published in July 2002, and in its very title, *Planning for Open Space, Sport and Recreation* (ODPM, 2002), a shift is explicit, from a concern with playing fields and pitches to a more holistic focus on the total provision in an area for sport and recreation. With the publication of the Scottish Executive Paper *Rethinking Open Space: Open Space Provision and Management: A Way Forward* (Scottish Executive, 2001) came a challenge to the central tenet of the NPFA, *The Six Acre Standard*, which is referred to as anachronistic, universalising and inappropriate (cited in Sport England, 2002a: 13). In effect, the original version of PPG17 was centred solely on sport and recreation rather than setting sport within a broader land-use policy context. The Scottish Executive study proved very influential in English Government thinking on open spaces.

Subsequently, the requirement that local authorities must consider, when a planning application is received for the disposal of a playing field, 'all the functions that open space can perform' (PPG17, paragraph 10; ODPM, 2002), rather than the narrower single focus on sport and recreation, and this signals a policy shift. It can be concluded that the revised PPG17 focuses on the quality and diversity of facilities offered rather than the quantity of open space. However, protectionists viewed the report as amounting to a 'developer's charter' and in reducing the amount of open space, what remains is less costly for local authority to maintain. Unsurprisingly, the NPFA stated that it 'does not carry the NPFA's full endorsement' (NPFA, 2003: 2) particularly given that the revised PPG17 does not refer to *The Six Acre Standard* at all. In this respect, a senior NPFA representative stated, 'The main problem is that PPG17 has institutionalised Sports England exception policies and Sport England are too frequently willing to accept a loss of outside facilities provided indoor sports facilities are put in place.'

The definition of the issue is therefore central to the policy process and in this respect the current government defines the issue more in terms of 'investing in sport as a whole', to 'widen participation' not only into formal competitive team games but also informal games and physical activity across a range of surfaces and facility settings (DCMS, 2002). This contrasts with the position of the NPFA and its coalition of support where the issue is defined in terms of the protection of grass playing fields marked as pitches for formal competitive team games such as football, cricket and rugby union, and to a lesser extent, spaces for informal recreation. Importantly, the revised PPG17 was grounded in a re-organisation of central government allowing it to gain institutional embeddedness, where greater central government coordination of land-use planning policy is the aspiration to be mirrored within local government. Cross-departmental working can be traced from the *Town and Country Planning (Playing Fields) Directive* (Department of Environment, Transport and the Regions, 1998b), being the first directive of its type to acquire cross-departmental support. By 2002, new organisational relationships had emerged that located playing fields as a policy concern within a broader set of interests that mirrored the thematic concerns of the *Game Plan* (DCMS, 2002).

Within a year of the revised PPG17, *Towards a Level Playing Field* (Sport England/CCPR, 2003) identified all of the recent policy guidance that impacts on the playing pitch issue and key national statistics, trends, issues and implications for future demand for playing pitches, in relation to eight pitch sports. In regard to football, for example, an expansion of mini-football is viewed as requiring a greater supply of both small-sided and junior-sized pitches (Sport England/CCPR, 2003: 2.7). *Towards a Level Playing Field* also identifies a revised methodology that accounts for a more holistic view of pitch provision as one element of open space in line with the revised PPG17. The guidance states, 'In essence, the planning and management of playing pitches is only one part of a wider issue of how best to conserve a finite open space resource for a diverse and sometimes conflicting range of needs' (Sport England/CCPR, 2003: 21).

Towards a Level Playing Field also highlights other factors affecting playing pitch provision, namely the rise in participation in small-sided games; a revised definition of a 'pitch'; the increasing role of artificial surfaces in some pitch sports; and a fuller understanding of issues of quality, capacity, accessibility and availability (Sport England/CCPR, 2003: 21–22). The guidance therefore seeks to establish 'pitch capacity' based on current and future supply and demand factors, as opposed to identifying a fixed number of pitches and current use only. It is noteworthy that within planning legislation, a playing field is 'the whole of the site which encompasses at least one playing pitch' (*Statutory Instrument 1817*, cited in Sport England/CCPR, 2003), where a pitch is 0.4 hectares (1 acre). However, DfES guidance defines a pitch size as 0.2 hectares (Sport England/CCPR, 2003: 40), where the pitch is either grass or an artificial surface marked as a pitch 'at least part of the year'. Clearly this presented difficulties in auditing playing pitch provision. Subsequently, Sport England, in line with the DfES, have adopted the 0.2 hectares definition, abandoning the prior 0.4 hectares definition, which perhaps again highlights the limited influence that Sport England has on the issue.

In sum, within the New Labour term in office, legislation and policy has made an increasing presumption towards retaining playing fields and pitches, albeit within a context of all possible open space land uses, and it could be argued that a significant gap remains between policy and practice. The advocates aiming to conserve all fields and pitches have gradually been marginalised by a discourse centred on change and practices centred on assimilating playing fields within a framework centred on 'community needs' including non-sport interests. This perhaps highlights the significant degree of influence that government departments, such as the ODPM, have on land-use policy, where 'sporting needs' are relatively marginal within a hierarchy of influence. The re-organisation of government to facilitate thematic working practices and an increasing emphasis on the utility of sport in meeting central government objectives around education, youth justice and health, for example, may indicate resurgence in the value placed on sport but not necessarily on pitch sports or protecting playing fields. Arguably, sport-specific interests have been compromised at the grass-roots level of sports, but the case for protection of all fields and pitches has also been weakened by a declining trend in pitch sports participation.

ANALYSIS: THE NATIONAL CONTEXT

The playing fields issue can be understood through an analysis of the relationships between key policy actors and clusters of interests, who place a greater or lesser value on protecting playing fields and pitches within a context of competing policy priorities for land use. It is argued that the strategy of central government since 1997 has been to re-define the parameters of the debate and re-organise the policymaking process so that the core non-sport interests of government shape the agenda. In this context, playing fields may or may not be retained dependent on a number of local factors and influences. Policy change is seen to be the outcome of competing interests, where non-sport government interests have arguably gained greater influence at the expense of sport interests within government and voluntary sector sport. This section develops this line of argument by exploring patterns of interests, relationships between key organisations and coalitions, and funding issues. A brief summary concludes this section prior to the Liverpool case study.

In terms of organisational arrangements, a cluster of interests aiming to conserve and protect playing fields and pitches has emerged whose common goal is protection of all sites ideally from any development, but more pragmatically against any change of usage away from sport and recreation, and whose advocacy has raised awareness of the issue among the media and public. At the core of this coalition is the NPFA, CCPR and sections of the media, who view both central and local government bodies as placing a low value on conserving land for sport and recreation. The second cluster of interests is within the public sector, consisting of the DCMS, Sport England, local authority sport representation and allies within other government departments and agencies. However, significant tensions exist between and within both central and local governments in respect of sport and its relative utility. A third cluster of interests is centred on land development and consists of private sector interests and elements of central and local governments.

It is argued that central government has expanded its influence since 1997 over this policy concern. For example, the role and influence of Secretaries of State is pivotal, facilitating a degree of 'ministerial activism' (Taylor, 1997). The introduction of arms-length advisory panels may be viewed as providing checks and balances on the influence wielded by Secretaries of State where planning applications are 'called in', or alternatively viewed as a 'legitimising mechanism' facilitating, if not extending, the influence of central government ministers. Also, the new cross-departmental working arrangements are not only intended to better coordinate policy and actions and reduce the costs of policy duplication but also ensure the priorities of the ODPM are the core priorities. This re-organisation is expected to be mirrored in local government despite the absence of historical working practices between, for example, Leisure Services, Planning, Health and Education (see Liverpool case study). Further, with the increasing interconnectedness between government and business interests, the agenda of the ODPM sets the parameters of the debate around land use, where sport is one component.

Thus, in land-use planning policy, Sport England does not ultimately have the power to shape strategic planning decisions. For example, where Sport England has objected to disposal or change of use, it has been overruled on a regular basis by the ODPM 'for local strategic reasons' (DCMS, 2003). In other words, pressures for new housing or retail expansion, for example, ultimately are prioritised above sport and recreation needs. Therefore policy impacting on playing fields and pitches is largely founded outside of the specific issue in wider debates about open space. Further, within planning for urban regeneration, although the government has recognised the importance of playing fields, with, for example, the establishment of an *Urban Green Spaces Task Force* with the objective of influencing local authority policy and strategies for open space, the extent to which playing fields and pitches played a significant role remained debatable.

Central government was concerned with both the 'development of sport' and 'development through sport', where sport is an instrument for social policy goals, with the consequences that the *revised PPG17* drew upon the PAT10 report on 'sport and social exclusion' (DCMS, 1999). However, the revision to PPG17 may also have been influenced by the Labour government's lack of empathy with the core beliefs of the NPFA and its allies that were not only ideologically aligned to traditional Conservatism but which also viewed sport-specific interests as their core concern, with little value placed on sport as an instrument of social policy. It can be argued that this divide along the lines of core beliefs and normative preferences has in part shaped the policy process for the playing fields issue where the debate has become highly emotive.

For example, the former director of the NPFA stated, 'by suggesting that funds received from playing fields are ploughed back into sport or education, they [the Government] may even be exacerbating the situation as schools can see the short-term gains available more clearly' (NPFA, 2003: 1). In contrast, the chief executive of the YST at the time stated, 'It's frustrating to keep on hearing the same old arguments … There are still one or two examples of sports field's sales to be concerned about, but the reality is that we are seeing improved sports facilities in schools' (*Times Higher*, 11 November 2003). The DCMS Secretary of State goes further in describing the NPFA media campaign as 'perverse' and 'irresponsible scaremongering' (*Times Higher*, 11 November 2003).

The legitimacy and credibility of the NPFA has been called into question by government, for example in respect of the NPFA list of 'fields under threat' that is viewed as inaccurate. Statistics produced by the NPFA and government differs as to playing field 'losses' in part due to the methodology used, but also in part due to the divide over what constitutes a 'loss'. Further, the channels of communication between the NPFA, CCPR and central government, established during the Major administration, have been broken. For example, the CCPR state that 'It is felt that the Regional Offices of Sport England could do more to bring statutory consultations to our attention' (PMP, 2001: 12) indicating weak channels of communication, and at the county level, the County Playing Fields Association state, 'We have had no opportunity to contribute to any particular campaign against a loss of a pitch' (PMP, 2001: 17) implying that the planning and policy process excludes some organisations who do not share government priorities. In sum, the conservation coalition has become increasingly marginalised and outmanoeuvred by government, so that the issue is one of open space planning and not specifically planning for playing fields.

Given that at the local level, maintaining playing fields can be costly for local authorities already subject to land-use development pressures and that new funding for sports provision via the National Lottery such as the *Green Spaces* initiative is conditional on meeting central government priorities, local authorities have moved further away from the core policy concerns of the protectionist coalition. Given the non-statutory status of sport provision in local authorities, sports interests tend to be relatively marginal and arguably it is planning departments that control the local agenda in line with national policy directives originating in the ODPM (replaced by a department for local government and communities in 2006). This analysis is explored further through a case study of playing fields policy in Liverpool.

SPORT AND PLAYING FIELDS POLICY IN LIVERPOOL

This case study, first, traces the evolution of playing fields policy (incorporating playing pitches) in Liverpool; second, highlights the key influences shaping policy change including relationships between interests both internal to LCC and between LCC and external interests; and third, draws a number of conclusions around interests, influence and policy change.

THE EVOLUTION OF LOCAL PLAYING FIELDS POLICY

Although many English cities have experienced rapid urbanisation and increasing population growth, Liverpool, in the post-war era, saw a steady decline in population that reduced development pressures on the city's open spaces. As of 2001, the city fell only fractionally below the NPFA's *Six Acre Standard* per one thousand people. However, by 2008, the population was stabilising and land development pressures, particularly around the city centre, were beginning to increase, on account of inward investment and the regeneration of Liverpool via the vehicle of *European Capital of Culture*. The loss of one part of Stanley Park to Liverpool Football Club for the planned construction of a new stadium and the recent sale of university playing fields to a retail chain may signal emerging pressures on land used for sport and recreation.

The land-use context in Liverpool has been fluid since the 1970s given population shifts, the need for housing renewal, and re-organisations of the education sector resulting in a number of school closures. A well-developed infrastructure existed until the Second World War, but post-war investment suffered. The slum clearances of the 1960s and 1970s resulted in a decline in the inner city population with one consequence being a long period of neglect of spaces for sport and recreation. Even in the mid-1980s, when a Militant-controlled local government gave a new impetus to public leisure and sport, the focus was in recycling money away from playing fields and into leisure facilities. A *Review of Open Space* (LCC, 1987) conducted by the departments of Leisure, Education and Planning acted as the catalyst for disposal of 'sites suitable for alternative development' given the context of wider city regeneration. Specifically, the report identified a large stock of detached school playing fields that served inner city schools that could be targeted for disposal.

Historically, the inner city population was expected to travel to the suburbs to access playing fields, and this was LCC strategy. Many inner city (primary) schools had stopped playing football and other pitch sports as a result of poor access to playing fields and the costs associated with transport to suburban sites.

It can also be noted that throughout Merseyside in the 1980s, capital monies used for building on open spaces was not supported with the revenue funding to maintain sites. In the 1980s, many sites were lost to developers to raise capital for a local authority in significant financial difficulties (see chapter 4). Without the funding to maintain sites, many were neglected, or in some cases vandalised, to facilitate disposal.

A senior NPFA officer states that local authorities 'have let sites deteriorate then negotiated improvements in return for the sale of part of the land '. Moreover, the interviewee added that 'Under-investment leads to deteriorating facilities, which people do not want to use. They are allowed to get worse and change of use kicks in later.'

In respect of ownership of, and control over (ADD *playing fields*), (ADD *responsibility*) has shifted between departments over time, and although policy overseeing playing fields and pitches is now within the sport and recreation remit, this was not always the case. The period from 1988 to 1990 saw a re-structuring of LCC that impacted on the protection of playing fields, where previously the Environment Department controlled all green spaces in the city, and many sites were lost; Sport and Recreation Services gained control of this function from the mid-1990s having managed to convince the politicians that playing fields should be transferred to sport services. 'Sport' however, did not feature in city-wide planning until the first UDP for the city was written in the mid-1990s, with provision for sport and recreation being a small component in city-wide planning. Following this, the *playing fields review* of 1998 (LCC, 1998) found that the demand for playing field use was declining as the number of sports teams and leagues declined. This fact continued to place spaces to play sport under threat of disposal.

Currently, there are three strands to open spaces policy within LCC represented by three different departments, namely *land-use planning* (Planning department, with policy linked to the goals of city-wide planning within national policy guidelines); *public parks* (Parks and Grounds Maintenance department); and *Playing fields/pitches* (Sport and Recreation Services within the Leisure Services department). A senior Planning officer noted that 'in terms of policy process and general governance, Planning and Parks have a history of working together, but Leisure Services have been separate', adding that 'with the current division of functions, there is a need to knit together existing but separate plans'. However,, interviewees across departments agreed that 'PPG17 is very current and will help to break down barriers.'

A further review of open space that took place in 2002 (Leisure and Tourism Select Committee, 11 April; LCC, 2002c) was to be written into the UDP for 2005, but with the Local Development Framework (LDF) replacing the UDP approach, land-use planning now has a 'spatial approach' to account for other policy concerns in education and health. The revised

PPG17 required local authorities to take a holistic approach to planning, but until recently, a corporate view of open space in terms of needs, strategy, management or agreement on the value placed on space for sport was absent. Nonetheless, control over the sale and disposal of playing fields has not ultimately rested with Sport and Recreation Services. At the Executive Board meeting of 15 December 2000, it was noted that 'the disposal of land and premises is now dealt with corporately and as such all recommendations relating to disposals must be referred to the Resources Portfolio'(Exccutive Board, 15 December, LCC, 2000b).

This fundamental policy shift, coupled with the introduction of the revised PPG17, underpinned a comprehensive review of land use, open spaces, parks and playing fields, and pitches. Subsequently, the consultancy brief (LCC, 2003c) noted that 'Playing fields may well pose one of the greatest challenges for open space policies' adding 'the retention of land specifically for use as playing pitches must be related to the local community's needs for organised sport.' Provision was thercfore to shadow need. However, defining 'need' given the changing demographics in Liverpool with an aging, smaller population, and lifestyle changes, falling school rolls, and taking account of the physical activities young people want to pursue, questions were raised within LCC around the continued relevance of parks and playing fields in the city.

The final report was subject to a number of delays due to Sport and Recreation Services and the government body, English Heritage being 'unhappy with the fieldwork conducted by the consultants', changes of staff in the Planning department, and the size of the task in mapping all open space and its uses in line with PPG17. Following a lengthy period of auditing provision, departmental negotiations and reviews, given the complexity of the debate and competing agendas, the Open Spaces Review (LCC, 2007) was finally published. This statement represents a compromise between the various local authority departmental interests with existing playing fields and pitches largely protected. This outcome was in part a result of the skilled brokering of the former policy officer in sport services responsible for the site protection and development.

In terms of current provision for pitch sports and outdoor recreation, with the population size halving in Liverpool since the 1960s and changes in demographics and lifestyles, the city arguably has adequate overall space to play sport. An abundance of playing fields and pitches exists across the county that compares favourably with provision across Greater Manchester (unpublished LCC data, 2004) although a more detailed analysis raises questions about the location, size and quality of sites. In terms of the adequacy of school playing fields, a former school head notes that the 'grass not being cut was a bigger problem' than the loss of fields, where 'quality' and 'access' were 'the real issues', not the amount of sites, giving the example of pupils of a specialist sport college in Liverpool having to travel a mile to access playing fields. In Liverpool, the pattern of provision appears uneven, with inner city areas experiencing a deficit and the suburbs a surplus. However, access has improved following the introduction of SSCs that facilitated the use of SSC sites by feeder schools (see Chapter 7). The economic and independent status of schools is a factor in pitch retention, where in the case of Bluecoats Selective School, grass pitches were purchased from the LEA in 2002. In contrast, the poorer inner city schools have been less able to defend sites from LEA disposal.

In terms of the disposal of sites, most of the fields that have been lost in the last few years have been to extend educational provision rather than for housing or other needs, and if a playing field was sold, it was replaced by one of better quality. In fact, there have been very few losses of sites in the last 5 years with losses related to school closures, which is perhaps indicative of the impact of the revised, more robust, PPG17. In terms of the growing presumption towards site retention, the thrust of national policy had an impact; with interviewees highlighting the fact that processes are 'more robust now than in prior years', where Sport England as a statutory Consultee 'has had a marked effect'. However, a senior officer adds that in recent years, 'The loss of playing fields … (has) … not been significantly arrested (but) has improved … whereas under the Conservatives sales went unchecked.'

In sum, sites are better protected than a decade ago, but the layers of protection within legislation and policy guidance do not necessarily conserve sites from disposal. In fact, the Merseyside Playing Fields Association (MPFA) highlight the 'small battles' fought in defence of land owned by the NPFA and leased to local authorities, and 'larger battles are fought where MPFA do not own the land'. For example, in recent years, 'battles' were fought where Liverpool University sold some of its playing fields to a supermarket, a site at Jericho Lane 'in good condition' and experiencing sport and recreation usage was sold for new housing despite 'huge protest', and the Lee Valley School site and playing fields were agreed to be sold in 2002, despite the site lying within the green belt area (as noted in the Executive Board minutes, 26 April 2002; LCC, 2002a). This is reflected in the demise of *The Six Acre Standard*, where a former planning officer confirms that '*The Six Acre Standard* is not adopted … the guidance in *Towards a Level Playing Field* is followed.'

A policy officer observed that 'The old NPFA *Six Acre Standard* which most local authorities used to work to, or try to emulate, effectively has gone out of the window.' The MPFA representative notes that the NPFA has recently 'fell out of favour with government ministers' and this too has affected local relationships. In terms of the relationship between LCC and the MPFA, arguably, the influence of the MPFA is marginal, where the local association is relatively inactive in opposing the loss of sites, as accepted by the Chair of the body, adding that 'the focus of MPFA's work has shifted from sport to play in recent years'. A MPFA officer notes that the MPFA 'have no particular rapport with the leisure (department) … the NPFA hear of LCC plans before we do'.

Moreover, the 'MPFA have not been consulted (by LCC) in the last 10 years', the time in which the current Chair has been in post. The interviewee states that LCC are 'not committed to working with the voluntary sector' and LCC 'do not support middle-men', that is representative bodies, preferring a direct relationship with voluntary sector groups. Further, LCC want to fund projects rather than organisations and 'if it doesn't fit their plan, they won't put themselves out to do it'. Although a senior officer of the NPFA claims to have had some success of late in influencing national DfES policy guidance that 'will have a drip down impact on many school sites', locally, the MPFA has had little impact on LCC policy, being resource dependent on local authorities (the MPFA receives funding from the five local authorities supplemented by fundraising activities) and not being embedded in decision-making processes affecting playing fields. In effect, the MPFA are 'tolerated' by LCC who remain indifferent to their activities, given that the MPFA has almost no influence on playing fields policy.

Within LCC, Sport and Recreation Services have recently engaged in developing new sites. This has been possible as a result of investment through NOF and by the Football Foundation totalling over £8m as the budget for sport and recreation alone was not adequate given budgetary constraints. A senior policy officer notes that Sport and Recreation Services have been 'trying to be proactive for a long time' and now are actively creating a reserve stock and therefore the capacity 'to counter shifts' in demand, demographics and population.

However, according to a number of interviewees, it was the influence of the former SAZ manager and regeneration agencies that prompted LCC to improve inner-city playing spaces through accessing non-sport specific funding streams. The fact that it has taken an exogenous intervention to take action perhaps indicates that local authorities are not sure which agenda they are following in respect of playing fields and open spaces. This in part may be due to the conditions in which playing fields policy is made and implemented, where regeneration is driven by programmes, the pursuit of funding, and meeting timescales within a constantly shifting policy context where policy statements and guidance dates quickly.

ANALYSIS: THE LOCAL CONTEXT

The research undertaken indicates that a number of inter-departmental and inter-organisational relationships influence playing fields policy, including central–local government, between LCC departments, the local authority and Sport England, non-sport agencies in the regeneration sector, voluntary sector bodies seeking to protect sites, and developers.

It is noteworthy that not only do decision-making processes exclude influence from the voluntary sector, but the decisions themselves are based on altogether different assumptions, understandings and values. LCC decisions are based on an analysis of supply and demand and data on trends. The issue is therefore defined as one of 'distribution'. There is pragmatism in policymaking where the level of LCC provision was not sustainable given the costs of ownership and maintenance, and this had an impact on LCC behaviour with LCC making the 'best' decisions under the circumstances. In practice, sites are considered for re-development 'as opportunities arise'. The revised PPG17 emphasis on compensatory developments and taking a 'flexible approach' locally do not square with the conservatism of the NPFA and regional representatives. Indicative of the difference in viewpoints between local authorities and the NPFA are comments made by a senior LCC policy officer who stated that 'Protectionists tend to fossilise the situation.'

In practice, the core working relationship on this issue is between LCC and Sport England, whose guidance is given greater significance than that offered by the NPFA. Partnerships are therefore made with other professionals in the public sector, excluding the voluntary sector. For example, the Open Spaces consultancy brief (LCC, 2003c) acknowledges the 'close working relationship' between LCC and English Heritage, whose guidance is central to LCC policy for open spaces, unlike the NPFA and its county representatives.

Despite the increasing control of the issue by the public sector to the exclusion of the voluntary sector and communities, significant yet familiar implementation problems remain, which in turn influence the policy process for playing fields. An officer involved in the recent Open Spaces Review noted that local authorities LCC commission consultants to do 'blue sky thinking' and master plans, but these just sit on the shelf and no one takes ownership of the open space issue. Other interviewees observed that organisations are 'chasing the money with little idea as to what to do with it', 'establishing initiatives that duplicate work elsewhere' and 'lack a strategic overview'.

In fact, the catalyst and spur for action in decisions concerning land use tends to originate from commercial sector pressure. In terms of private sector interests, perhaps the most high-profile sale of land in the last few years has ironically been the loss of part of Stanley Park, one of the first Victorian parks built in the city, for the purpose of building a new stadium for Liverpool Football Club denoting the strength of commercial sports interests by comparison with grass-roots sport interests.

A senior policy officer stated that 'The City Council Regeneration section (Parks Department) does not want to look after any more open space as they are strapped for money' hence as of late 2005, LCC were tendering for management of its own parks. LCC were not in a position to invest in parks (LSF, 2005b) given the level of subsidy to Leisure Services and the rising costs of grounds maintenance. In working with the private sector, many LCC senior officers and members argue that the benefits of such a partnership outweigh the costs in terms of city-wide regeneration, in respect of which, the value of open spaces is recognised by Liverpool First and the LPG (the strategic bodies that oversee city-wide regeneration) in relation to increasing tourism and inward migration. However, development pressures have increased in Liverpool since the allocation of *Capital of Culture* status in 2003, where the increased emphasis on housing via Housing Market Renewal Initiative (HMRI) monies may put pressure on existing open spaces. The ongoing major housing renewal programme in the city is likely to be the key regeneration initiative to impact on playing field retention. A policy consultant observed that 'If it is not defined as open space it will become a housing development area.' Arguably the housing regeneration bodies have little interest or commitment to developing good quality open space or public realm areas.

Considering the future, the pattern of interests and relationships is set to change again via a number of forthcoming exogenous events outside of 'sport' that shape the playing fields issue. First, in respect of change in education policy, with so many schools in Liverpool, the problem is finding anywhere suitable for the new schools meaning green spaces may be lost to development via the *Building Schools for the Future* (DfES, 2005b) initiative. Second, in terms of demographics, Liverpool has an aging population, potentially impacting on the type of sports provision offered by LCC. Third, given the trend away from pitch sports participation, playing fields again may be lost.

CONCLUSIONS

Liverpool as an urban area has a relatively high number of spaces to play sport and recreate, given its legacy of public park provision, sporting culture and history of outward migration. Yet, it also has a history of neglecting its playing fields, and questions remain around distribution, quality and access. In terms of key interests, playing fields policy cuts across a number of local government departmental priorities, with policy a compromise between interests, although it is arguably a discourse framed by economic priorities. Although the 'modernisation' of local government has encouraged inter-departmental working practices around the 'spatial planning' model, departmentalism remains embedded within LCC.

In this context, Sport and Recreation Services has sought to defend its playing fields and pitch programmes from departmental interests within Education, Planning and Resources, who have greater influence over decision-making processes underpinning playing fields policy. In short, the playing fields issue is not determined to any significant degree by sport-specific interests, either within LCC or external to it. Sport and Recreation Services has adopted a pragmatic stance, making policy decisions based on changes in supply and demand, demographic factors and by anticipating trends in sport participation. Policy processes appear to be officer-driven within LCC, where councillors, despite making promises to protect playing fields in election statements, are compromised once in office. Nonetheless, where key decisions regarding land-use in the city are on the agenda, the ruling political party executive has significant scope for intervention.

In sum, policy concerns and issues around playing fields are historically embedded in disputes concerning the use of space for recreational and sporting purposes. Arguably, it is a case of how the issue is defined that underpins subsequent policy actions and defining the parameters of the issue are competing interests each with differing core policy priorities. The framing of the issue is complicated by the fact that so many organisations have an interest in this issue. These include a number of central and local government departments and agencies, regeneration agencies, voluntary sector bodies, private sector businesses and schools. It is suggested that the balance of influence between these bodies and sectors has changed over time as political ideologies and policy rationales, in particular, have changed.

Policy change for this issue is therefore, at least in part, the result of coalitions of interests competing to define and orientate policy to mirror their core beliefs and policy priorities. In particular, the 'protectionist' coalition, with the NPFA at its core, has been in direct competition with the 'development' coalition supported by government and business interests. It can also be noted that decisions regarding playing fields are shaped locally by relationships between public sector body professionals to the exclusion of the voluntary sector for sport, where an ineffective loose coalition of interests in and around playing fields conservation exists.

In respect of the playing fields issue, legislation and policy guidance may be viewed therefore as little more than a record of the bargains struck within a policy area that includes sport, recreation, education, planning and commercial development interests. The close relationship both locally and centrally between government and commercial interests, particularly in Liverpool given the ongoing regeneration around culture, tourism, education and housing, has served to highlight the tensions between the many interests seeking to shape policy affecting spaces to play.

The ambiguity embedded within policy affecting pitch sports is evident with, on the one hand, the more robust PPG17, an increasing value placed on sport or at least physical activity, by central government, the increasing emphasis on the importance of school sport and PE and new funding streams, and the requirement for local authorities to conduct local needs assessments, all of which would suggest that the retention of playing fields and pitches appears to have become a greater concern of national and local policymakers over the last decade. On the other hand, development pressures, particularly for new housing, retail expansion, and even new stadia for commercial sector football clubs, suggest that playing fields and other public spaces to play, even parks, are ultimately expendable. Further, the complexities of the planning system and its relative interconnectedness with charity law, contract law and potential new legislation affecting school playing fields may impact on policy outcomes and produce unintended consequences.

The muddled implementation of policy is further compromised by the capacity of LCC to act. For example, in respect of the requirement on local authorities to undertake local audits, a policy officer stated 'the move towards local assessments is welcome for all forms of open space but experience indicates that the assessments may not be comprehensive and that they will not be kept up to date.' Indeed, assessment of playing pitch quantity, quality, access and sustainability has been infrequent and often conducted as a response to 'crisis' or policy in adjacent policy sectors. As the national PMP survey indicated, local authorities have been less than effective or accountable, despite proclamations of *Best Value*, in implementing a coherent and workable strategy for playing fields and pitches. This survey also notes that local authorities have little incentive to prepare needs assessments and quality audits of provision for sport, with relatively few sites allocated to sport/recreation in development plans. Moreover the system 'is hampered to some extent by current national planning policies and by reluctance amongst local planning authorities to allocate sufficient land for these purposes' including sport (Independent Sports Review Group, 2005: 74).

Finally a senior representative of the NPFA concluded that as locally elected members, Directors of local authority Departments, School Governors and Heads are all in place for a relatively short time, they all feel the need to effect change, and they need resources for this. Often the easiest and biggest resources come from changing land use and disposal.

Note: *The Six Acre Standard* consists of a range of spaces fit for 'outdoor sport' and 'children's playing space', including playing pitches, and also athletics tracks, greens, courts, playgrounds, 'training areas', 'casual or informal playing space within housing areas' and 'miscellaneous sites' irrespective of ownership type, whether local authorities or facilities within the education, voluntary, private, industrial and commercial sectors (NPFA, 2001: 7).

CHAPTER 10

Sport and Community Regeneration

CHAPTER CONTENTS

INTRODUCTION

This chapter will describe and analyse sport policy and practice within an area-based community-level initiative in south Liverpool where sport is a component of social policy objectives (see Chapter 3). The particular focus is the use of sport, recreation and related physical activity in addressing social exclusion defined in terms of a combination of linked problems such as unemployment, poor skills, low incomes, poor housing, high crime, ill health and family breakdown (Collins and Kay, 2003; DCMS, 1999, 2002). As a result of this policy concern, SAZs were established on the premise that 'Sport and recreational activity can contribute to neighbourhood renewal and make a real difference to health, crime, employment and education in deprived communities' (DCMS, 1999: 8). This area-based approach to policy intervention was already established in the form of

Education Action Zones (EAZs) and HAZs, for example, with Merseyside being one such HAZ prior to the introduction of PCTs (see Chapter 8).

Sport Action Zones located in areas of socio-economic deprivation embody a partnership-based approach to policy implementation that cuts across policy areas such as sport, education, health, youth justice and employment. Initially twelve were identified, including an area of inner-city Liverpool around Granby and Toxteth. The socio-economic and political history of the area and its relationship with local sport policy, particularly in regard to the urban unrest of 1981 and the subsequent construction of Toxteth Sports Centre, is documented in Chapter 5.

LIVERPOOL SPORT ACTION ZONE

The Liverpool SAZ was established in the year 2000 with a remit to operate for 5 years. The area has a population of approximately 55,000 and can be characterised in terms of high levels of socio-economic deprivation, poor health and low levels of participation in sport and physical activity. The SAZ was the outcome of negotiations involving central government, Sport England and LCC Sport, whose former head lobbied for the original geographical boundaries to be altered so as to include the facilities at the Wavertree Playground site in order to increase the possibilities for raising participation. With social policy goals at its core, a 5-year plan was created, centred specifically on increasing participation and impacting on social exclusion through establishing a series of programmes that linked sport and physical activity with social policy. This is demonstrated in identifying the key partners and their core business. The partners included LCC Sport (the accountable body), Parks Options (regeneration), NACRO (community safety with a focus on young people), Dingle Opportunities (employment) and Liverpool PCT (health). Over its 5-year term, £2.6m was received from Sport England (including funding for the SAZ manager's post) and £14.4m of external funding was generated (4.8 revenue and 9.6 capital) from government, trusts and European sources. In fact, 52% of the funding generated to underpin programme development and implementation was from non-sporting sources.

The significant management challenges facing a small core team of staff included establishing credibility with local communities; building capacity into a weak infrastructure; effective partnership-working across policy areas; acquiring and sustaining funding; and assessing, disseminating and demonstrating good practice. Notable capital projects undertaken within the SAZ include the establishment of new dual-use sport facilities at Shorefields School (Starrfields), refurbishment of the BCAC, use of *Space for Sport and the Arts* monies to upgrade the play area at Beaufort Park School, a new sports centre in Kensington, a community tennis club based at Belvedere

School and upgrades of Admiral Street Recreation Ground and Botanic Park. Revenue projects included setting up of after-school sports clubs; boxing-based initiatives at BCAC; various health-related schemes; utilising sport in employment schemes such as Skills Training and Employment Programme for Sport (STEPS); and in tackling youth crime, for example the Dingle Youth Sport Project. Four of these projects are detailed in this chapter. Specific target groups for interventions included young people, ethnic minorities and people with disabilities in areas of low income. In terms of resource distribution, SAZ community grants were allocated to a range of local organisations including youth clubs, sport-specific clubs (including those for martial arts, boxing and basketball) and organisations representing specific social or ethnic groups in an area characterised by multi-cultural diversity. In order to build capacity, SAZ management worked with existing and entrenched community sports organisations including the long-standing Toxteth Tigers basketball club (now known as Everton Tigers).

At the completion of the 5 years, a review by Ipsos MORI commissioned by Sport England found that 'overall regular participation in sport and physical activity increased by five per cent (60% to 65%) although more significantly it increased 12 per cent among the over 50 age group (36% to 48%) and among socio-economically deprived (C2DE) groups it increased by 10 per cent (43% to 53%)'. Specific 'success factors' identified in the report included a highly motivated and skilled leader and team of local paid staff and volunteers, taking a 'bottom up' approach to empower local people and providing small grants to help build goodwill in the community, utilising people's sense of identity and community in developing programmes, offering a variety of physical activities (not only a narrow range of sports) with low-cost or free taster sessions, investing in appropriate facilities and open spaces, promoting and supporting volunteering by local residents, and engaging effectively with a wide range of partnerships within and outside of the sport sector in order to pool resources and influence. These findings mirror those identified in the PAT10 report (DCMS, 1999), where good practice was identified as effective partnership-working involving the community; locally trained leaders and youth workers; sustainable schemes that are adequately resourced; monitoring and evaluating success and/or problems in programmes; and learning from good practice elsewhere. The relative success of the SAZ can be located within the context of a city with poor participation levels and high levels of poor health, particularly in the north of the city as identified in Sport England's *Active People* survey (Sport England, 2006).

The success of the SAZ resulted in the area-based approach being replicated across Liverpool from 2007 to 2008 through five SPAAs with the former SAZ forming one part of two SPAAs. Each alliance has been geographically constructed around the five NMAs in the city, each incorporating six local authority wards. Further, the four SSCs form partnerships with the five alliances (although one school may not acquire full SSC status at the time of writing). The policy emphasis of SPAAs is primarily on physical activity as opposed to sport *per se*, but sports can feature in delivering physical activity in communities. As of 2008, the size of the challenge remains very high, where sport, in practice, may only play a minor, albeit important, role in community regeneration and building social inclusion (Coalter, 2007). Arguably, the infrastructure within the sport policy area does not currently have the capacity to deliver significant, long-term social change. Building this capacity is the key objective of the SPAAs. However, this, as the case studies to follow demonstrate, requires adequate sustainable resourcing, leadership, expertise and political will.

PROGRAMMES AND PROJECTS

This section consists of four case studies that describe, analyse and attempt to explain policy processes and practices. Of particular interest are, first,

Starrfields

Starrfields is a capital project based at Shorefields Comprehensive School in the Dingle area of Toxteth and aimed to provide sport facilities for both the school and wider community in an area of the city with few facilities for young people. An interviewee charged with acquiring the funding for the project noted that a prior The Office for Standards in Education, Children's Services and Skills (OFSTED) report had cited the poor quality of the outdoor space for sport at the school. The idea of the project was effectively to extend the school site by acquiring the derelict space adjoining the school that was regularly used for anti-social activities by a small number of youths.

In 2001, NOF monies became available to support a number of capital projects across Liverpool. In the case of Shorefields School, the facility was funded primarily by NOF with a financial contribution made by the school itself. Starrfields, as the facility was named (after the Beatles musician Ringo Starr who once lived in the area), was a phase-two project that was led by the SAZ with key partners being the school, a regeneration agency and Youth Services (within LCC), Sport and Recreation Services and

representation from the EAZ that has since been dissolved. The NOF funding was delivered in two phases, with phase-one projects given priority. One successful project resulting from phase one was the construction of a new tennis centre at Archbishop Beck Specialist Sports College. Unfortunately, as the phase-one projects overspent, some phase-two projects were cut, including Starrfields. However, fortunately for the project, a phase-one project in the Gateacre area of the city subsequently failed given the problems with the site survey, resulting in Starrfields being reinstated. The new facility was eventually opened in 2007.

A number of inter-related issues can be identified in this project that provides insight into policy processes and political practices. First, the problems associated with obtaining planning permission for the change of use of an open space can delay projects. Second, change of use was resisted by a small but vocal minority of residents given fears that the sports facility would attract young people, which was perceived as a threat by a small number of residents whose property adjoined the site. Third, the intervention of ward councillors in 'support' of a few residents and against the policy content, including the nature of policy problems; second, the key policy actors, their partners and/or networks of influence and their policy priorities; third, policy determinants (factors or influences shaping stability and change in policy and practice); fourth, instruments utilised by local actors seeking to achieve organisational objectives; fifth, the local organisational and funding context in which policy is formulated and implemented; and sixth, policy outcomes and impacts that may inform policy re-formulation and policy learning. Each study highlights *components* of these complex policy processes rather than attempting to provide a comprehensive account.

It is intended that the cases will illuminate policy and practice at the level of implementation and the findings can be employed in constructing a theoretical framework for understanding local sport policy (in this case as an element of social policy).

the wider benefits of the project to the area, and young people in particular, serves only to illustrate the regressive nature of local politics in the city. The fact that ward boundaries changed during the term of project development and the fact that the project is located in a ward that borders two others, overseen by different councillors and, latterly, by different political groups, has resulted in disputes over who are the benefactors of the project. Compounding the politics of parochialism is the fact that funding allocations to wards differ on the basis of indices of deprivation leading to disagreements over which ward should support the project and to what extent.

Fourth, there were significant challenges for SAZ management in working with the partner agencies that demonstrated weak commitment, energy and leadership. This resulted in the SAZ having to commit greater human resources to the project at the expense of other activities. Fifth, tensions emerged around community use of the site outside of school hours. In essence, community sport groups wanted free usage of the site and the school and other partners believe the facility will be more highly valued by participants who pay a nominal amount to use the site. Moreover, the school pays for the site to be open in the evenings and for its maintenance. However, the culture of dependence on 'the state' is deeply entrenched in the mindset of poorer communities, and the expectation among community groups is one of non-payment given an inflated sense of entitlement. Sixth, as with almost all facilities across the city, there are security issues relating to misuse and vandalism including, most prominently, the costs of securing buildings and open spaces. These costs reduce funding for delivering a higher quality of sports facility.

It can be added that the preferential allocation of monies by the NOF steering group to 'favoured projects' illustrates the lobbying capacity of dominant interests and individuals involved in shaping policy and practice. It cannot be said that the merits of a bid alone will win support. In the final analysis, the project was fortunate ever to have been approved and but for the efforts, brokering and negotiation skills, funding knowledge, and strong leadership of the SAZ management, this project would not have been realised.

Botanic Park

The aim of this project was to stimulate greater use of a public park through building a new community facility to serve an existing junior football league (Edge Hill) that has a long history of using the park's pitches, Edge Hill Youth Club, and for other community uses. The core funders were the European Regional Development Fund (ERDF) and the Football Foundation with support from a regeneration agency, Sport England, LCC (NRF monies) and a housing association; to be delivered through the SAZ; maintained by LCC Sport; and managed by a community group.

The SAZ faced a number of significant challenges over a period of almost 6 years from project proposal to completion in 2008. First, the SAZ met with significant resistance from Parks and Environmental Services (Parks) within LCC that did not approve the plans for 2 years due to the SAZ seeking a 'stand alone project', whereas Parks thought of Botanic park in terms of a wider restoration plan, in line with *Rethinking Open Space. Open Space Provision and Management: A Way Forward* (see Chapter 9). Further, there are the financial costs to the local authority of owning and maintaining a facility in the context of existing budget commitments. Second, difficulties were encountered with securing access to monies released through Section 106 of the *Town and Country Planning Act 1990* that 'allows local authorities to negotiate agreements with developers that require them to make some form of financial commitment if planning permission is obtained' (London Assembly, 2008: 8). A component of the wider park that hosts the Littlewoods building (formerly used for administering the football pools) had been purchased by developers *Urban Splash* in 2006. In return, the financial guaranted of the developers was to commit to improving the park for recreational purposes.

Belvedere Boy's and Men's Boxing Programme

The BCAC, formerly a boys' club formed in 1898, is a venue for a number of sport-based community programmes in L8. Commonly known as 'the Belve', the facility also hosts the *Golden Gloves* Amateur Boxing Club. One boxing-based programme was founded on the 'lads and dads' concept that aims to re-establish family values, provide role models for young men, increase the employability of participants, and rebuild communities affected by poor health, high unemployment and other aspects of social exclusion. The Working Neighbourhood Fund (WNF that replaced NRF) which operates on a rolling 1-year cycle underpins the programme that is managed through the SPAA for south-central Liverpool. The SPAA manager has therefore to continually pursue funding to sustain this programme alongside many others. One such funding source is the PCT health grants in a partnership that cuts across policy areas. The key stakeholders include the SPAA, LCC boxing development, the LCC Youth Offending Team (YOT), the boxing club and the local community.

In regard to the implementation of the programme, the pilot was initially unsuccessful for a number of reasons including difficulties with the distrust within the local community of 'external' interventions and professionals; the internal politics of the community centre; levels of staff expertise in managing conflict; and not least, in recruiting participants. However, within a short time period, the programme expanded rapidly and gained community support. The 'tipping point' was the recruitment of an ex-professional boxer to the programme, who was a youth worker and is a local resident, and therefore holds a high level of respect within the community. The subsequent recruitment of a current professional boxer to host 'exhibition' sessions and the linking of boxing-based activities to an on-site 'breakfast club' for local families has strengthened the sustainability of the programme. Moreover, the strategic role of the SPAA manager combined with the brokering role of the project leader has engendered trust in a community defined by low levels of social capital.

Nonetheless, the future success of the programme is dependent on a number of factors. First, support from local councillors with a partial control over local resource allocation is important. A key source of conflict that exists around

Third, a key partner delayed committing funds until a 'window of opportunity' arose for their funds to be released. The threat of 'claw-back' by central government incentivised the agency to support the project, albeit belatedly. Fourth, a community group was initially resistant to the proposed facility until misunderstandings were resolved. One specific difficulty related to the costs associated with commissioning a feasibility study. A combination of these influences resulted in significant delays that could have resulted in the project being discontinued particularly as the costs of the project escalated. Moreover, it is unusual for ERDF to fund sport-based projects, and delays almost derailed the project.

To a considerable extent, it was the SAZ senior management that negotiated the project through these obstacles. Without highly skilled management demonstrated in brokering interests and knowledge of funding acquisition

processes, the community facility would not have materialised. This and other projects involving a relationship between LCC and external agencies in the 'development through sport' policy area (Houlihan and White, 2002) highlight competing understandings of 'sport in the community'. Although LCC Sport view community sport as centring on making available sport facilities in local communities, the SAZ and similar agencies view their remit in terms of outreach work where sport is an instrument of community engagement and meeting social policy outcomes. Whereas the SAZ remit is defined in terms of pro-active development, facilitating and enabling communities to be self-managing, LCC Sport see their role as providing *for* the community. Arguably, the local authority has a narrow understanding of community sport and this undermines progressive discourse and action in the local policy area.

community programmes centres on identifying the beneficiaries, particularly where clubs attract participants across ward boundaries (as with the Starrfields project). Second, competition for participations between organisations in the community, such as youth clubs, where funding retention is linked to the number of service users, can undermine programme objectives and reduce trust between organisations with similar objectives. Third, a low value is allocated to sport by non-sport organisations, including youth services and detached youth workers. Without recognition of the positive impact of sport on communities, programme sustainability is compromised. Critically, it is established and effective relationships between organisations that facilitate funding acquisition, project management and the retention of participants. Fourth, the relatively low level of monitoring and evaluation in addition to the difficulties associated with quantifying programme effectiveness does not support the case for sport in meeting social policy objectives (Coalter, 2007). This programme has subsequently established a partnership with a local university to assist in programme assessment. However, it is often the case that non-sport

bodies such as those in the local health sector do not always insist on detailed and qualitative programme evaluation in the distribution of grants. The release of funds has more to do with the stage of the organisation's funding cycle.

Sixth, the success of programmes of this type appears to depend on the skills and commitment of a few individuals who hold respect in local communities. Rolling out the programme to other areas of the city could be problematic without individuals who hold this profile. However, given the 'old boys network' around community boxing clubs in the city, an opportunity exists for the dissemination of good practice and policy learning. Seventh, without an effective partnership between community leaders and policy brokers with strong communication skills in public sector bodies such as SPAAs, tensions between community factions and individuals can undermine programmes. However, the benefits and costs associated with utilising community members in the shaping of programmes needs careful consideration. Given the multi-ethnic and multi-racial nature of the L8 area, it has proved to be important that clubs and programmes do not acquire a single-group status as one strand of intra-community tension centres on who can be identified as the users and beneficiaries of the centre. In sum, this revenue-based, community sport–based programme, as with others across the city, operates in a complex policy environment that is not predisposed to supporting policy actors seeking to tackle elements of social exclusion through sport and physical activity. Despite this, anecdotal evidence suggests that these type of projects can and do 'make a difference' to individuals and local communities. It is unfortunate that the work of community sport clubs goes largely unrecognised by those responsible for steering public policy.

Dingle Youth Sport Project

The aim of this project, founded in 2004 and operational in the Dingle area of Toxteth, was to utilise sport in conflict resolution between youth gangs divided by 'boundary disputes' relating to components of social exclusion (DCMS, 1999) and the legacy of sectarianism in the area. One programme objective was to establish a youth forum in order to provide a voice for disaffected young people, with a particular focus on extending recreational opportunity. The project was developed by the SAZ and managed through the Dingle Community Regeneration Trust (DCRT) until it folded and was replaced by the Merseyside Youth Association (MYA). The project was funded by Sport Relief and the SAZ Magnet Fund.

The challenges facing the SAZ are similar to the challenges faced by the other programmes identified in this chapter. First, there are difficulties of public sector bodies such as the SAZ working with voluntary sector groups that demonstrate weak organisational capacity and leadership in the delivery of project objectives. The leadership of projects such as these is critical to the sustainability and impact of the project. Second, community 'buy-in' is essential where communities can and do resist 'external' initiatives on account of 'intervention fatigue' following years of agencies delivering short-term, unsustainable initiatives. Active intervention is required of public sector agencies to appease funding bodies, even if it is inappropriate, and this has had a negative impact on social capital, itself a scarce resource in many local communities across Liverpool. Third, the community politics of the area is divisive and regressive, and sport-based youth projects have limited capacity to mediate adversarial inter-organisational relations in attempting to implement social policy goals.

ANALYSIS

Understanding policy processes in the implementation of community-based programmes, originating in national policy, that utilise sport and physical activity requires an analysis of the resources and relationships located within a local socio-economic and political context. Policy actors attempt to pursue their organisational and personal objectives in the context of scarce resources. Their actions are mediated by a range of partner organisations with similarities and differences in priorities, resources, the extent to which they can mobilise influence, and the extent of their entrenchment within local communities. As the case study demonstrates, the relative success in achieving policy goals, where it is to be found, is in large part the result of skilled brokering, expertise and commitment of a few individuals operating in a hostile policy environment.

The case study illustrates how policy actors, such as the SAZ management, are constrained in attempting to implement policy by a combination of factors. First, the necessity to pursue monies to support programmes and staffing in the absence of mainstreamed funding undercuts the quality of delivery. The requirements, conditions, timescales and inflexibility of funding bodies serve only to impede capacity-building. Second, weak leadership demonstrated by key partner organisations inhibits successful policy outputs and outcomes. Partner agencies have consistently failed to support innovation, development and core costs. In part, these issues stem from neither LCC Sport nor regeneration agencies placing a value on the work of sport-based organisations involved in delivering sport within the 'community-regeneration' remit.

Third, there are significant weaknesses in the local, sport-related facility infrastructure that impedes programme delivery resulting from significant long-term under-investment in community sport across the city, particularly where many community leisure centres, clubs, school sites and open spaces are no longer 'fit for purpose'. Fourth, political-party and personal agendas of local politicians and their varying levels of budgetary control can cut across programme objectives. Fifth, community negativity, isolationism and defensiveness resulting in part from relentless public sector interventions have served only to reinforce a pre-existing culture of resource dependence. Sixth, the variable quality of human resources in programme delivery can militate, and has in some cases militated, against programme success. It can be added that community regeneration agency objectives tend to prioritise organisational benefit and survival ahead of community benefit. Senior SAZ personnel also cited difficulties in implanting new thinking and ideas into a policy area with weak learning capacity. In part, this is due to the costs associated with new developments; hence there is little incentive to innovate. Where organisations such as the local authority are increasingly resources-driven, the disincentive to innovate is magnified and therefore 'buy-in' to expanding community provision is limited.

It is perhaps surprising that some sport-based community-regeneration programmes can and do result in positive outcomes and impacts. Although not detailed here, the STEPS project, for example, has delivered employment in the sport sector for many long-term unemployed people and this has had a 'knock-on effect' on families and local communities. Again, however, it was strong leadership and skilled personnel that was critical to developing a successful project in a constructive partnership with *Everton in the Community* (Everton Football Club's community project). Nonetheless, many programmes, unsurprisingly, given the policy context as outlined, have little or no positive impact on communities, and the dissemination of good practice, where it exists, is not extensive. Moreover, policy learning cannot be said to be a feature of most projects and evaluation; where it exists, it is limited in scope and quality (see Coalter, 2007). Instead, it is political agendas that drive community regeneration. Organisations such as the SAZ and latterly the SPAAs that embody policy priorities around 'development through sport' (Houlihan and White, 2002) require skilled policy brokers to navigate the overlapping interests of issue networks at the margins of local public policy concerns.

PART 5

Discussion

Analysing Sport Policy in Liverpool

INTRODUCTION

Based on the case study research outlined in previous chapters, this chapter provides, first, a summary analysis of the key dimensions of local sport policy, and second, relates the findings to understandings of local government and governance. The following chapter will then seek to explain local sport policy and practice through the use of policy theory as set out in Part 1 of this book.

DIMENSIONS OF SPORT POLICY IN LIVERPOOL

In brief, the study of sport policy in a single local authority area found evidence of a relatively mature elite sport policy community or advocacy coalition, whose members include the local authority sport/recreation department; elite sport interests within six governing bodies for sport, representing athletics, boxing, football, gymnastics, swimming and tennis; and commercial representation for each sport. A nascent policy advocacy coalition exists, based loosely around school sport and those involved in utilising sport in community regeneration, with other diverse interests associated with sport spanning a range of issue networks, including those concerned with the competitive grass-roots sport (a number of schools and voluntary sector bodies that may represent a minor advocacy coalition), and bodies concerned with sport's role in health promotion. There is evidence of competition between these clusters of interests in the making and implementation of policy. This competition is exacerbated by interventions from central government and its agencies. These themes are explored further in the following section that analyses core dimensions of policy processes, including policy priorities; the organisational and funding context; relationships between policy actors; patterns of interests and exogenous factors influencing sport policy at the local level.

Policy priorities: influence, stability and change

Since the early 1980s, public policy for sport at the local level has been driven by the local authority sport/recreation department with a more limited direct input into sport policymaking from voluntary sector sport bodies. Specific policy priorities have become embedded in the decision-making processes and organisational culture of LCC, where the dominant and persistent policy concern locally has been the showcasing of the city through elite sport competition and delivery of high-profile events. Voluntary sector voices are recognised and assimilated into these priorities for at least six sports. Outside of this 'inner circle' of influence, few voices in a diverse and extensive local voluntary sector have found a similar level of recognition and resourcing.

Although competing policy concerns, such as community/grass-roots sport, have enjoyed limited support at specific times, in part as a response to central government priorities of the day; political control of the local authority; and as a response to local events such as the urban unrest of the early 1980s, there is little evidence to support a claim that a sustainable approach to investment and development exists in regard to *Sport for All* objectives, and the commitment to social policy goals is almost wholly dependent on external funding sources. The local authority does own and operate a number of community facilities, but almost all are poorly used and increasingly subject to threats of closure. In sum, the core policy priority remains the organisation and promotion of an annual calendar of elite sport events to highlight the city and its local authority, underpinned increasingly by a commercial sector ethos.

The Sport and Recreation department within LCC has effectively defended its core priorities in part through the strategic action and tactics of key policy actors within the department, including creating a critical mass locally for elite sport around six specific sports to raise the profile of Liverpool and acquire local political support; assimilation of alternative local voices into existing programmes; resistance to or modification of central government-led sport policy priorities; ensuring policy processes remain officer-driven in the absence of pro-active councillors; retaining control of information and diverting debate concerning priorities; and maintaining the resource dependency of voluntary sector sport bodies. In fact, until the late 1990s, the sport/recreation service was managed in the style of a 'benevolent dictatorship' where the voice of sport within LCC was distinct.

However, the long-standing strategy of raising the profile of sport through events and sporting success in order to win political favour with local councillors has had diminishing success in recent years as, ironically, the political salience of sport has increased. The representation of sport interests within the local authority, despite re-organisations that appeared to favour sport, by comparison with other interests is relatively weak, despite the recent election of a council leader who places a value on sport. Although LCC Sport has control over sport policy, a number of other departments within the City Council increasingly shape the policy context. These include education (see Chapter 7), planning (see Chapter 9), resources (that oversees the leisure budget), service areas connected with regeneration (see Chapter 10) and the health authority (see Chapter 8). Further, public–private bodies responsible for the economic renewal of the city including the LPG and Liverpool First directly influence sport policy through context setting and shaping. The key reason, however, for the diminishing autonomy of Sport and Recreation Services over the last decade is the increasing influence of central government and its intermediaries.

Increasing intervention from central government, is in a sense welcomed where policy priorities are coterminous, such as around elite sport. However, government pressures around the social inclusion agenda receive a mixed reception at the local level. Although government requires local authority sport/recreation departments to work thematically and meld departmental priorities with those of other departments, the entrenched departmentalism of the local authority is unlikely to dissolve willingly. However, those policy actors concerned with health promotion and pre-care intervention have developed a constructive relationship with LCC Sport, in part, to off-set the limited capacity of local health policy actors to achieve unrealistic government policy goals and targets, particularly in a city facing significant health-related challenges.

Far from a 'hollowing out' of the state (Rhodes, 1994), it is argued that the central state has extended its influence given the increasing dependency of local sport interests on central state resources. The 'modernisation' of local government has impacted on relationships between departments and between the City Council and external bodies, particularly schools. For example, the re-invigoration of school sport locally (at secondary level) in the last decade has not been the result of LCC sport policy, but central government policy, which, to an increasing extent, has bypassed local authority funding mechanisms in shaping of school sport. In effect, a combination of sanctions and inducements has been used by central government to effect change in line with its policy priorities. Although sport/recreation services have fought to retain control of local sport policy, the ongoing 'modernisation', coupled with the rising costs of maintaining local provision (facilities, playing fields, events), and the high subsidy of Leisure Services, creating an internal resource dependency, have significantly reduced the local control over sport that sport/recreation services once enjoyed. Nonetheless, it is clear that the *old regime* has resisted and continues to resist change and protect its interests. As Houlihan (1997: 51) observes, 'attempts by government, or parts of government, to determine policy can be successful, but they are extremely difficult to sustain without an infrastructure of support'.

The significance of policy actors: structure and agency

A persistent theme of the findings emerged around the influence of key individuals in the sport policy area, who, although operating in an increasingly constrained policy context, have had an impact at the local level. For example, up until the late 1990s, the policy process for sport appears to have been strongly influenced by the former head of Sport and Recreation Services. The policy priorities he established and embedded within the department continue to shape current priorities, although aspects of his innovation that had little time to become entrenched before his retirement, such as the attempts to build a sustainable relationship with the voluntary sector, via the LSF, have faltered. This indicates that leadership and skilled brokering are scarce resources in the local sport policy area.

It is also important to acknowledge the significance of the career histories of key personnel within LCC, almost all of whom, especially the Sport and Recreation Service officers, were first employed by LCC in the 1980s.

One consequence is that priorities have become institutionalised and this, in part, explains the incremental nature of policy change and resistance to new ideas. The personal preferences of individuals are important in policy processes and aspects of the service area have been 'personality-driven' that has impacted on relationships across the policy area. The culture of the department is widely perceived by policy actors outside of LCC as 'inward-looking' and bureaucratic, but this is not an untypical outcome of local authority administrative and funding arrangements.

Although other influential individuals operating outside of LCC policy processes have arguably had an impact on policy in the last few years, up until the late 1990s, these alternative voices have been marginalised. For example, individuals instrumental in advocating CSPs met with significant resistance from LCC in attempting to introduce alternative priorities to those of elite sport in Liverpool. This is demonstrated in the collapse of *Active Sports* and, more recently, the resistance to any social policy agenda for sport unless it fitted LCC goals. In this respect, Green and Houlihan (2005a: 59) note, 'the expectation that ... welfare goals should permeate all public services has to be reconciled with the existence of entrenched service specific policy priorities'.

Nonetheless, where the directive capacity of senior personnel within LCC Leisure Services has been weakened by central government pressure, a new type of influential individual has emerged who operates within the spaces between competing interests. These individuals have career histories closely connected to Sport England policy priorities and are part of a broader network of professionals who share common interests around core social policy objectives. Further, their influence is extended into school sport, particularly in two local SSC. However, the opportunities for 'policy brokers' to influence the status quo has in large part been the result of increasing government pressure on local authorities and their control over, or access to, central government resources.

In sum, individuals continue to drive or resist policy change, in the mediation of the policy context in which they operate. It is perhaps unique to fragmented policy areas such as sport for individual preferences to have had a relatively high degree of influence, which perhaps demonstrates the lack of systemic embeddedness of sport within local authorities. However, this type of influence may decline as sport interests develop an interdependent or 'corporate' relationship with the state, particularly around elite sport.

Relationships between local policy actors

Another theme to emerge from the study is the significant level of conflict between policy actors, which appears to be an important dimension of sport policy stability and change. These conflicts exist within the local authority, between the public and voluntary sectors and between 'clusters of interests', each having a historical dimension underpinning current tensions. These tensions centre on the priorities of the competing interests that represent embedded beliefs and the structure of resource allocations. As identified in the case studies, particular tensions exist between sport/recreation within LCC and the voluntary sector for sport, outside of elite sport across six specific sports, but also significant tensions exist between sport/recreation priorities and other LCC priorities across a range of departments. These tensions tend to surface with the intervention of central government where the parameters for policymaking and implementation are changed; most notably in respect of organisation and funding. The consequences of the tensions are important as, rather than a positive dynamic being created that can lead to issue resolution and policy changes for the mutual benefit of policy actors, the tensions result in policy stagnation. Where 'the system seems frozen', as one interviewee stated, policy implementation has been weak, resulting, for example, in claw-back from funding bodies, particularly central government, and increasing distrust across the policy area.

A consensus on the value of sport and core priorities has therefore not emerged in Liverpool. For example, within LCC, conflict between the former council leader and former chief executive led to delays in building the 50 metre swimming pool (see Chapter 6). The existing council leader has greater sympathies for sport, given his former role as executive officer for the Leisure portfolio. However, interviewees did not believe that the incoming chief executive (formerly head of education) shared this perspective. Only time can tell as to whether the new council leader can raise the profile and resourcing of sport within LCC and city-wide. Apart from leadership, tensions exist between officers and members (councillors), where, as interviewees observed, 'it's the only local authority in the country where officers tell [elected] members what to do'. As noted in Chapter 4, councillors have a benign influence on sport policy and practice but cannot be described as 'proactive' in their support of sport/recreation interests in the city, particularly given the largely indiscriminate cuts in the leisure budget over time, where other service areas are prioritised. In this sense, sport/recreation is a marginal policy concern within the local authority.

Further, this study identified significant tensions between departments, given different priorities, as noted, and tensions exist between the different agendas within Leisure Services (that includes culture/arts, libraries and sport) and within Sport and Recreation Services (between functions representing parks, indoor/outdoor facility management and sports development/event organisation). The internal City Council tensions have recently been exacerbated with the introduction of the Culture Company (that oversees a programme of events within the *Capital of Culture* framework) which to an extent has attempted to incorporate some of the responsibilities of the sports development unit into its programmes.

External to the local authority, a plethora of organisations compete for recognition and resources, with particular tensions between LCC and the voluntary sport sector, as documented. Of particular note is that the representative body for the voluntary/public sectors has been largely ineffective in shaping policy. As a consequence of these tensions, collective action in the sport policy sector has been weak. Further, clusters of interests spanning LCC departments and external organisations such as schools, regeneration-led agencies and voluntary sector bodies represent another layer of potential and actual conflict into a fragmented policy area.

Patterns of interests

By comparison with the relatively mature elite sport policy community and the nascent policy community based loosely around school sport and the activities of the SAZ, other interests span a range of issue networks, including those concerned with sport's role in health promotion (Chapter 8) and sport in youth work and crime reduction. A further cluster of interests exists in the voluntary sector around competitive grass-roots sport, which has a long historical association with school sport, particularly at primary level, but this coalition has a weak voice locally, with the LSF the only organisational feature of the network that includes public sector representation. As demonstrated in the case studies, particular tensions exist between the two main 'coalitions' around the purpose of school sport and PE where more than one specialist school sport network in the city does not engage with LCC Sport priorities. It is only relatively recently that sport/recreation services have worked with sectors and organisations concerned with 'regeneration', most notably the health sector (see Chapter 8), as the current central government social policy agenda for sport is not rooted within existing provision, apart from the example of *SportsLinx* where health promotion meets sports development, and even in this case, tensions remain over the goals of the programme and its location within the local authority. *Figure 11.1* highlights three clusters of interests in the Liverpool sport policy area, where the dominant coalition is based around the elite sport interests of LCC and six NGBs of sport.

Although an emergent coalition has gained in influence as the local authority-led coalition has begun to decline, it cannot be claimed that this is indicative of the lobbying capacity of the education/regeneration coalition, but more a result of central state support for these interests, often

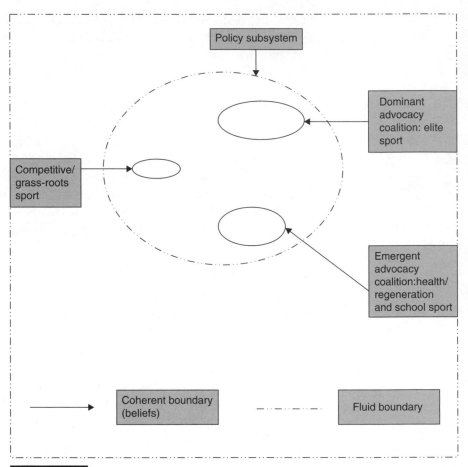

FIGURE 11.1 *The sport policy subsystem (area) in Liverpool.*

with funding that bypasses sport/recreation services within LCC. Central state departments and agencies have been pivotal in constructing networks through which its objectives can be realised at the local level, sustained through resource control and dependency.

The priorities of LCC around elite sport events do not, however, sit easily with the increasing focus on elite sport development at the national level (Green, 2004a, b), which emphasises the pursuit of sporting success 'from playground to podium'. Moreover, LCC have not engaged in sport development that links schools, clubs and other bodies to any significant extent, and only the engagement with health objectives through sport has gathered momentum in recent years.

Sport in Liverpool is in effect a struggle between two policy elites, that of the local authority and its coalition of vested interests, and central government that seeks to control local government and its priorities. Green and Houlihan (2005b) explore the notion of governmentality in analysing governmental attempts to steer policy processes, via shaping, channelling and guiding the conduct of NGBs of sport and the context these bodies operate within. The study of sport policy in Liverpool found evidence of these practices in the local voluntary sector for sport (see Chapter 6); in the re-organisation of sport in secondary schools in conjunction with financial incentives to achieve compliance with core objectives (Chapter 7); and in terms of utilising sport in social policy (Chapters 8 and 10).

Prior to examining the utility of the neo-pluralism and three meso-level theoretical frameworks for sport policy in Liverpool in Chapter 12, the following section links the key findings to institutional analysis and the theories of urban politics, local government and governance (see Chapter 2) in order to provide a context to this analysis.

SPORT POLICY: AN ANALYSIS OF GOVERNANCE

Thelen and Steinmo (1992: 2) observe how institutions 'shape how political actors define their interests and … structure their relations of power to other groups'. It is clear from the research that the *culture* of LCC Sport/ Recreation Services (and the Leisure Services department) is embedded with beliefs, norms and values around elite sport, in part, a strategy to retain control over internal decision-making processes. Institutionalism also highlights the relationship between the behaviour of policy actors and the structures within which they make decisions (Hall, 1986). Here, the research demonstrates the importance of the location of sport within LCC, giving it a relatively marginal status, in part a result of its non-statutory status. The organisational and political infrastructure of LCC has therefore been significant in shaping policy, where sport remains subject to funding reductions and its priorities compromised by other service area priorities. Institutional analysis can therefore sensitise the researcher to the structural and cultural dimensions of sport policy processes within LCC, that in part explain the behaviour of policy actors and the strategic action adopted.

As stated in Part 1 of this book, the focus of the research also invites theories of urban politics, local government and governance into the study (cf. Judge, Stoker and Wolman, 1995; Stoker, 1991, 2000). Within LCC, a 'regime' defined as a 'relatively stable group *with access to institutional resources* that enable it to have a sustained role in making governing decisions'

(Stone, 1989: 4; original emphasis) and can be identified around the elite sport priorities for sport, where business interests such as sponsors of sports events have become embedded into these priorities. Without private sector support, it is unlikely that these priorities could be sustained, given the finances of Leisure Services. A degree of cooperation exists therefore within this network of public/private interests, as indicated in regime theory, where interests 'blend their capacities to achieve common purposes' (Stone, 1989: 55; original emphasis). Regime theory highlights the strategies of policy actors in sustaining the capacity to influence policy, in which respect, interests outside of the regime are not cooperated with to any significant extent. At a broader level, regime theory can be related to the regeneration objectives of LCC, central government and local business partners, but within the *Capital of Culture* framework, as indicated in the case study, sport plays a minor role. Further, in respect of land-use planning, a land-use development regime, connected to the wider regeneration of the city, appears to have little specific interest in playing fields and sport per se (see Chapter 9).

Importantly for this study, regime theory offers a framework for analysing power relations. As identified in Chapter 2, the theory identifies four types of power. In relating these types of power to the research undertaken, it is evident that sport has weak systemic power given its location within LCC, as noted. The wider regeneration-based regime clearly has a dominant position, where sport events with commercial backing are viewed as being of value, but less so those services that need subsidy around community sport. Regime theory also has utility in highlighting command or social control, where Leisure Services is engaged in the active mobilisation of resources towards elite sport priorities. In terms of coalition power, where actors engage in bargaining in search of consensus, there is little evidence locally of consultation and negotiation in the setting of sport-related policy priorities. The LSF has in effect provided a venue for LCC to inform the voluntary sector of its activities and discuss how other policy actors might 'fit into' LCC priorities. Finally, in terms of pre-emptive power, where leadership is critical in complex policy areas, until the retirement of the former head of sport/recreation, this intentional aspect of power was important in steering local sport policy. However, in the last 5 years in particular, leadership of this nature has been missing, in part, due to increasing central state intervention in local authorities. In sum, the coalition within LCC around elite sport is embedded and can retain influence, but in respect of other sport policy concerns, it is weak.

As identified in Chapter 2, the key dimensions of the diverse literature around local government and governance may be of value in the study of sport policy in Liverpool. These dimensions are central-local government relations; the literature around local government financing and spending control; the internal politics of local government; and relation between local interest groups and local authorities, where each dimension is a component of a historical account of local government. Each of these dimensions is related to the empirical research as follows.

LCC has a history of conflict with central government (see Chapter 4). The recent 'modernisation' agenda is a continuation of this struggle. Specific policy instruments used to steer LCC sport policy processes have included the use of legislation, particularly in regard to education (see Chapter 7) and land-use planning (see Chapter 9), re-organisations, audits and increasingly conditional funding arrangements. However, as Rhodes (1981) observes, an 'implementation gap' exists between central state policy and local state delivery. Until the last decade, although the education policy area experienced significant change (Ranson, 1986), areas such as sport, given minimal political salience until recently, experienced relatively little central government intervention. Hence the relative freedom of the former head of sport/recreation to deliver policy objectives, in a context where LCC have strongly resisted central state intervention. However, in the last decade in particular, greater political salience has been given to 'sport' with consequences for central-local government relations. At the core of this changing relationship has been the 'battle' over local spending. Central government has sought to set the agenda for local spending needs through greater control over local capital expenditure. Funding allocations to sport are increasingly connected with welfare-led priorities around education, health and social inclusion, and increasingly ring-fenced, particularly in respect of school sport.

In respect of the internal politics of local authorities, throughout the 1970s and 1980s, it was generally accepted that a policy elite controlled policy (Saunders, 1979). Although Stoker (1991) argues that multiple sources of influence within local government have replaced elite control in recent years, the findings do not suggest that this plurality of organisations operating in the sport policy area represents a pluralist arrangement of power locally. Although many conflicts exist between departments, in terms of local politics, and between LCC and other local policy actors, it is the elite sport advocacy coalition that retains influence over sport priorities. However, where conflict exists between 'elite' officers and councillors over the construction of the 50 metre swimming pool for example (see Chapter 6), the goals and influence of this policy elite can be checked.

The relationship between local authorities and local interest groups is also of relevance to this study. Stoker (1991) identified four types of interest groups. The research indicates that it is producer groups, including business and public sector professionals, that dominate sport policy. Local

Table 11.1	Summary of the Case Study Findings		
Theme	**Structural Context**	**Strategic Action of Policy Actors**	**Outcomes (Consequences)**
Prior policy priorities and current core policy priorities	Robust support for elite sport events programme over time.	Use of high-profile events to retain internal political support – use of media to highlight sporting success.	Increasing costs associated with service provision and control.
	Variable support for community sport and school sport.	Policy processes are largely officer-driven.	The resistance to central government intervention has weakened in recent years.
	Instrumental support for 'development through sport' objectives.	Resistance to central government social policy agenda if it threatens core priorities.	Interests outside of the 'sphere of influence' continue to thrive where financially autonomous.
		Assimilation of alternative voices.	
Organisational and administrative arrangements	The status and location of 'sport' in local authority policy processes is historically weak but increasingly politically salient. Sport remains a marginal policy concern.	Service protectionism and survival strategy.	Difficulties in planning. Little 'joined-up' delivery; duplication.
		Resistance to new ideas, nepotism	
		Lobbying for sport has limited impact	
Organisational culture	An ethos of local authority as 'provider' remains.	Limited focus on partnership-working	Significant tensions within LCC and between sport/recreation and external bodies.
	Departmentalism: resistance to cross-department or thematic working. Embedded priorities and practices (and human resources) with sport/recreation.		

(Continued)

Table 11.1	(Continued)		
Theme	**Structural Context**	**Strategic Action of Policy Actors**	**Outcomes (Consequences)**
Local politics	Low value placed on sport by senior personnel with funding and policy control, for example senior LCC officers.	Benign influence of councillors. Little proaction in support of sport.	A 'longer view' of sport compromised by short-term-ism of the political system.
Funding context	Leisure budget subject to continual pressure and cuts. Increased economic rationales of local authority within regeneration agenda.	Pursuit of local political support. Reliance on retaining the departmental subsidy, financial reserves and unsecured borrowing.	Likely introduction of private sector into facilities management. Threats to recreational space from developers.
	Facilities and recreational spaces aging and costly to maintain. Capital projects experience significant delays and spiralling costs.	Attempts to gain status and funding via *Capital of Culture* and other policy areas, for example health.	Increasing resource dependence on non LCC funding sources.
	A resource-driven context: short-term funding arrangements for revenue-based projects.	Attempts to maintain direct management control of facilities. Conversion of facilities into 'health-based' gymnasia.	Lack of trust between levels of government. Instrumental/contractual relationships dominate.
		Attempts to bend funding towards core priorities.	Funding 'claw-back' by central government and other bodies. Diminishing control over areas such as school sport.
			Direct funding (ring-fencing) to local bodies from central government and other organizations.
Relationships between interests	Significant tensions between central and local government over priorities and funding. Central-local political party control puts a strain on agreeing priorities.	Two advocacy coalitions have emerged around (1) elite sport and (2) school sport and welfare-led goals, and a number of weak issue networks.	A restructuring of the policy area since 1997 has reduced local autonomy (across public and voluntary sectors).

(Continued)

Table 11.1 (Continued)			
Theme	**Structural Context**	**Strategic Action of Policy Actors**	**Outcomes (Consequences)**
Patterns of interests	Long-standing tensions between the public and voluntary sectors for sport outside of elite sport interests within specific sports.	Protectionist and development interests compete for playing fields.	Increasing central government influence – brokers/entrepreneurs are a scarce resource.
	Inter-departmental tensions, particularly between Leisure, Education and Planning, reflected in sport/recreation services tension with school sport and disputes over uses of recreational spaces.	LCC defend priorities – limited proactive engagement with other bodies in sport policy area.	Partnerships do not acquire ownership, for example, collapse of LSF.
Exogenous factors mediating the sport policy area	Factors: changing central government priorities and macro-level socio-economic factors. Local economic context (high poverty, poor health) and turbulent local political history.	A mix of adaptation and resistance. Instrumentalism 'chasing the money'.	No overarching strategy for sport.
		Instrumental alliance between sport and health sector/interests for funding acquisition. Ambiguous response to sport's uses in regeneration agenda.	Increasing expectations and responsibilities placed on sport in a context of decreasing autonomy.
	Better organised and resourced competing lobby groups and pressures from other policy areas – policy spill-over.		Negative impact on local relationships – particularly for school sport.
	'Focusing events': for example urban unrest in early 1980s; the introduction of the National Lottery; *Capital of Culture* award.	Unsustainable policy responses – policy-taking	Sport's role in *Capital of Culture* reduced.

'cause' groups, such as the area playing fields association, community groups; and not-for-profit groups such as sports clubs and associations, area representatives of NGBs of sport; and representative fora for sport in the voluntary sector such as the LSF, have minimal influence on sport policy outside of elite sport, indicating weak lobbying capacity and also the relative strength of the LCC 'showcasing' coalition.

In respect of the pluralist/elitist 'debate' around group influence, it can be concluded that the local authority has been an enclosed organisation – 'unresponsive, oligarchic and inward-looking' (Dunleavy, 1980: 150), where power is concentrated at senior officer level, and producer group interests sustain privileged access to policy processes. This implies an elite pluralist arrangement of power. The 'insider groups' (Grant, 1989) are business interests that support LCC sport priorities rather than voluntary sport bodies. In sum, the body of literature around local government offers many insights that have utility for understanding local sport policy. At the very least, these theoretical approaches sensitise the researcher to key 'themes' and influence shaping the local sport policy area.

CONCLUSIONS

In sum, as a result of its structural location, non-statutory status, weak formal representation and poor leadership, Sport and Recreation Services has limited control of policy direction, outside of elite sport, and even here programmes are compromised by non-sport interests and the increasing influence of central government. Nonetheless, until recently, power and resource control have been monopolised by holders of formal offices at the local level, for elite sport interests, challenging pluralist assumptions. As Blom-Hansen (1999) observes, local government policy actors pursue sectoral policy goals, economic control and local autonomy in the context of intergovernmental policy networks that both constrain and facilitate interests. *Table 11.1* is a summary of the key findings of the study that precedes a discussion of theory as it relates to these findings in Chapter 12. A number of 'themes' are identified, namely policy priorities, patterns of interests, the organisational and funding context, local politics, relationships between interests, and exogenous influences impacting on the local sport policy area. Each theme is related to the strategic action taken by LCC sport/recreation within the 'structural context' for such action. Further, the consequences of the actions of policymakers are identified. This analysis forms the basis for the subsequent discussion of policy theory and the conclusions in the following chapter.

Theorising Sport Policy at the Local Level

INTRODUCTION

This chapter is structured as follows: first, it is contended that an understanding of sport policy cannot be fully captured by any single policy framework, theory or model, but those identified in this book do nonetheless offer a degree of descriptive, analytical and potential explanatory utility. Second, the key findings of the case study of sport policy and practice at the local authority area level, as summarised in Chapter 11, are related to neo-pluralist understandings of policy and each of three meso-level policy frameworks (as detailed in Chapter 2) in order to assess their relative utility for explaining policy processes.

It is intended that this analysis will form the basis for further comparative research of sport policy and practice in local authority areas and urban areas in particular. *Table 12.1* summarises the strengths and weaknesses of each framework for explaining local sport policy. Recent studies of sport policy have drawn on these theoretical frameworks (e.g. Green and Houlihan, 2005a; Houlihan, 1997, 2005; Houlihan and White, 2002) and insights from these texts are drawn upon. Third, a number of conclusions are drawn and recommendations for future areas of research identified.

FRAMEWORKS, THEORIES AND MODELS

The differences in definition between 'frameworks', 'theories' and 'models' need to be defined when analysing the policy process. Ostrom (1999) defines a *framework* or *conceptual framework* as one that identifies a set of variables and relationships that are examined to explain a set of phenomena. Such a framework may or may not identify critical hypotheses. A *theory* provides a denser, more logically coherent set of relationships including direction of relationship and hypotheses. It applies values to some variables. A *model* is a representation (usually mathematical) of a specific situation and is narrower in scope than a theory. It contains specific assumptions about critical variables and relationships. Therefore, as Sabatier (1999) observes, these concepts can be thought of on a continuum of increasing logical interconnectedness and specificity of values and relationships, from framework to model, but decreasing in scope.

In regard to the meso-level of analysis, the ACF may meet the criteria of a 'theory', where Sabatier (1999: 261) defines a *theory* as 'a logically related set of propositions that seeks to explain a fairly general set of phenomena'. A 'theory', according to Sabatier (1999: 262), should be logically coherent, possess clear causal drivers, major propositions should be empirically falsifiable, the intended scope of the theory should be clear and relatively broad, and it should generate research beyond its original scope giving rise to non-obvious implications. In the study undertaken of sport policy, the hypotheses of the ACF are not specifically tested, and the ACF is treated as a theoretical framework alongside the multiple streams and policy network 'frameworks'. These frameworks are selected in line with Houlihan (2005: 167), who notes that each theory has already stimulated empirical application; and each has demonstrated intellectual robustness, having received critical evaluation.

Table 12.1 Strengths and Limitations of Meso-Level Theoretical Frameworks

Frameworks	Strengths	Limitations
Policy networks	The spectrum of policy networks from policy community to issue network is useful for understanding the influence of interests, the extent of policy consensus and the degree of policy stability – the context for strategic action. The approach recognises the complexity of the sport policy area (fragmented/fluid).	The approach may over-emphasise policy stability and the significance of resource dependency in policy processes/mediation. Little attention paid to how endogenous change occurs – although the dialectical 'model' (Marsh and Smith, 2000) does capture the dynamics of policy change.
Multiple streams	The three policy streams help to conceptualise complex policy processes. The notions of 'policy entrepreneurs' and their role in policy change is supported. Ideas and ambiguity, are given prominence – this is plausible given that rational models of policy bear little resemblance to 'reality'.	The framework places too much of a focus on the agenda-setting stage of the policy processes in earlier versions of the frameworks. The framework may embody cultural specificity – being centred on political systems in the USA. Applicability can be problematic.
Advocacy Coalition Framework	The ACF helps to illustrate dynamic processes in complex policy areas such as 'sport'. The framework is useful for characterising the sport policy 'subsystem' as complex, fluid, multi-layered and fragmented. Policy change does appear in part to result from competition between 'advocacy coalitions' (clusters of interests) who share sets of beliefs. The role of exogenous events in policy change is supported: specifically, change in governing coalitions, socio-economic factors and as a result of policy spill-over. Longitudinal studies are supported – change can be understood approximately over a decade.	There are difficulties in identifying and delimiting 'coalitions' and 'policy subsystems' or areas. Also, mapping belief systems presents empirical difficulties. The ACF may attempt to include too many variables and potential explanations of policy. An understanding and explanation of 'power' is limited unless linked to neo-pluralism. The notion that public pressure s a significant exogenous factor in policy change is unsupported. The notion that 'policy learning' produces change is questionable.
Meso-level frameworks as a whole	The frameworks offer utility for descriptive–analytical research. When set within the parameters of neo-pluralism, these approaches offer explanatory insights into power/influence, change/stability, and the possibilities for agency. Strategic action can be contextualized. The unit of analysis (policy area, sector, network, subsystem) has utility as a point of entry for research and as a 'mapping' device. The significance of policy brokers/entreprerteurs in policy processes is supported. The approach has utility for comparative research.	The explanatory potential in understanding power/influence and policy change/stability may be limited – combining these approaches to a macro-level theory of power is important. Delimiting boundaries between policy areas is problematic in areas subject to policy spill-over. A greater focus on policy instruments may be required for an explanation of power/influence. The micro-level of policy analysis is largely omitted – a model of 'human nature/behaviour' may be needed to complement meso-level analysis. The different origins and terminologies employed serve only to confuse.

Source: Adapted from Bulkeley (2000); Green (2003); Marsh and Rhodes (1992); Sabatier (1999)

MACRO-LEVEL THEORY

This study claims that a persuasive account of sport policy processes can be gained via a meso-level analysis of policy processes only when combined with the assumptions underpinning a macro-level theory of the state such as neo-pluralism (see Chapter 2). It is argued that the macro-level of analysis underpinning this study has utility in respect of understanding the configurations of power found in state/government to non-state/civil society relations. More specifically, the organisational structure of the state and the support given by the central state to specific interests mediates policy at the local level. In this study, local government sport interests and non-sport interests have attempted to shape local sport policy within a context of increasing central government involvement in sport policy processes. This 'intervention' has taken the form of context-shaping and conduct-shaping, manifested via strategies of governance that attempt to ensure consensus at the local level for meeting central government policy priorities. 'Power thus conceived, centres on the capacity of actors to redefine the parameters of what is socially, politically and economically possible for others' (Green and Houlihan, 2005a: 182).

The case study of sport policy in Liverpool has revealed how the dominant discourse of central government around sport emerged and shaped local action. However, the study also served to illustrate the dominance of local government interests in the city and how the local authority has retained its priorities despite a series of 'focusing events', exogenous influences and state intervention through a 'modernisation' programme. The re-structuring of the national sport policy area in the last decade has presented opportunities for local sport interests to extend influence but also constrained the influence of some interests. Nationally, elite sport interests have been the major beneficiaries of policy originating in central government (Green, 2004a). At the local level, the coalition of interests centred on LCC priorities around 'showcasing' the city remains the dominant policy concern.

Another insight from the literature around neo-pluralism centres on conflict between interests as the 'core' of politics, as reflected in the case study analysis of relationships between policy actors, and this in part explains policy outcomes. In sum, 'political outcomes are ... the product of conflict between interests ... for the allocation of scarce resources in a context characterised by structural inequality' (Marsh, 1995: 273). Marsh (1995: 283) concludes that there are four questions that any theory of power needs to address, namely 'Who exercises power?'; 'How do they exercise power?'; 'Why do some people have privileged access to power?' and 'In whose interest do they rule?' In the case of sport policy processes in

Liverpool, within the changing national sport policy context, it is evident that power is exercised locally through the local authority, albeit increasingly mediated by national policy interests. Power is exercised by strategic action that resembles the steering strategies of central government. The use of resources is central to these strategies, where embedded practices limit the influence of alternative voices. Privileged access to power is dependent on historical processes that have shaped the contours of contemporary processes. These interests 'rule' to defend the status quo, and the beneficiaries of these processes are the local authority and its core partners.

A neo-pluralist approach to research prompts an analysis of the 'strategic action' selected by actors, considered necessary for understanding the 'structures of influence' shaping sport policy. Local authority policy actors in sport/recreation have sought for the most appropriate means to retain core priorities. Although central government has set the parameters for policy actor's activities, in attempting to ensure that discourse and action is dominated by narratives and meanings that serve the interests of the central state, strategically calculating agents have re-interpreted national policy to retain priorities and local autonomy, despite an increasingly conditional funding environment.

Also in line with neo-pluralism, a 'manipulated consensus' exists in the local sport policy area, maintained by powerful public sector interests, where the voluntary sport bodies have limited influence unless assimilated into local authority priorities. Lukes' third dimension of power (see Ham and Hill, 1993: 23) may be instructive here, as the strategic action of the local authority has to some extent excluded alternative voices. Neo-pluralism recognises a significant role for elites in shaping policy but emphasises that elites themselves are often 'internally divided'. In Liverpool, the policy elite within sport/recreation, and more broadly, leisure services, is, as identified, divided across sub-areas of the service. Nonetheless, despite a plurality of interests across the service area, mediated by inter-departmental conflict and exogenous influences, the embedded core priorities imply a neo-pluralist understanding of power. Finally, there is evidence of incrementalist notions of policy processes in local sport policy (Lindbolm, 1960, 1977, 1986), compatible with the idea that powerful interests constraining policy change.

MESO-LEVEL THEORY

In this section, three meso-level theoretical frameworks for understanding sport policy processes are related to the findings of the study.

Policy networks

The policy networks literature highlights processes of negotiation and bargaining, coalition building, resource dependencies, and interest mobilisation in policymaking and implementation (see Chapter 2). It is argued that the networks approach to understanding policy is useful for a descriptive–analytical account of sport policy and a number of examples are provided to support this argument.

First, the policy networks approach recognises the complexity of policy-making, and the fragmented and differentiated environment in which policy is made and implemented, as demonstrated in this study, where a large number of interests co-exist in uneasy relationships and in some cases 'marriages of convenience'. Second, the networks perspective asserts that policy is the product of the interaction between government and 'clusters' of interests, where the type of relationship that exists varies across policy sector (or area) over time. When aligned to a neo-pluralist position, groups can be viewed as unequal participants in the policy process. These insights are helpful in understanding sport policymaking in Liverpool, most notably where Sport and Recreation Services is the lead actor in one of two clusters of interests in the local policy area.

Third, in relation to pressure groups, Grant (1995: 152) concludes, 'if we are interested in finding out who wins and who loses in the political process, and why they win and lose, the question of [interest] effectiveness cannot be ignored by … analysts'. In this regard, interests outside of the dominant policy concerns in LCC sport are relatively ineffective, particularly in the voluntary sector, but also in public sector bodies and even within LCC Leisure Services itself, although the emerging network or community based around 'development through sport' priorities supported by national government and regional bodies has become increasingly influential over the last decade. However, the fact that it has taken a decade to only partially dislodge dominant interests around 'showcasing' the city is testament to the embedded power of this agenda.

Grant (1989: 14–15) distinguishes between 'insider' and 'outsider' groups. However, insider status does not guarantee substantive influence over policy. The LSF is a case in point where its 'insider' status has not resulted in any change in policy direction. Although some indication of influence can be gained through analysis of a group's resources, lobbying skill and capacity, and the policy environment, Smith (1993: 4) claims, 'The influence of pressure groups does not derive from how they use their resources but from the historical, ideological and structural context within which they operate.' In this regard, the evolution of LCC itself, its resistance to external influences, particularly central government priorities and the 'modernisation' agenda act as the context to the construction of sport policy and the attempt to retain its 'jealously guarded programme' of elite sport and event organisation. Further, Smith (1993: 228) contends that rather than pressure groups 'capturing' government, 'State actors have incorporated groups in order to achieve their own goals', as governments need groups as a source of policy ideas and expertise, to implement policy, and to secure legitimacy for policy preferences. In this regard, LCC sport has sought to 'incorporate' other local sport actors into its priorities.

Fourth, the networks approach highlights the institutionalisation of beliefs and values in addition to rules and routines, most clearly evidenced with LCC Leisure Services located at the hub of a network associated with elite sport priorities. Houlihan (1997: 16) observes that probably *the* defining characteristic of policy communities is 'the emergence of a core set of values that will inform the way in which problems are identified and defined, and also the way in which solutions are selected'. As Richardson (1982: 22) argues, policy communities are less concerned to solve policy problems and more concerned with creating stable relationships of self-interest, thus avoiding conflict and policy change, and arguably policy learning. The elite sport policy network within LCC can perhaps be best described as a policy community rather than a network, where Rhodes (1988: 78) defines policy communities as characterised by a 'stability of relationships, continuity of a highly restrictive membership, vertical independence based on shared service delivery responsibilities and insulation from other networks and invariably from the general public ... They are highly integrated'.

Although not all of the components of a policy network were quantified in the case study, the primary characteristics of the elite sport policy network have been highlighted and include most of the key components of a policy community, specifically a limited number of members; some groups consciously excluded; membership, values and outcomes persistent over time; professional interests dominate; the basic relationship is an exchange relationship; hierarchical decision-making processes; and one group dominates. Thus the elite sport policy network can effectively rebut influences that may challenge its core beliefs and policy priorities.

Fifth, a number of issue networks exist in the local sport policy area that exhibit the characteristics identified by a number of writers (e.g. Marsh and Rhodes, 1992; Marsh and Smith, 2000; Smith, 1993). These large and diverse networks encompass a range of interests, where access fluctuates significantly and a measure of agreement exists over policy goals, although conflict is ever present. Smith (1993) sees issue networks as developing, where low political priority is given to the policy area in question or by contrast where there has been high political controversy (and therefore potential costs for government of intervention), or where a new issue has not been institutionalised. Clearly, in the case study, interests outside of elite sport are not institutionalised and are given low political priority at the local level. A local issue network has emerged around concerns over the poor health, particularly in young people (see Chapter 8), but despite LCC involvement, these priorities are not systemically embedded. In this study of Liverpool, it is clear that the emerging policy community around the SAZ and school sport has had limited capacity to influence the core interests of LCC sport/recreation services, despite recent central government support.

Sixth, in line with the policy networks literature, the case study highlights a number of resource dependencies, most notably found in, first, the relationship between departments within LCC, where sport is subsidised and subject to budgetary reductions at short notice depending on policy concerns and priorities in other sectors; second, between local and central government, where, for example, the additional resources from DfES into school sport in recent years has impacted on departmental relations and arguably weakened the influence of sport interests; and third, between local government and the voluntary sector for sport, who increasingly are 'squeezed' by both local and central governments.

Further, with policy spill-over evidenced from the Health and Education sectors, sport interests as a whole are increasingly dependent on non-sport interests for recognition and survival. Houlihan (1997: 269) identifies that 'in many policy areas the initiative in the formation of policy communities and networks rests with governments and their emergence depends on whether governments have a need for them in terms of legitimising policy choice or cooperation in policy implementation'. For school sport and sport's role in health policy, networks have been established and directed by central government. However, for elite sport, the network or policy community has emerged from the local sport policy area. Although the current government places a high value on elite sport (Green, 2004a; Green and Houlihan, 2005a), local authorities are valued more for their potential welfare remit, which raises a number of questions concerning the local elite sport policy focus evident in Liverpool and whether there has been a balance between elite and community sport policy and practice.

Seventh, Marsh and Smith's (2000) focus on the method by which networks change. Some authors stress endogenous factors (e.g. resource dependencies) and others exogenous factors (e.g. ideological or political context). Exogenous 'forces' mediate networks in shaping policymakers' choices in policy selection (Marsh and Rhodes, 1992; Smith, 1993). These insights are relevant for the study, as it is clear that socio-economic and political factors (as identified in Chapter 4) have mediated local sport policy, particularly, as stated, the political influence of local and central governments. As Marsh and Smith (2000) observe, it is political authority that is the most significant external factor in determining network change. From the findings of the case study, it is clear that 'exogenous changes can affect the resources, interests and relationships of the actors within networks' (Marsh and Smith, 2000: 8). In terms of policy spill-over as identified in Chapters 7–10, 'the consequences produced by one policy are increasingly likely to interfere with the working of other policies' (Majone, 1989, cited in Houlihan, 2000: 180).

Eighth, the networks literature has utility in providing insights into the strategic action of policy actors, most notably in this study, the actions of central and local government. Kickert et al. (1997) highlight government 'steering' strategies to gain consent for policy priorities, including the use of legal instruments, economic instruments, communicative instruments, by creating a strategic consensus around a 'common purpose' (see Chapter 2). It is evident that both central and local government bodies responsible for sport have used a variety of policy instruments at different times to secure policy priorities, with variable degrees of success. Most notable perhaps are the conditional funding arrangements set by central government in an attempt to shape local authority policy and practice. Where this strategy has proved to be ineffective, the strategy of central government and its agencies has been to 'bypass' the local authority agenda in creating a parallel set of structures, resourced by government, particularly around school sport and community regeneration priorities.

Ninth, as Rhodes (in Thompson et al., 1991: 209) observes, policy networks have not supplanted party political channels of communication and influence, where 'The effects of party are pervasive. It spans levels of government and communicates a range of interests. Most important, it spans the policy network.' In central–local government relations, policy implementation relies on the cooperation of local authorities, where 'each of which has its own political priorities set by its elected members' (Houlihan, 2000a: 199). Nonetheless, the case study demonstrates that it is officers rather than members that have directed sport policy with councillors generally benign but lacking any expertise in sport-related policy issues. However, 'councillor activism' where it has occurred has shaped departmental priorities and budgets. The 'showcasing' agenda, however, is encouraged rather than opposed by members. Within LCC, the extent of the influence of council select committees is considered slight, where, as noted, there is no 'clear blue water' between the committee scrutinising sport policy and the department responsible for making and delivering sport policy.

In the final analysis, as Marsh and Stoker (1995: 293) claim, 'To explain the origins, shape and outcomes of a network it is necessary to examine why some interests are privileged in a given network or, if no interests are privileged, why the network is open.' Therefore a theory of power is needed to explain the relation between state and civil society. Although the policy networks approach offers a plausible account of policy processes, its strength may be in its descriptive and analytical capacity as opposed to its explanatory capacity. In a sense, networks are viewed as the manifestation of prior policies, ideologies and processes (Smith, 1993) and, therefore, when located in a neo-pluralist theoretical framework and theory of power, the strengths of the approach are accentuated, it is argued and the weaknesses diminished.

The multiple streams framework

The second approach utilised for this study of sport policy is the MSF (e.g. Kingdon, 1995). This approach focuses on agenda setting and choice between policy alternatives, where argument, persuasion and reasoning are central in policy formation, although under conditions of ambiguity.

The MSF has a number of strengths for the study of sport policy that can be related to the study. First, the approach emphasises the complexity, fluidity and fuzziness of policy processes. As identified in the case study, the sport policy area can be characterised as complex where ambiguity is a feature of decision-making given that the area is subject to policy spill-over. Policy is in practice more to do with policytaking rather than policymaking (Dery, 1999). Second, the MSF identifies time and resources as key constraints in policy choice. Timing has been crucial in local sport policy process, where differences in funding cycles, for example, exacerbate tensions between key policy actors. Further, delays in sport/recreation services and other bodies allocating funding have led to 'claw-back' where central government departments lose faith in local government (see Chapter 4 for an analysis of the funding context). Moreover, deadlines are regularly missed as events external to the policy area impact on attempts to develop policy and strategy. For example, LCC Sport delayed strategy for 2003–2008 remained unpublished. Moreover, capital projects are delayed by years in some cases, for example the 50 metre swimming pool.

Third, the approach recognises that not all is happenstance, by emphasising that political ideology is central to policy formation as it provides meaning to action and a guide to identifying which issues are seen as important. Zahariadis (1999: 80) maintains that 'The ideology of the governing party shapes the kind of issues that will rise to the agenda and demarcates the solutions available for adoption.' Policy selection criterion in the MSF is based on 'value acceptability' as well as feasibility, where not only unfeasible policy options but less favoured policies (and ideologies) are likely to be rejected. In Liverpool, the dominant policy priority has been elite sport, although pragmatism shapes policy priorities as much as a 'belief' in elite sport.

Fourth, as with policy networks, the role and influence of policy elites are important in shaping policy. The MSF views higher rank and status as increasing influence, as does membership of multiple arenas or 'venues' (Baumgartner and Jones, 1993). A policy elite can perhaps be identified in Liverpool consisting of senior local authority officers who have retained influence over time. However, their influence is compromised by senior non-sport policy actors within the City Council and central government sport policy actors. Fifth, the explanation of policy change within the MSF is instructive for this analysis. Baumgartner and Jones (1993) and Sabatier and Jenkins-Smith (1993) suggest that policy change is incremental (as in the policy networks framework) although punctuated by occasional 'paradigm shifts'. In Liverpool, these shifts relate to exogenous factors such as the urban unrest of the 1980s that gave birth to sports development and accelerated the facility building programme or the more recent award of *Capital of Culture*.

In terms of policy change, the MSF identifies three streams, namely 'politics', 'policy problems' and 'policy solutions', which interact to produce change (see Chapter 2 for more detail). The three streams normally operate independently except in the event of a 'window of opportunity', where policy entrepreneurs act to couple the streams. The concept of 'policy entrepreneur' who can be found in an institutionally weak policy area, such as 'sport', has utility in this case study. In the study, interviewees, as noted, identified individuals who acted as entrepreneurs (or brokers) where policy windows present 'opportunities for advocates of proposals to push their pet solutions, or to push attention to their special problems' (Kingdon, 1995: 165). The former head of Sport and Recreation Services was perhaps the most significant 'policy entrepreneur' in the local context.

In sum, the MSF highlights aspects of policy processes that can be applied to the sport policy area. A partial explanation of sport policy can be achieved using this approach and when integrated with a theory of power, such as neo-pluralism, it has utility for theory construction. However, the approach can over-emphasise the role of ideas, beliefs and 'muddle' in policy processes, and underplay institutional and socio-economic factors (see Parsons, 1995).

The advocacy coalition framework

A third approach to understanding local sport policy can perhaps be gained by utilising the ACF (e.g. Sabatier, 1999) that is primarily concerned with policy change and stability. Although having much in common with the policy networks approach, the ACF 'is a broader set of processes than that evoked by the network metaphor' (John, 1998: 169). It is contended that the ACF offers many insights into the policy process and can assist in developing a theoretical frame to more fully capture the complexities of policymaking, implementation and change. However, it also has many limitations as illustrated in this section.

The ACF provides a starting point for research in identifying a unit of analysis, the policy subsystem (or area). Sabatier (1999: 119) states, 'A subsystem consists of those actors from a variety of public and private organisations who are actively concerned with a policy problem or issue ... and who regularly seek to influence public policy in that domain.' Thus, the sport policy subsystem in Liverpool can be mapped inclusive of the many policy actors, their beliefs and values, resources and relationship to other actors. Further, the ACF makes a distinction between a *nascent* subsystem (one in the process of forming) and a *mature* subsystem (one that has existed for approximately 10 years or more). In this regard the subsystem around elite sport can be treated as mature in Liverpool. The utility of this distinction is that in a mature subsystem, relationships, processes, systems and structures are relatively embedded, meaning policy change tends to be incremental and change is resisted if it threatens policy core beliefs, policy priorities and resource allocations.

Second, Sabatier (1991) and Sabatier and Jenkins-Smith (1993) maintain that it is the relationships between actors in policy subsystems that is key to understanding how policy processes work. This is borne out in the case study that explored relationships between sectors, organisations and actors internal and external to Liverpool. In conducting the research, it was the interview questions that related to relationships which produced the greatest insight into local sport policy. Third, the ACF (as with policy networks and the MSF) states that policymaking is dominated by elite opinion, although not necessarily *stable* elites, where nonelites have 'neither the expertise, nor the time, nor the inclination to be active participants in the policy subsystem' (Sabatier and Jenkins-Smith, 1993: 223). In the case of sport policy in Liverpool, it is clear that LCC Sport has driven policy, albeit mediated by other City Council interests, such as those embedded in the planning department (see Chapter 9), at least until the last 5 years, from when central government has exerted greater influence. It would be difficult to conclude that voluntary sector interests, outside of those association with the 'priority sports' at the level of performance/competition, have influence in LCC sport policy.

Fourth, the ACF emphasises that to understand policy change, a time period of at least a decade is needed in order to complete at least one 'formulation–implementation–reformulation' *policy cycle*. Importantly, the historical emphasis of the case study analysis, in tracing policy change over time, is coterminous with the premises of the ACF and does assist in contextualising contemporary policy processes and priorities. Fifth, the ACF has utility in recognising two causal drivers in policy change, namely the core beliefs of actors and exogenous 'perturbations' in shaping policy. Sabatier (1999) conceives of two sets of exogenous variables that impact upon the constraints and opportunities of subsystem actors. These are relatively stable 'parameters' (see Chapter 2) including socio-cultural values and the political system, and relatively dynamic 'external events' including changes in socio-economic conditions, public opinion and governing coalitions. In respect of 'relatively dynamic external events', Liverpool as a city has experienced rapid economic decline, significant outward migration and political upheaval over the last 30 years. These 'external events' have impacted significantly on LCC where sport has been a marginal policy concern within LCC as a whole, on account of its non-statutory status. In terms of 'stable parameters', the adversarial nature of the political system, both at national and local levels, and changes in the socio-cultural context, such as demographics and lifestyle, have also strongly influenced policy and practice.

In respect of the core beliefs of policy actors, as stated in Chapter 2, Sabatier (1999) organises the belief systems of each coalition into a hierarchical tripartite structure. The study of sport in Liverpool has identified the beliefs of policy actors for sport, as manifested in the two clusters of interests and finds, as Sabatier (1999: 130) states that 'actors are driven by a set of policy-oriented goals comprising value priorities and conceptions of whose welfare should be of greatest concern'. In the case study, the central tension is between those focused on the 'development of sport', particularly elite sport, and those concerned with 'development through sport'. It appears that the 'deep core beliefs' have not changed, where particular divisions exist between the public and voluntary sectors around the role of the state, and the purposes and nature of sport, and between elite and welfare sport-related objectives. The ACF claims that coalitions will resist information that challenges deep core beliefs. It may therefore be exogenous factors to produce change, notably the increasing influence of central government.

Sixth, the ACF assumes that actors can be aggregated into a number of 'advocacy coalitions' (clusters of interests that share common beliefs) composed of various government and private or voluntary sector organisations. Each coalition shares both a set of normative and causal beliefs, and engages in 'a non-trivial degree of co-ordinated activity over time'. In this respect, Liverpool has two distinct advocacy coalitions, one based around elite sport inclusive of LCC and selected sports bodies, and the other smaller coalition based around education and regeneration. However, this latter coalition has significant support from national, regional and county bodies, including DCMS, DfES, Sport England, YST, NWSB, the MSP, and to a lesser extent, other education and regeneration bodies across Liverpool.

In the ACF it is policy core beliefs that provide the principal glue of coalitions of interests (Zafonte and Sabatier, 1998). It can be argued that although membership of coalitions has changed over time, as has coalition influence, the core beliefs of individuals and organisations have remained largely unchanged and the sport policy subsystem remains ideologically polarised. However, as Green (2006) observes, with reference to Daugbjerg and Marsh (1998: 71), the ACF 'cannot explain policy outcomes simply by reference to the structures of coalitions or the behaviour of actors therein. We need to understand why coalitions take the form they do, how they relate to the broader political system and thus how policy outcomes might be facilitated/constrained'. Therefore the role of exogenous factors gains in significance in any analysis of sport policy, as does the 'structured context' in which policy is made and implemented.

Seventh, the ACF maintains that 'policy brokers' act to mediate between competing coalitions. In the study undertaken, it is clear that brokers have sought to work in the spaces between the two advocacy coalitions, similar to the concept of the policy entrepreneur in the MSF. The case study provides evidence of the influence of 'brokers', as noted. However, the ACF implies that policy brokers are 'neutral' in negotiating policy, which is clearly not the case. Eighth, the ACF contends that policy change is in part due to a process of 'policy-oriented learning'. Learning subsequently feeds back into the beliefs and resources of coalitions. However, Parsons (1995) questions whether successful coalitions are those that learn 'better' than others, or those which hold the greater resources and power. Parsons argues that coalitions may change as they advance core interests; hence no rational learning process is required. Although some 'learning' can be identified in the case study in sport policy formulation and in practice, in agreement with Parsons (1995), the evidence supports change through the 'advance of core interests'.

In sum, the ACF has significant potential for a description, analysis, and where coupled with neo-pluralism, an explanation of sport policy. The ACF highlights and contextualises the strategic action of local sport interests in mediating national policy initiatives, for example. Nonetheless, there are weaknesses too as identified. *Table 12.1* summarises the key strengths and limitations of the ACF and the other meso-level theoretical approaches used in this book.

CONCLUSIONS

This book has highlighted the key influences shaping policy processes in a specific location and within a specific time period. It has foregrounded the strategic action of policy actors (primarily local authority sport policy actors) seeking to pursue policy priorities in a context mediated by a range of endogenous and exogenous influences shaping public policy. It has focused primarily on relationships and resources as a method to acquiring insight into the politics of sport policy in local contexts, and it has sought to explain sport policy through an engagement with theory. Fundamentally, it is an exploratory study of sport that recognises sport policy as a political and socio-cultural construct. *Table 12.2* relates the objectives of the study with the key findings.

A number of conclusions can be drawn from this summary. First, public policy for sport can be best understood through an investigation of the relationships between policy actors. The tensions in these relationships revolve

Table 12.2	Relationship Between the Research Objectives and Key Findings	
Objectives of the Study	**Specific Areas of Research**	**Findings**
To identify the main sport policy actors	Their interests, beliefs, values, resources, policy priorities	Ideologically polarised clusters of interests
To evaluate the relationships between sport interests	Public–voluntary sector relations Departmental relations within Liverpool City Council Central–local government relations and regional–local relations	Significant tensions outside of elite sport for six sports Inter-departmental tensions impact on policy Tensions around 'modernisation' exacerbated by party politics
To trace the evolution of sport policy processes	Changes in the political and socio-economic context that may impact on sport interests	Impact of changes in government priorities, governance, local economic context and watershed events
To assess exogenous influences that may shape the sport policy area	The impact of interests in adjacent policy areas, particularly education, land-use planning and health	Sport-related interests and issues are mediated by non-sport interests
To identify and evaluate the strategies adopted by sport interests	The activities of policy actors The policy context in which actors pursue their goals	A combination of reactive strategies, based on resistance to change, instrumentalism. Innovation is increasingly constrained

around competing priorities in a context of scarce resources. Second, the study explained the strategic action of interests in the pursuit of resources, recognition and other goals, through exploring the dialectical relationship between structure and agency. Third, the study revealed the significance of structural privilege where policy elites exercise control over policy processes. The basis of this control is in part found in the resources actors can mobilise. Also, vested interests are embedded within organisational and administrative structures that serve to highlight the importance of historical processes. Fourth, two local coalitions of interests in the public sector compete for control over the direction of sport policy in Liverpool, although on an uneven playing field. Fifth, the sport policy area in the city can be characterised by increasing public sector intervention at the national and local levels; fragmentation representing plurality but not evidence of pluralism (but a neo-pluralist or elite pluralist arrangement of power); and significant exogenous influences including, notably, policy spill-over from policy areas including education, health, community regeneration and land-use planning.

AREAS FOR FUTURE RESEARCH

In attempting to explain sport policy processes at the local level, there are a number of dimensions to investigate, including, first, the local historical, socio-cultural, economic and political context; second, the institutional or organisational context, policy networks, coalitions or patterns of interests; third, the funding context, mechanisms, processes and resource dependencies; fourth, relationships between organisations and individuals, both within the sport sector and between policy sectors, between the public, voluntary and commercial sectors, and between the local, county/regional and national or international levels of governance; and fifth, the role of skilled policy brokers and entrepreneurs, and their capacity of policy actors to mobilise influence given their embeddedness within institutions and networks.

Given these dimensions of analysis, studies could centre on policy ideas and values or regimes; policy actors and their interests, alliances and networks of influence; policy content including priorities and strategic planning; policy instruments utilised by actors in pursuing goals; policy determinants or the endogenous and exogenous factors shaping policy processes including perceived crisis and 'focusing events'; policy stability and change over time; and policy learning. In studies of policymaking, dynamic relations between these variables are many and can include, as in this book, a focus on how changes in the national policy and resourcing context impact on relationships at the local level, and vice versa. In studies of policy implementation and evaluation, the importance of the local infra-structure for delivering policy goals cannot be neglected, hence an audit and assessment of facilities, financial and human resources, partnerships and political support could be undertaken in any analysis. In practice, it is problematic to separate studies of policymaking from implementation and evaluation.

More specifically, future areas of research at the local level could include comparative studies of local authority sport policy between cities or between authorities within specific counties. Longitudinal studies of single authority or between authorities would also offer the scope for fur-ther understanding of local level sport policy stability and change. In this sense, the research underpinning this text should be viewed as an ongoing process or 'work in progress' rather than an end point. Continued research into local authority sport policy is viewed as critical to understanding the politics of sport both locally and nationally, not least, because of the signifi-cant levels of public monies allocated to sport and the role of authorities in shaping our opportunities to take part. The distinctiveness of place clearly shapes and re-shapes policy, and therefore the extent to which we bene-fit from public policy is to a large extent as result of *where* we live. More broadly, exploring the local level of sport policy cannot be disconnected from the fundamental question that underpins all of policy studies and is not a question that researchers can lose sight of, namely 'Who gets what, how and why?'

References

Acheson, D. (1998) *Independent Inquiry into Inequalities in Health*. London: HMSO.

Activity Coordination Team, ACT (2003a) *Minutes of Meeting*, 27th November.

Activity Coordination Team, ACT (2003b) *Minutes of Meeting*, 2nd October.

Adams, L. and Cunning, F. (2002) Promoting social and community development in Sheffield: a reflection on ten year's work. In L. Adams, M. Amos and J. Munro (Eds.), *Promoting Health. Politics and Practice*. London: Sage.

Adams, L., Amos, M. and Munro, J. (2002) *Promoting Health. Politics and Practice*. London: Sage.

Alford, R. (1975a) *Health Care Politics*. Chicago, IL: University of Chicago Press.

Alford, R. (1975b) Paradigms of relations between state and society. In L.N. Lindberg, R. Alford, C. Crouch and C. Offe (Eds.) *Stress and Contradiction in Modern Capitalism*. Lanham, MD: Lexington Books.

Allied Dunbar (1992) *National Fitness Survey*. London: Author.

Altheide, D. (1996) *Qualitative Media Analysis*. London: Sage.

Anderson, J. (1984) *Public Policy Making*. New Holt: Rinehart and Winston.

Armitage, M. and Povall, S. (2003) Practical issues in translating evidence into policy and practice. In A. Oliver and M. Exworthy (Eds.) *Health Inequalities: Evidence, Policy and Implementation. Proceedings of a Meeting of the Health Equity Network*. London: Nutfield Trust.

Atkinson, M. and Coleman, W. (1992) Policy networks, policy communities and the problems of governance. *Governance*, 5(2), 154–180.

Audit Commission (1988) *Sport for Whom? Clarifying the Local Authority Role in Sport and Recreation*. London: Author.

Audit Commission (2002) *Best Value Review of Liverpool City Council*. London: Author.

Audit Commission (2003) *Achieving the NHS Plan*. London: Author.

Bacchi, C. (2000) Policy as discourse: What does it mean? Where does it get us?. *Discourse: Studies in the Cultural Politics of Education*, 21(1), 45–57.

Bachrach, P.S. and Baratz, M.S. (1962) Two faces of power. *American Political Science Review*, 56, 947–952.

Bachrach, P.S. and Baratz, M.S. (1970) *Power and Poverty: Theory and Practice*. New York: Oxford University Press.

Ball, S.J. (1992) *Politics and Policymaking in Education – Explorations in Political Sociology*. London: Routledge.

Ball, S.J. (1993) What is policy? Texts, trajectories and toolboxes. *Discourse: Studies in the Cultural Politics of Education*, 13(2), 10–17.

Bauld, L. and Judge, K. (Eds.) (2002) *Learning from Health Action Zones*. Chichester: West Sussex: Aeneas Press.

Baumgatner, F. and Jones, B. (1993) *Agendas and Instability in American Politics*. Chicago, IL: Chicago University Press.

Becker, G. (1970a) *What Is a Case? Exploring the Foundations of Social Inquiry*. Cambridge: Cambridge University Press.

Becker, G. (1970b) *The Economic Approach to Human Behaviour*. Chicago, IL: University of Chicago Press.

Benson, J.K. (1979) *Inter Organisational Networks and Policy Sectors: Notes Towards Comparative Analysis, Mimeo*. University of Missouri.

Benson, J.K. (1982) Networks and policy sectors: a framework for extending inter-governmental analysis. In D. Roger and D. Whitton (Eds.) *Inter-Organisational Coordination*. Ames, IA: Iowa State University.

Bentley, A. (1967) *The Process of Government*. Chicago, IL: Chicago University Press.

Bergmann Drewe, S. (1998) Competing conceptions of competition: implications for physical education. *European Physical Education Review*, 4(1), 5–20.

Bergsgard, N.A., Houlihan, B., Mangset, P., Nodland, S.I., and Rommetvedt, H. (2007) *Sport Policy: A Comparative Analysis of Stability and Change*. Oxford: Butterworth-Heinemann.

Berridge, V. (2003) The black report: interpreting history. In A. Oliver and M. Exworthy (Eds.) *Health Inequalities: Evidence, Policy and Implementation. Proceedings of a Meeting of the Health Equity Network*. London: Nutfield Trust.

Bevir, M. and Rhodes, R.A.W. (1998) *Interpreting British Governance*. London: Routledge.

Bianchini, F. and Parkinson, M. (1993) *Cultural Policy and Urban Regeneration: The Western European Experience*. Manchester: Manchester University Press.

Biddle, S., Markland, D., Gilbourne, D., Chatzisarantis, N. and Spakes, A.C. (2001) Research methods in sport and exercise psychology: quantitative and qualitative issues. *Journal of Sport Sciences*, 19, 777–809.

Blaikie, N. (1993) *Approaches to Social Enquiry*. Cambridge: Polity Press.

Blaikie, N. (2000) *Designing Social Research: The Logic of Application*. Cambridge: Polity Press.

Blom-Hansen, J. (1999) Policy-making in central–local government relations: balancing local autonomy, macroeconomic control, and sectoral policy goals. *Journal of Public Policy*, 19, 237–264.

Bramham, P. (1991) Explanations of the organisation of sport in British society. *International Review of the Sociology of Sport*, 26, 139–154.

Bramham, P. (2001) Sport policy. In K. Hylton, P. Bramham, D. Jackson and M. Nesti (Eds.) *Sports Development: Policy, Process and Practice*. London: Routledge.

Brewer, G. (1974) The policy sciences emerge: to nurture and structure a discipline. *Policy Sciences*, 5(3), 239–244.

British Heart Foundation, BHF (2000) *Couch Kids – The Growing Epidemic*. London: BHF.

Brittan, S. (1975) The economic consequences of democracy. *British Journal of Political Science*, 5, 129–159.

Brittan, S. (1987) *The Role and Limits of Government*. Aldershot: Wildwood House.

Bryman, A. (1988) *Quantity and Quality in Social Research*. London: Unwin Hyman.

Bryman, A. (2001) *Social Research Methods*. Oxford: Oxford University Press.

Bulkeley, H. (2000) Discourse coalitions and the Australian climate change policy network. *Environment and Planning C: Government and Policy*, 18, 727–748.

Bulmer, S. (1984) Facts, concepts, theories and problems. In M. Bulmer (Eds.) *Sociological Research Methods: An Introduction*. London: Macmillan.

Bunton, R. (1992) More than a woolly jumper: health promotion as social regulation. *Critical Public Health*, 3(2), 4–11.

Burrell, G. and Morgan, B. (1979) *Sociological Paradigms and Organisational Analysis*. London: Heinemann.

Cale, L. (2000) Physical activity promotion in secondary schools. *European Physical Education Review*, 3(2), 71–90.

Carrington, B. and McDonald, I. (2003) The politics of 'race' and sports policy. In B. Houlihan (Ed.), *Sport and Society: A Student Introduction*. London: Routledge.

Castles, F. (1982) *The Impact of Parties*. London: Sage.

Cavill, N., Dugdill, L. and Porcellato, L. (2005) *Physical Activity in the North-West of England*. Manchester: Cavill Associates/University of Salford.

Central Council for Physical Recreation, CCPR (1985) *Sports Fields and Recreational Facilities Threatened with Disposal*. London: Author.

Central Council for Physical Recreation, CCPR (2000) *Active Britain*. London: CCPR.

Central Council for Physical Recreation, CCPR (2003) *Saving Lives, Saving Money: Physical Activity – The Best Buy in Public Health*. London: CCPR.

Chalip, L. (1995) Policy analysis in sport management. *Journal of Sport Management*, 9(1), 1–13.

Chalip, L. (1996) Critical policy analysis in sport: the illustrative case of New Zealand sport policy development. *Journal of Sport Management*, 10(3), 310–324.

Charmaz, K. (2002) Qualitative interviewing and grounded theory analysis. In, J.F. Gubrium and J.A. Holstein (Eds.), *Handbook of Interview Research: Context and Method*. Thousand Oaks, CA: Sage.

CIPFA (2006) *Sport and Recreation Statistics for Liverpool City Council*. London: Author. Personal correspondence.

Coalter, F. (1990) The 'mixed economy' of leisure: the historical background to the development of the commercial, voluntary and public sectors of the leisure industries. In, I.P. Henry, (Ed.), *Management and Planning in the Leisure Industries*. Basingstoke: Macmillan.

Coalter, F., Allison, M. and Taylor, J. (2000) *The Role of Sport in Regenerating Deprived Areas*. Edinburgh: SECRU.

Coalter, F. (2007) *A Wider Social Role for Sport. Who's Keeping the Score?*. London: Routledge.

Coalter, F., Long, J. and Duffield, B. (1988) *Recreational Welfare*. Aldershot: Gower.

Cobham Report (1973) *Second Report of the Select Committee of the House of Lords on Sport and Leisure (Select Committee Report)*. London: HMSO.

Coghlan, J. and Webb, I.M. (1990) *Sport and British Politics Since 1960*. London: Falmer Press.

Cohen, M., March, J. and Olsen, J. (1972) A garbage can model of organisational choice. *Administrative Science Quarterly*, 17, 1–25.

Collins, M.F. and Kay, T. (2003) *Sport and Social Exclusion*. London: Routledge.

Couch, C. (2003) *City of Change and Challenge: Urban Planning and Regeneration in Liverpool*. Aldershot: Ashgate.

Couch, C. and Dennemann, A. (2000) Urban regeneration and sustainable development in Britain: The example of the Liverpool Ropewalks Partnership. *Cities*, 17(2), 137–147.

Council of Europe (1976) *European Charter for Sport: Sport for All*. Strasbourg: Author.

Council of Europe, COE (1993) *The European Sports Charter*. Strasburg: Author.

Crenson, M.A. (1971) *The Un-Politics of Air Pollution: A Study of Non-Decision Making in the Cities*. Baltimore, MD: John Hopkins University Press.

Crick, M. (1986) *The March of Militant*. London: Faber and Faber.

Crotty, M. (1998) *The Foundations of Social Research*. London: Sage.

Dahl, R. (1961) *Who Governs? Democracy and Power in an American City*. New Haven, CT: Yale University Press.

Dahl, R. (1967) *Pluralist Democracy in the United States*. Chicago, IL: Rand McNally.

Dahl, R. (1971) *Polyarchy: Participation and Opposition*. New Haven, CT: Yale University Press.

Dahl, R. (1982) *Dilemmas of Pluralist Democracy*. New Haven, CT: Yale University Press.

Dahl, R. (1985) *A Preface to Economic Democracy*. Cambridge: Polity Press.

Dahlgren, G. and Whitehead, M. (1991) *Policies and Strategies to Promote Equity in Health*. Stockholm: Institute of Future Studies.

Daugbjerg, C. and Marsh, D. (1988) Explaining policy outcomes: integrating the policy network approach with macro-level and micro-level analysis. In, D. Marsh (Ed.), *Comparing Policy Networks*. Buckingham: Open University Press.

Deacon, E., Hulse, M. and Stubbs, P. (1997) *Global Social Policy: International Organisations and the Future of Welfare*. London: Sage.

De Leon, P. (1999a) *Democracy and Policy Sciences*. Albany: State University of New York Press.

De Leon, P. (1999b) The stages approach to the policy process: What has it done? Where is it going?. In, P.A. Sabatier, (Ed.), *Theories of the Policy Process*. Boulder, CO: Westview Press.

Denscombe, M. (2003) *The Good Research Guide for Small-Scale Social Research Projects*. Maidenhead: Open University Press.

Denzin, N.K. (1970) *The Research Act in Sociology*. London: Butterworths.

Department of Culture, Media and Sport, DCMS (1999) *Report to the Social Exclusion Unit – Arts and Sport, Policy Action Team 10*. London: Author.

Department of Culture, Media and Sport, DCMS (2000) *A Sporting Future for All*. London: Author.

Department of Culture, Media and Sport, DCMS (2001a) *The Government's Plan for Sport*. London: Author.

Department of Culture, Media and Sport, DCMS (2001b) *A Sporting Future for All: Action Plan*. London: Author.

Department of Culture, Media and Sport, DCMS (2003) *Planning for Play. Playing Fields and Positive Gains for Sport 2001/02*. London: Author.

Department of Culture, Media and Sport (2004) *First Game Plan Delivery Report*. London: Author.

Department of Culture, Media and Sport/Strategy Unit (2002) *Game Plan: A Strategy for Delivering Government's Sport and Physical Activity Objectives*. London: Author.

Department for Education and Employment (1996) *The Education Act 1996*. London: HMSO.

Department for Education and Employment, DfEE (1996b) *Area Guidelines for Schools, Building Bulletin 82*. London: HMSO.

Department for Education and Employment (1998a) *The Education Reform Act*. London: HMSO.

Department for Education and Employment (1998b) *Specialist Schools: Education Partnerships for the 21st Century*. London: Author.

Department for Education and Employment, DfEE (1998c) *Sports Colleges: A Guide for Schools*. London: Author.

Department for Education and Employment (1998d) *The School Standards and Framework Act*. London: The Stationery Office.

Department for Education and Employment (1999 a) *The Education (School Premises) Regulations 1999, Statutory Instrument No. 2*. London: Author.

Department for Education and Employment (1999 b) *The School Playing Fields General Disposal and Change of Use Consent 1999*. London: Author.

Department for Education and Employment (1999 c) *Protecting School Playing Fields: A Brief Guide*. London: Author.

Department for Education and Employment (June 1999 d) *Circular 3/99: The Protection of School Playing Fields*. London: Author.

Department for Education and Employment (2000) *Protection of School Playing Fields and Land for City Academies*. London: Author.

Department for Education and Science (1991) *The National Curriculum for Physical Education*. London: HMSO.

Department for Education and Skills, DfES (2001) *Guidance for the Protection of School Playing Fields*. London: Author.

Department for Education and Skills, DfES (2003) *Learning through PE and Sport: A Guide to the Physical Education, School Sport and Club Links Strategy*. London: Author.

Department for Education and Skills, DfES (2004) *Learning through PE and Sport: An Update on the National PE, School Sport and Club Links Strategy*. London: Author.

Department for Education and Skills, DfES (2005 a) *Every Child Matters*. London: Author.

Department for Education and Skills, DfES (2005 b) *Building Schools for the Future*. London: Author.

Department of the Environment, DoE (1975) *Sport and Recreation (White Paper, Cmnd. 6200)*. London: HMSO.

Department of the Environment, DoE (1977) *A Policy for the Inner Cities*. London: HMSO.

Department of the Environment, DoE (1980) *Circular 9/80. Land for House Building*. London: HMSO.

Department of the Environment, DoE (1989) *Sport and Active Recreation: Provision in the Inner Cities*. London: HMSO.

Department of the Environment, DoE (1990) *This Common Inheritance. White Paper*. London: Author.

Department of the Environment, DoE (1991) *Planning Policy Guidance for Sport and Recreation*. London: Author.

Department of the Environment, DoE (1996) *Town and Country Planning (General Development Procedure (Amendment) Order*. London: Author.

Department of Environment, Transport and the Regions (1998 a) *The Effectiveness of Planning Policy Guidance on Sport and Recreation*. London: The Stationary Office.

Department of Environment, Transport and the Regions (1998 b) *The Town and Country Planning (Playing Fields) (England) Direction 1998*. London: The Stationery Office.

Department of Environment, Transport and the Regions (2001a) *Draft Revised Planning Policy Guidance Note on Sport, Open Space and Recreation (PPG17): For Public Consultation*. London: The Stationary Office.

Department of Environment, Transport and the Regions (2001b) *Rethinking Open Space*. London: Author.

Department of Health, DH (1989) *Working for Patients, and the NHS*. London: HMSO.

Department of Health (1992) *The Health of the Nation*. London: HMSO.

Department of Health (1990) *Community Care Act*. London: HMSO.

Department of Health, DH (1996) *Health Survey for England 1994. A Survey Carried Out on Behalf of the DH, by Social and Community Planning Research*. London: HMSO.

Department of Health, DH (1997) *A New NHS*. London: HMSO.

Department of Health, DH (1998) *The Health of the Nation: A Policy Assessed*. London: HMSO.

Department of Health, DH (1999a) *Saving Lives: Our Healthier Nation – Executive Summary*. London: HMSO.

Department of Health, DH (1999b) *Health Survey for England: Cardiovascular Disease '98. A Survey Carried Out on Behalf of the DH*. London: HMSO.

Department of Health (1999c) *Health Survey for England 1998*. London: HMSO.

Department of Health, DH (2000) *Health Survey for England: Report of the AusDiab Study, 2000; National Centre of Health Statistics, 1999–2000*. London: HMSO.

Department of Health, DH (2001) *Exercise Referral Systems: A National Quality Assurance Framework*. London: HMSO.

Department of Health, DH (2002) *Tackling Health Inequalities: Consultation on a Plan for Delivery*. London: HMSO.

Department of Health, DH (2003) *Tackling Health Inequalities: A Programme for Action*. London: HMSO.

Department of Health, DH (2004a) *Choosing Health: Making Healthier Choices Easier*. London: Author.

Department of Health, DH (2004b) *Choosing Health: A Consultation on Action to Improve People's Health*. London: Author.

Department of Health, DH (2004273c) *White Paper on Public Health*. London: HMSO.

Department of Health, DH (2004d) *At Least Five a Week*. London: HMSO.

Department of Health, DH (2005a) *Choosing Health? Choosing Activity*. London: Author.

Department of Health, DH (2005b) *Choosing Activity: A Physical Activity Action Plan*. London: Author.

Department for Health and Social Security, DHSS (1976) *Prevention and Health: Everybody's Business*. London: HMSO.

Department for Health and Social Security, DHSS (1980) *The Black Report: Inequalities in Health*. London: HMSO.

Department of National Heritage, DNH (1995) *Sport: Raising the Game*. London: Author.

Dery, D. (1999) Policy by the way: when policy is incidental to making other policies. *Journal of Public Policy*, 18(2), 163–176.

Devine, F. (1995) Qualitative analysis. In D. Marsh and G. Stoker (Eds.) *Theory and Methods in Political Science*. Basingstoke: Macmillan.

DfEE (1988) *The Education Reform Act*. London: Author.

Dietz, W.H. (2001) The obesity epidemic in young children. *British Medical Journal*, 322, 313–314.

Dolowitz, D. and Marsh, D. (1996) Who learns what from whom? A review of the policy transfer literature. *Political Studies*, 44, 343–357.

Dowding, K. (1994) Policy networks: don't stretch a good idea too far. In P. Dunleavy and J. Stanyer (Eds.) *Contemporary Political Studies*. pp. 59–78. Belfast: Political Science Association.

Dowding, K. (1995) Model or metaphor? A critical review of the policy network approach. *Political Studies*, 45, 136–158.

Downs, A. (1972) Up and down with ecology: the issue-attention cycle. *Public Interest*, 28, 38–50.

Dunleavy, P. (1980) *Urban Political Analysis*. London: Macmillan.

Dunleavy, P. and O'Leary, B. (1987) *Theories of the State: The Politics of Liberal Democracy*. London: Macmillan.

Dye, T. (1972) *Politics, Economics and Public Policy*. Chicago, IL: Rand McNally.

Easton, D. (1953) *The Political System*. New York: Alfred A. Knopf.

Easton, D. (1965) *A Framework for Political Analysis*. Englewood Cliffs, NJ: Prentice Hall.

English Sports Council (1991) *The Playing Pitch Strategy*. London: ESC/CCPR/NPFA.

English Sports Council, ESC (1993) *Planning Obligations for Sport and Recreation – A Guide to Negotiation and Action*. London: Author.

English Sports Council, ESC (1994a) *Factfile 2: Planning and Provision for Sport*. London: Author.

English Sports Council (1994b) *Planning Obligations for Sport and Recreation. Factfile 2: Planning and Provision for Sport*. London: Author.

English Sports Council (1995) *Assessing Playing Pitch Requirements at the Local Level: Factfile 2, Planning and Provision for Sport*. London: Author.

English Sports Council (1996) *Playing Fields for Sport*. London: Author.

English Sports Council, ESC (1997a) *A Sporting Future for the Playing Fields of England: Policy on Planning Applications for Development on Playing Fields*. London: Author.

English Sports Council (1997b) Playing Fields for Sport. *Planning Bulletin*, Issue 1. London: Author.

English Sports Council (1997c) *England: The Sporting Nation*. London: Author.

English Sports Council, ESC (1998a) *Strategic Planning for Sport*. London: Author.

English Sports Council (1998b) *More People, More Places, More Medals*. London: Author.

Ericson, R., Baranek, P. and Chan, J. (1991) *Representing Order: Crime, Law, and Justice in the News Media*. Milton Keynes: Open University Press.

Evans, D. (2003) Implementing policies to tackle health inequalities at local level. In A. Oliver and M. Exworthy (Eds.) *Health Inequalities: Evidence, Policy and Implementation. Proceedings of a Meeting of the Health Equity Network*. London: Nutfield Trust.

Evans, M. (1995) Elitism. In D. Marsh and G. Stoker (Eds.) *Theory and Methods in Political Science*. Basingstoke: Macmillan.

Evans, M. (2001) Understanding dialectics in policy network analysis. *Political Studies*, 49, 542–550.

Evans, J. and Penney, D. (1995) Physical education, restoration and the politics of sport. *Curriculum Studies*, 3(2), 183–196.

Evans, J. and Penney, D. (1998) Policy, process and power. In K. Green and K. Hardman (Eds.) *Physical Education: A Reader*. Oxford: Meyer and Meyer.

Evans, J. and Penney, D. (2005) Policy, power and politics. In K. Green and K. Hardman (Eds.) *Physical Education: Essential Issues*. London: Sage.

Exworthy, M. (2003) The Acheson report: the aftermath. In A. Oliver and M. Exworthy (Eds.) *Health Inequalities: Evidence, Policy and Implementation. Proceedings of a Meeting of the Health Equity Network*. London: Nutfield Trust.

Finer, S.E. (1966) *Anonymous Empire*. London: Pall Mall.

Fischer, F. and Forester, J. (Eds.) (1993) *The Argumentative Turn in Policy Analysis and Planning*. London: UCL Press.

Flick, U. (1998) *An Introduction to Qualitative Research*. London: Sage.

Flintoff, A. (2003) The school sport coordinator programme: changing the role of the physical education teacher? *Sport, Education and Society*, 8(2), 231–250.

Foster, A. (2004) *Moving On: A Review of the Need for Change in Athletics in the UK*. London: UK Sport and Sport England.

Fox, D. (1986) *Health Policies, Health Politics*. Princetown University Press.

Garrett, R. (2004) The response of voluntary sports clubs to Sport England's lottery funding: cases of compliance, change and resistance. *Managing Leisure*, 9(1), 13–29.

Gavanta, J. (1980) *Power and Powerlessness*. Oxford: Clarendon Press.

Geertz, C. (1973) Thick description: toward an interpretive theory of culture. In C. Geertz (Ed.) *The Interpretation of Cultures*. New York: Basic Books.

Giddens, A. (1998) *The Third Way. The Renewal of Social Democracy*. Cambridge: Polity.

Goodin, R.E. and Klingemann, H.D. (1996) Political science: the discipline. In R.E. Goodin and H.D. Klingemann (Eds.) *A New Handbook of Political Science*. Oxford: Oxford University Press, pp. 3–49.

Gough, I. (1979) *The Political Economy of the Welfare State*. London: Macmillan.

Goverde, H. and Tatenhove, J.V. (2000) Power and policy networks. In H. Goverde et al. (Eds.), *Power in Contemporary Politics: Theories, Practices and Globalisations*. London: Sage.

Government Office for the Regions NW, GONW (2003) *Investment for Health: A Plan for North-West England*. Manchester: Author.

Gramsci, A. (1971) *Selections from the Prison Notebooks of Antonio Gramsci. Q. Hoare and G. Nowell-Smith*. London: Lawrence and Wishart.

Granovetter, M. (1985) Economic action and social structure: the problem of embeddedness. *American Journal of Sociology*, 91, 481–510.

Grant, W. (1989) *Pressure Groups, Politics, and Democracy in Britain*. London: Sage.

Grant, W. (1995) *Pressure Groups, Politics, and Democracy in Britain* (2nd ed.). London: Sage.

Gratton, C. and Henry, I.P. (Eds.) (2001) *Sport in the City. The Role of Sport in Economic and Social Regeneration*. London: Routledge.

Gratton, C. and Jones, I. (2004) *Research Methods for Sport Studies*. London: Routledge.

Greckhamer, T. and Koro-Ljungberg, M. (2005) The erosion of a method: examples from grounded theory. *International Journal of Qualitative Studies in Education*, 18(6), 729–750.

Green, M. (2003) *An analysis of elite sport policy change in three sports in Canada and the UK*. Doctoral thesis, Loughborough University.

Green, M. (2004a) Changing policy priorities for sport: the emergence of elite sport development as a key policy concern. *Leisure Studies*, 23(4), 365–385.

Green, M. (2004b) Power, policy and political priorities: elite sport development in Canada and the UK. *Sociology of Sport*, 21, 376–396.

Green, M. (2006) *Integrating macro- and meso-level approaches: a comparative analysis of elite sport development in Australia, Canada and the UK*. Unpublished paper, Loughborough University.

Green, M. and Houlihan, B. (2004) Advocacy coalitions and elite sport policy change in Canada and the UK. *International Review for the Sociology of Sport*, 39(4), 387–403.

Green, M. and Houlihan, B. (2005a) *Elite Sport Development: Policy Learning and Political Priorities*. London: Routledge.

Green, M. and Houlihan, B. (2005b) Governmentality, modernisation and the 'disciplining' of national sport organisations: an analysis of athletics in Australia and the UK. Unpublished paper, Loughborough University.

Greenaway, J., Smith, S. and Street, J. (1992) *Deciding Factors in British Politics: A Case Study Approach*. London: Routledge.

Greenleaf, W.H. (1983) *The British Political Tradition: The Rise of Collectivism*. London: Methuen.

Grimshaw, P. and Prescott-Clarke, S. (1978) *Sport, school and the community*. Sports Council Working Paper Number 9. London: Sports Council.

Grix, J. (2002) Introducing students to the generic terminology of social research. *Politics*, 22(3), 175–186.

Guba, E. (1990) The alternative paradigm dialogue. In E. Guba (Ed.) *The Paradigm Dialogue*. London: Sage.

Guba, E. and Lincoln, Y. (1981) *Effective Evaluation*. San Francisco, CA: Jossey-Bass.

Guba, E. and Lincoln, Y. (1987) *Competing Paradigms in Qualitative Research*. San Francisco, CA: Jossey-Bass.

Haas, P.M. (1992) Introduction: epistemic communities and international policy coordination. *International Organisation*, 46(1), 1–35.

Hall, P. (1986) *Governing the Economy*. Cambridge: Polity Press.

Ham, C.J. (1977) Power, Patients and Pluralism. In K. Barnard and K. Lee (Eds.) *Conflicts in the NHS*. Croom Helm.

Ham, C.J. (2000) *The Politics of NHS Reform 1988–97*. London: Kings Fund.

Ham, C.J. (2004) *Health Policy in Britain. The Politics and Organisation of the NHS* (5th ed.). Basingstoke: Palgrave Macmillan.

Ham, C. and Hill, M. (1993) *The Policy Process in the Modern Capitalist State* (2nd ed.). New York: Harvester-Wheatsheaf.

Hammersley, M. (1992) *Deconstructing the Qualitative–Quantitative Divide*. London: Routledge.

Hammersley, M. and Atkinson, P. (1983) *Ethnography: Principles and Practice*. London: Tavistock.

Hancock, M.D. (1983) Comparative public policy: an assessment. In A. Finifter (Ed.) *Political Science: The State of the Discipline*. Washington, DC: American Political Science Association.

Harvey, L. (1990) *Critical Social Research*. London: Unwin Hyman.

Hawkesworth, M. (1992) Epistemology and policy analysis. In W. Dunn and R. Kelly (Eds.) *Advances in Policy Studies*. New Brunswick, NJ: Transaction Books.

Hay, C. (1995) Structure and agency. In D. Marsh and G. Stoker (Eds.) *Theory and Methods in Political Science*. Basingstoke: Macmillan.

Hay, C. (1996) *Re-stating Social and Political Change*. Buckingham: Open University Press.

Hay, C. (1997) Divided by a common language: political theory and the concept of power. *Politics*, 17(1), 45–52.

Hay, C. (2002) *Political Analysis: A Critical Introduction*. Basingstoke: Palgrave.

Health Education Authority, HEA (1998) *Young and Active? Policy Framework for Young People and Health-Enhancing Physical Activity*. London: Author.

Heclo, H. (1974) *Modern Social Politics in Britain and Sweden: From Relief to Income Maintenance*. New Haven and London: Yale University Press.

Heclo, H. (1978) Issue Networks and the Executive Establishment. In A. King (Ed.) *The New American Political System*. Washington, DC: American Enterprise Institute.

Heclo, H. and Wildavsky, A. (1981) *The Private Government of Public Money* (2nd ed.). London: Macmillan.

Heidenheimer, A.J., Heclo, H. and Carolyn, T. (1990) *Comparative Public Policy: The Politics of Social Choice in America, Europe and Japan*. New York: St Martin's Press.

Held, D. (1996) *Models of Democracy* (2nd ed.). Cambridge: Polity Press.

Henry, I.P. (1993) *The Politics of Leisure Policy*. London: Macmillan.

Henry, I.P. (2001) *The Politics of Leisure Policy* (2nd ed.). Houndmills: Palgrave.

Henry, I.P. and Bramham, P. (1986) Leisure, the local state and social order. *Leisure Studies*, 5(2), 189–209.

Henry, I.P. and Bramham, P. (1993) Leisure policy in Britain. In P. Bramham, I.P. Henry, H. Mommass and H. Van der Poel (Eds.) *Leisure Policies in Europe*. Wallingford: CAB International.

Hewitt, C.J. (1974) Elites and the distribution of power in British society. In A. Giddens and P. Stanworth (Eds.) *Elites and Power in British Society*. Cambridge: Cambridge University Press.

Hill, M. (1997) *The Policy Process: A Reader* (2nd ed.). London: Prentice Hall/Harvester-Wheatsheaf.

Hill, M. and Hupe, P. (2002) *Implementing Public Policy*. London: Sage.

Hogwood, B. and Gunn, L. (1984) *Policy Analysis for the Real World*. Oxford: Oxford University Press.

Horne, J., Tomlinson, A. and Whannel, G. (1999) *Understanding Sport: An Introduction to the Sociological and Cultural Analysis of Sport*. London and New York: E&FN Spon.

Houlihan, B. (1991) *The Government and Politics of Sport*. London: Routledge.

Houlihan, B. (1992) The politics of school sport. In J. Sugden and C. Knox (Eds.) *Leisure in the 1990s: Rolling Back the Welfare State*. LSA, 46, 59–80.

Houlihan, B. (1997) *Sport, Policy and Politics: A Comparative Analysis*. London: Routledge.

Houlihan, B. (2000 a) Sporting excellence, schools and sports development: the politics of crowded policy spaces. *European Physical Education Review*, 6(2), 171–193.

Houlihan, B. (2000b) Theorising sport policy-making: problems of globalisation and marginalisation. *Paper presented at the pre-Olympic Congress*, Brisbane.

Houlihan, B. (2002) Political involvement in sport, physical education and recreation. In A. Laker (Ed.) *The Sociology of Sport and Physical Education*. London: Routledge-Falmer.

Houlihan, B. (2003) Politics, power, policy and sport. In B. Houlihan (Ed.) *Sport and Society*. London: Routledge.

Houlihan, B. (2005) Public sector sport policy: developing a framework for analysis. *International Review for the Sociology of Sport*, 40(2), 163–185.

Houlihan, B. and Green, M. (2006) The changing status of school sport and physical education: explaining policy change. *Sport, Education and Society*, 11(1), 73–92.

Houlihan, B. and White, A. (2002) *The Politics of Sports Development: Development of Sport or Development through SPORT?*. London: Routledge.

Howarth, D. (1995) Discourse Theory. In D. Marsh and G. Stoker (Eds.) *Theory and Methods in Political Science*. Basingstoke: Macmillan.

Howlett, M. and Ramesh, M. (2003) *Studying Public Policy. Policy Cycles and Policy Subsystems*. Oxford: Oxford University Press.

Hunt, H. and Lamble, K. (2007) City's swimming shame. *Liverpool Echo*, 17th September.

Hunter, D. (1983) Centre–periphery relations in the NHS: facilitators or inhibitors of innovation?. In K. Young (Ed.) *National Interests and Local Governments*. Heinemann.

Hylton, E., Branham, P., Jackson, D. and Nesti, M. (2001) *Sports Development: Policy, Process and Practice*. London: Routledge.

Hylton, K. and Bramham, P. (Eds.) (2008) *Sports Development. Policy, Progress and Practice* (Second Edition). London: Routledge.

Independent Sports Review Group (2005) *Raising the Bar. The Final Report of the Independent Sports Review*. London: Greenaways.

Jackson, D. and Nesti, M. (2001a) Sports practice. In K. Hylton, P. Bramham, D. Jackson and M. Nesti (Eds.) *Sports Development: Policy, Process and Practice*. London: Routledge.

Jackson, D. and Nesti, M. (2001b) Resources for sport. More people, more places, more medals – and more money?. In K. Hylton, P. Bramham, D. Jackson and M. Nesti (Eds.) *Sports Development: Policy, Process and Practice*. London: Routledge.

Jenkins, W.I. (1978) *Policy Analysis: A Political and Organisational Perspective*. London: Martin Robertson.

Jenkins, B. (1997) Policy Analysis: Models and Approaches. In M. Hill (Ed.) *The Policy Process: A Reader* (2nd ed.). London: Prentice Hall/Harvester-Wheatsheaf.

Jenkins-Smith, H.C. and Sabatier, P.A. (1993a) The dynamics of policy-oriented learning. In P.A. Sabatier and H.C. Jenkins-Smith (Eds.) *Policy Change and Learning: An Advocacy Coalition Approach*. Boulder, CO: Westview Press.

Jenkins-Smith, H.C. and Sabatier, P.A. (1993b) The study of public policy processes. In P.A. Sabatier and H.C. Jenkins-Smith (Eds.) *Policy Change and Learning: An Advocacy Coalition Approach*. Boulder, CO: Westview Press.

Jessop, B. (1990) *State Theory: Putting Capitalist States in Their Place*. Cambridge: Polity.

John, P. (1998) *Analysing Public Policy*. London: Pinter.

John, P. and Cole, A. (1995) Models of local decision-making in Britain and France. *Policy and Politics*, 23(4), 303–312.

Johnson, T., Dandeker, C. and Ashworth, C. (1984) *The Structure of Social Theory*. Basingstoke: Macmillan.

Jones, P. and Wilks-Heeg, S. (2004) Capitalising culture: Liverpool 2008. *Local Economy*, 19(4), 341–360.

Jordan, A., Maloney, W. and McLaughlin, A. (1992) Characterising agriculture policy making. *Public Administration*, 72(4), 502–526.

Jordan, A.G. and Richardson, J.J. (1983) *Government and Pressure Groups in Britain*. Oxford: Clarendon.

Jordan, A.G. and Richardson, J.J. (1987) *British Politics and the Policy Process*. London: Unwin Hyman.

Judge, D., Stoker, G. and Wolman, H. (Eds.) (1995) *Theories of Urban Politics*. London: Sage.

Kay, W. (1998) *The New Right and physical education: a critical analysis*. Doctoral thesis, Loughborough University.

Keat, R. and Urry, J. (1975) *Social Theory as Science*. London: Routledge and Kegan-Paul.

Kickert, W.J.M., Klijn, E.H. and Koppenjan, J.F.M. (Eds.) (1997) *Managing Complex Networks: Strategies for the Public Sector*. London: Sage.

King, N. (2006) *The role and remit of the Liverpool Sports Forum*. Unpublished report to the LSF Executive.

King, G., Keohane, R.O. and Verba, S. (1994) *Designing Social Enquiry: Scientific Inference in Qualitative Research*. Princeton: Princeton University Press.

Kingdon, J.W. (1984) *Agendas, Alternatives and Public Policies*. Michigan: Harper Collins.

Kingdon, J.W. (1995) *Agendas, Alternatives and Public Policies* (2nd ed.). New York: Harper-Collins.

Kirk, D. (1992) *Defining Physical Education: The Social Construction of a School Subject in Post-War Britain*. London: Falmer Press.

Kirk, D. (2003) Sport, physical education and schools. In B. Houlihan (Ed.) *Sport and Society*. London: Routledge.

Kirk, J. and Miller, M. (1986) *Reliability and Validity in Qualitative Research*. Beverly Hills, CA: Sage.

Klein, R. (2000) *The New Politics of the NHS* (4th ed.). London: Prentice Hall.

Klein, R. (2003) Commentary: making policy in a fog. In A. Oliver and M. Exworthy (Eds.) *Health Inequalities: Evidence, Policy and Implementation. Proceedings of a Meeting of the Health Equity Network*. London: Nutfield Trust.

Labour Party (1996) *Labour's Sporting Nation*. London: Labour Party.

Lakatos, M. (1978) The methodology of scientific research programmes. In J. Worral and G. Currie (Eds.) *Philosophical Papers*. Cambridge: Cambridge University Press, 1, 1–104.

Lansley, S., Goss, S. and Wolmar, C. (1989) *Councils in Conflict: The Rise and Fall of 'Local Socialism'*. London: Macmillan.

Laski, H.J. (1939) *The Danger of Being a Gentleman and Other Essays*. London: George Allen and Unwin.

Laswell, H.D. (1956) *The Decision Process: Seven Categories of Functional Analysis*. College Park, MD: University of Maryland Press.

Laumann, E.O. and Knoke, D. (1987) *The Organizational State*. Madison, WI: University of Wisconsin Press.

Lave, C. and March, J. (1975) *An Introduction to Models in the Social Sciences*. New York: Harper Row.

Layder, D. (1985) Power, structure and agency. *Journal of the Theory of Social Behaviour*, 15(2), 131–149.

Lehmbruch, C. and Schmitter, P. (Eds.) (1982) *Patterns of Corporatist Policymaking*. London: Sage.

Lentell, B. (1993) Sports development: goodbye to community recreation?. In C. Brackenbridge (Ed.) *Body Matters: Leisure Images and Lifestyles*. Eastbourne: Leisure Studies Association.

Lewis, P.A. (2002) Agency, Structure and Causality in Political Science: a comment on sibeon. *Politics*, 22(1), 17–23.

Lincoln, Y. (1990) The making of a constructivist: a remembrance of transformations past. In E. Guba (Ed.) *The Paradigm Dialogue*. London: Sage.

Lindbolm, C.E. (1960) The science of muddling through. *Public Administration Review*, 19(2), 79–88.

Lindbolm, C.E. (1977) *Politics and Markets*. New York: Basic Books.

Lindbolm, C.E. (1986) *Democracy and Market System*. Oslo: Norwegian University Press.

Liverpool City Council, LCC (1984) *Sport and Recreation Statement*. Liverpool: Author.

Liverpool City Council, LCC (1987) *Review of open space in Liverpool*. Planning Department, unpublished report.

Liverpool City Council, LCC (1997) *On the Right Track*. Liverpool: Author.

Liverpool City Council, LCC (1998) *A review of playing fields provision*. Leisure Services and Planning, unpublished report.

Liverpool City Council, LCC (2000) *Liverpool SportsLinx Project: Report on health and fitness: for 9–10 year olds*. Liverpool: Author.

Liverpool City Council, LCC (2000b) Minutes of the Executive Board, 15th December.

Liverpool City Council, LCC (2000c) Swimming Strategy 2000–05.

Liverpool City Council, LCC (2001) Minutes of the Executive Board, 20th July.

Liverpool City Council, LCC (2002a) Minutes of the Executive Board, 26th April.

Liverpool City Council, LCC (2002b) *A review of playing fields provision*. Leisure Services and Planning, unpublished report.

Liverpool City Council, LCC (2002c) Minutes of the Leisure and Tourism Select Committee, 11th April.

Liverpool City Council, LCC (2003a) *Realising the potential*. Unpublished strategy for sport and recreation in Liverpool, 2003–08. Liverpool: Author.

Liverpool City Council, LCC (2003b) *European Capital of Culture: The Bid*. Liverpool: Author.

Liverpool City Council, LCC (2003c) *Liverpool open spaces study: consultancy brief*. Liverpool: Author. Unpublished report.

Liverpool City Council, LCC (2005) *Active City*. Liverpool: Author.

Liverpool City Council, LCC (2006a) Minutes of Leisure and Tourism Select Committee, 9th January.

Liverpool City Council, LCC (2006b) Minutes of Leisure and Tourism Select Committee, 27th March.

Liverpool City Council, LCC (2007) *Liverpool SPAA Delivery Plan for 2007–10*. Liverpool: Author.

Liverpool City Council, LCC (2008a) *Sport and Recreation Strategy for 2008–12*. Liverpool: Author. A Draft.

Liverpool City Council (2008b) The Indices of Deprivation 2007. Regeneration Policy Programmes and Performance Division. Publication Number PMD 376. Liverpool: Author.

Liverpool First for Health (2002 a) *Liverpool City Health Plan*. Liverpool: Author.

Liverpool Sports Forum (2002a) Minutes of the Meeting of 4th April.

Liverpool Sports Forum (2002b) Minutes of the Meeting of 16th May.

Liverpool Sports Forum (2002c) Minutes of the Meeting of 12th June.

Liverpool Sports Forum (2002d) Minutes of the Meeting of 24th September.

Liverpool Sports Forum (2002e) Minutes of the Meeting of 19th November.

Liverpool Sports Forum (2003) Minutes of the Meeting of 21st October

Liverpool Sports Forum (2004a) Letter to LSF Membership, 10th February.

Liverpool Sports Forum (2004b) Letter to LSF Membership, 4th March.

Liverpool Sports Forum (2004c) Minutes of the Meeting of 22nd March.

Liverpool Sports Forum (2004d) Minutes of the Meeting of 7th July.

Liverpool Sports Forum (2004e) Letter to LSF Membership, 14th October.

Liverpool Sports Forum (2004f) Minutes of the Meeting of 28th October.

Liverpool Sports Forum (2004g) Minutes of the Meeting of 23rd November.

Liverpool Sports Forum (2005a) Minutes of the Meeting of 12th June.

Liverpool Sports Forum (2005b) Minutes of the Meeting of 27th September.

London Assembly (2008) *Who gains? The Operation of Section 106 Planning Agreements in London*. Planning and Spatial Development Committee, London, Author.

London Council for Sport and Recreation, LCSR (1990) *A Playing Field Strategy for London*. London: Author.

Loftland, J. and Loftland, L. (1984) *Analyzing Social Settings: A Guide to Qualitative Observation and Analysis*. Belmont: Wadsworth.

Lord Carter of Coles (2005) *Review of National Sport Effort and Resources*. London: Sport England.

Lottery Monitor (1998) Smith's Annual Report Sets Lottery Agenda, August, 8–11.

Lowndes, V. and Wilson, D. (2003) Balancing revisability and robustness? A new institutionalist perspective on local government modernization. *Public Administration*, 81(2), 275–298.

Lowi, T.J., (1972) *The End of Liberalism*. New York: Norton.

Lukes, S. (1974) *Power: A Radical View*. London: Macmillan.

Lukcs, S. (1997) Three distinctive views of power compared. In M. Hill (Ed.) *The Policy Process: A Reader* (2nd ed.). London: Prentice Hall/Harvester-Wheatsheaf.

Mackie, T. and Marsh, D. (1995) The comparative method. In D. Marsh and G. Stoker (Eds.) *Theory and Methods in Political Science*. Basingstoke: Macmillan.

Majone, G. (1989) *Evidence, Argument and Persuasion in the Policy Process*. New Haven, CT: Yale University Press.

March, J. and Olsen, J. (1976) *Ambiguity and Choice in Organisations*. Oslo: Universitieforlaget.

March, J. and Olsen, J. (1984) The new institutionalism: organisational factors in political life. *American Political Science Review*, 78, 734–749.

March, J. and Olsen, J. (1989) *Rediscovering Institutions: The Organisational Basis of Politics*. Free Press.

Marinetto, M. (1999) *Studies of the Policy Process: A Case Analysis*. London: Prentice Hall.

Marsh, D. (1995) The convergence between theories of the state. In D. Marsh and G. Stoker (Eds.) *Theory and Methods in Political Science*. Basingstoke: Macmillan.

Marsh, D. (1998) The utility and future of policy network analysis. In D. Marsh (Ed.) *Comparing Policy Networks*. Buckingham: Open University Press.

Marsh, D. and Rhodes, R.A.W. (1992) Policy communities and issue networks: beyond typology. In D. Marsh and R.A.W. Rhodes (Eds.) *Policy Networks in British Government*. Oxford: Clarendon.

Marsh, D. and Smith, M. (2000) Understanding policy networks: towards a dialectical approach. *Political Studies*, 48, 4–21.

Marsh, D. and Smith, M. (2001) There is more than one way to do political science: on different ways to study policy networks. *Political Studies*, 49, 528–541.

Marsh, D. and Stoker, G. (Eds.) (1995) *Theory and Methods in Political Science*. Basingstoke: Macmillan.

Marsh, D., Buller, J. and Hay, C. (1999) *Post-War British Politics in Perspective*. Cambridge: Polity Press.

May, T. (1997) *Social Research: Issues, Methods and Process*. Buckingham: Open University Press.

McDonald, I. (1995) Sport for All – 'RIP'. A political critique of the relationship between national sport policy and local authority sports development in London. In Enter S. Fleming (Ed.) *Policy and Politics in Sport, Physical Education and Leisure*. Eastbourne: Leisure Studies Association.

McDonald, I. (2000) Excellence and expedience? Olympism, power and contemporary Sports Policy in England. In M. Keech and G. McFee (Eds.) *Issues and Values in Sport and Leisure Cultures*. Oxford: Meyer and Meyer.

McFarland, A.S. (1987) Interest groups and theories of power in America. *British Journal of Political Science*, 17, 129–147.

McIntosh, P. and Charlton, V. (1985) *The impact of sport for all policy 1966–1984 and a way forward*. London: Sports Council.

McLennan, G. (1990) *Marxism, Pluralism and Beyond*. Cambridge: Polity Press.

McLennan, G. (1995) *Pluralism*. Milton Keynes: Open University Press.

McPherson, A. and Raab, C. (1988) *Governing Education: A Sociology of Policy Since 1945*. Edinburgh: Edinburgh University Press.

Merseyside Sport Partnership, MSP (2003) *Team Works in Merseyside: Together Everyone Achieves More. Strategy for 2003–08*. Liverpool: MSP.

Merseyside Sport Partnership, MSP (2006) *Merseyside Strategy for Sport and Physical Activity: 2006–10*. Liverpool: MSP.

Miles, M. and Huberman, A. (1994) *Qualitative Data Analysis*. Thousand Oaks, CA: Sage.

Milliband, R. (1969) *The State in Capitalist Society*. London: Weidenfield and Nicolson.

Mills, M. and Seward, M. (1994) Policy communities: theoretical issues. *Policy Studies Journal*, 20(3), 243–251.

Muccarioni, G. (1992) The garbage can model and the study of policy making: a critique. *Polity*, 24, 459–482.

Murden, J. (2006) City of change and challenge: Liverpool since 1945, Chapter 6. In J. Belchem (Ed.) *Liverpool 800: Culture, Character and History*. Liverpool: Liverpool University Press.

Naidoo, J. and Wills, J. (Eds.) (2000) *Health Studies: An Introduction*. Basingstoke: Palgrave.

National Playing Fields Association, NPFA (1986) *Space Requirements for the More Popular Outdoor Games*. London: Author.

National Playing Fields Association, NPFA (1989) *The State of Play*. London: Author.

National Playing Fields Association, NPFA (1991) *The Six Acre Standard: Minimum Standards for Outdoor Playing Space*. London: Author.

National Playing Fields Association, NPFA (2001) *The Six Acre Standard: Minimum Standards for Outdoor Playing Space*. London: Author.

National Playing Fields Association, NPFA (2003) Press release, June. www.npfa. co.uk, accessed in October 2004.

National Statistics Online: Census (2001) www.statistics.gov.uk, accessed in February 2005.

Newton, K. and Curran, T. (1985) *The Politics of Local Expenditure*. London: Macmillan.

Nordlinger, E. (1981) *On the Autonomy of the Democratic State*. Cambridge, MA: Harvard University Press.

North West Sports Board, NWSB (2004) *Regional Delivery Plan for Sport*. Manchester: Author.

Nutbeam, D. (2003) Tackling health inequalities in the UK: What is the government doing?. In A. Oliver and M. Exworthy (Eds.) *Health Inequalities: Evidence, Policy and Implementation. Proceedings of a Meeting of the Health Equity Network*. London: Nutfield Trust.

Oakley, B. and Green, M. (2001) Still playing the game at arm's length? The selective re-investment in British sport 1995–2000. *Managing Leisure*, 6, 74–94.

ODPM (2002) *Planning for Open Space, Sport and Recreation*. London: Author.

Offe, C. (1985) *Disorganised Capitalism: Contemporary Transformations of Work and Politics*. Cambridge: Polity Press.

Oliver, A. and Exworthy, M. (Eds.) (2003) *Health Inequalities: Evidence, Policy and Implementation. Proceedings of a Meeting of the Health Equity Network*. London: Nutfield Trust.

Olsen, M. (1965) *The Logic of Collective Action: Public Goods and the Theory of Groups*. Cambridge, MA: Harvard University Press.

Olsen, (1982) *The Rise and Decline of Nations: Economic Growth, Stagflation and Social Rigidities*. New Haven, CT: Yale University Press.

ONS (2007) National Population Statistics. Office of National Statistics website, accessed September 2008.

Ostrom, E. (1999) Institutional rational choice: an assessment of the institutional analysis and development framework. In P.A. Sabatier (Ed.) *Theories of the Policy Process*. Oxford: Westview Press.

Outshoorn, J. (1991) Is this what we wanted? Positive action as issue perversion. In E. Meetan and S. Svenhuijsen (Eds.) *Equality Politics and Gendre*. London: Sage.

Parkinson, M. (1985) *Liverpool on the Brink: One City's Struggle Against Government Cuts*. London: Policy Journals.

Parkinson, M. (1989) The Thatcher government's urban policy 1979–89. *Town Planning Review*, 60(4), 421–440.

Parkinson, M. Leadership and regeneration in Liverpool: confusion, confrontation or coalition? (1990). In D. Judd and M. Parkinson (Eds.) Leadership and regeneration: cities in North America and Europe. Urban Affairs Annual Reviews Vol. 37. London: Sage, pp. 241–257.

Parkinson, M. and Wilks, S. (1987) The politics of inner-city partnerships. In M. Goldsmith (Ed.) *New Research in Central–Local Relations*. Aldershot: Gower.

Parsons, W. (1995) *Public Policy: An Introduction to the Theory and Practice of Policy Analysis*. Cheltenham: Edward Elgar.

Pascal, G. (2003) Health and health policy. In J. Baldock et al. (Eds.), *Social Policy* (2nd ed.) Oxford: Oxford University Press.

Parrish, R. (2003) The politics of sport regulation in the European Union. *Journal of European Public Policy*, 10(2), 246–262.

Patton, M.Q. (1978) *Utilization-Focused Evaluation*. Newbury Park: Sage.

Penney, D. (1998) Positioning and defining physical education, sport and health in the curriculum. *European Physical Education Review*, 4(2), 117–126.

Penney, D. (2000) Physical education, sporting excellence and educational excellence. *European Physical Education Review*, 6(2), 135–150.

Penney, D. (2002) Equality, equity and inclusion in physical education and school sport. In A. Laker (Ed.) *The Sociology of Sport and Physical Education*. London: Routledge-Falmer.

Penney, D. (2004) Policy tensions being played out in practice – the specialist schools initiative in England. *Journal for Critical Evaluation in Policy Studies*, 2(1), 1–23.

Penney, D. and Evans, J. (1997) Naming the Game. Discourse and domination in physical education and sport in England and Wales. *European Physical Education Review*, 3(1), 21–32.

Penney, D. and Evans, J. (1999) *Politics, Policy and Practice in Physical Education*. London: E&FN Spon.

Penney, D. and Houlihan, B. (2001) Re-shaping the borders for policy research: the development of specialist sports colleges. *Australian Association for Research in Education Conference*, Freemantle, Australia, December 2001.

Penney, D., Houlihan, B. and Eley, D. (2002) Specialist Sports Colleges – National Monitoring and Evaluation Research Project: National Survey Report. Loughborough: Institute of Youth Sport.

Peters, B.G. (1998) *Comparative Politics: Theory and Methods*. Basingstoke: Macmillan.

Physick, R. (2007) *Played in Liverpool. Charting the Heritage of a City at Play*. Manchester: English Heritage.

Pickup, D. (1996) *Not Another Messiah: An Account of the Sports Council, 1988–93*. Edinburgh: Pentland Press.

PMP Consultancy (2001) *A review of the playing pitch strategy: survey analysis*. Unpublished report. London: Author.

Polsby, N. (1963) *Community Power and Democratic Theory*. New Haven, CT: Yale University Press.

Pressman, J. and Wildavsky, A. (1973) *Implementation*. Berkerley: University of California Press.

Ranson, S. (1986) Power relations in that new structure. In S. Ranson and J. Tomlinson (Eds.) *The Changing Government of Education*. London: Allen and Unwin.

Raphael, D. (2000) The question of evidence in health promotion. *Health Promotion International*, 15(4), 355–367.

Ravenscroft, N. (1992) *Recreation planning and development*. Basingstoke: Macmillan.

Ravenscroft, N. (1998) The changing regulation of public leisure provision. *Leisure Studies*, 17, 138–154.

Regan, P.M. (1993) Ideas or interests? Privacy in electronic communications. *Policy Studies Journal*, 21, 450–469.

Reich, R.B. (Ed.) (1990) *The Power of Public Ideas*. Cambridge, MA: Harvard University Press.

Rhodes, R.A.W. (1981) *Control and Power in Central–Local Government Relations*. London: Unwin Hyman.

Rhodes, R.A.W. (1988) *Beyond Westminster and Whitehall: The Sub-Central Governments of Britain*. London: Unwin Hyman.

Rhodes, R.A.W. (1991) Theory and methods in British public administration: the view from political science. *Political Studies*, XXXIX, 533–554.

Rhodes, R.A.W. (1994) The hollowing out of the state: the changing nature of the public service in Britain. *The Political Quarterly*, 65(2), 138–151.

Rhodes, R.A.W. (1995) The institutional approach. In D. Marsh and G. Stoker (Eds.) *Theory and Methods in Political Science*. Basingstoke: Macmillan.

Rhodes, R.A.W. (1996) Policy networks and sub-central government. In G. Thompson et al. (Eds.) *Markets, Hierarchies and Networks: The Coordination of Social Life*. London: Sage.

Rhodes, R.A.W. (1997) Forward: managing complex networks. Strategies for the public sector. In W.J.M. Kickert et al. (Eds.) *Managing Complex Networks: Strategies for the Public Sector*. London: Sage.

Rhodes, R.A.W. (2001) *Understanding Governance: Policy Networks, Governance, Reflexivity and Accountability*. Buckingham: Open University Press.

Richards, D. (1996) Elite interviewing: approaches and pitfalls. *Politics*, 16(3), 199–204.

Richardson, J.J. (1982) The concept of policy style. In J.J. Richardson (Ed.) *Policy Styles in Western Europe*. London: Allen and Unwin.

Richardson, J.J. (2000) Government, interest groups and policy change. *Political Studies*, 48, 1006–1025.

Richardson, J.J. and Jordan, A.G. (1979) *Governing Under Pressure: The Policy Process in a Post-parliamentary Democracy* (2nd ed.). Oxford: Martin Robertson.

Riley, (2004) A question of balance. *Recreation*, March, 54–55.

Robson, S. (2001) Sport and health. In K. Hylton, P. Bramham, D. Jackson and M. Nesti (Eds.) *Sport Development: Policy, Process and Practice*. London: Routledge.

Robson, S. and McKenna, J. (2008) Sport and health. In K. Hylton, P. Bramham, D. Jackson and M. Nesti (Eds.) *Sports Development: Policy, Process and Practice* (2nd ed.). London: Routledge.

Roche, M. (1993) Sport and community: rhetoric and reality in the development of British sports policy. In J.C. Binfield and J. Stevenson (Eds.) *Sport, Culture and Politics*. Sheffield: Sheffield Academic Press.

Rorty, R. (1980) *Philosophy and the mirror of nature*. Oxford: Basil Blackwell.

Rose, N. (1999) *Powers of freedom: reframing political thought*. Cambridge: Cambridge University Press.

Rose, R. (1984) *Do parties make a difference?*. London: Macmillan.

Rossi Committee (1986) *Environment Committee 2nd Report: Sports Council*. London: HMSO.

Rowe, N., Adams, R. and Beasley, N. (2004) *Sport, Physical Activity and Health: Future Prospects for Improving the Health of the Nation*. London: Sport England.

Sabatier, P.A. (1986) What can we learn from implementation research?. In K. Kaufman, G. Majone and V. Ostron (Eds.) *Guidance, Control and Evaluation in the Public Sector*. New York: deGruyter.

Sabatier, P.A. (1987) Knowledge, policy-oriented learning and policy change: an advocacy coalition framework. *Knowledge, Diffusion, Utilization*, 8(4), 649–692.

Sabatier, P.A. (1988) An adversary coalition framework for policy change and the role of policy-oriented learning therein. *Policy Sciences*, 2, 129–168.

Sabatier, P.A. (1991) Toward better theories of the policy process. *Political Science and Politics*, 24, 147–156.

Sabatier, P.A. (1993) Policy change over a decade or more. In P.A. Sabatier and H.C. Jenkins-Smith (Eds.) *Policy Change and Learning: An Advocacy Coalition Approach*. Boulder, CO: Westview Press.

Sabatier, P.A. (1998) The advocacy coalition framework: revisions and relevance for Europe. *Journal of European Public Policy*, 5(1), 98–130.

Sabatier, P.A. (1999) *Theories of the Policy Process*. Oxford: Westview Press.

Sabatier, P.A. and Jenkins-Smith, H.C. (1993) The advocacy coalition framework: assessment, revisions and implications for scholars and practitioners. In P.A. Sabatier and H.C. Jenkins-Smith (Eds.) *Policy Change and Learning: An Advocacy Coalition Approach*. Boulder, CO: Westview Press.

Sabatier, P.A. and Jenkins-Smith, H.C. (1999) The advocacy coalition framework: an assessment. In P.A. Sabatier (Ed.) *Theories of the Policy Process*. Oxford: Westview Press.

Salaman, G. (1981) *Class and the Corporation*. London: Fontana.

Saunders, P. (1979) *Urban Politics*. London: Hutchinson.

Saunders, P. (1980) *Urban Politics* (2nd ed.). London: Hutchinson.

Sayer, A. (1992) *Method in Social Science: A Realist Approach* (2nd ed.). London: Routledge.

Scambler, G. (2005) *Sport and Society: History, Power and Culture*. London: Blackwell.

Schlager, E. (1997) A response to Kim Quaile Hill's In Search of a Policy Theory. *Policy Currents*, 7(June), 14–15.

Scott, J. (1990) *A Matter of Record: Documentary Sources in Social Research*. Cambridge: Polity Press.

Scott, J. (1991) *Who Rules Britain?*. Cambridge: Polity Press.

Scottish Executive (2001) *Rethinking Open Space: Open Space Provision and Management: A Way Forward*. Edinburgh: Author.

Searle, C. (1999) *The Quality of Qualitative Research*. London: Sage.

Sibeon, R. (1997) *Contemporary Sociology and Policy Analysis: The New Sociology of Public Policy*. London: Kogan Page and Tudor.

Sibeon, R. (1999) Agency, structure, and social chance as cross-disciplinary concepts. *Politics*, 19(3), 139–144.

Silverman, D. (1985) *Qualitative Methods and Sociology*. Aldershot: Gower.

Skopcol, T. (1979) *States and Social Revolutions*. Cambridge: Cambridge University Press.

Smith, M.J. (1990) Pluralism, reformed pluralism and neo-pluralism. *Political Studies*, 38, 302–322.

Smith, M.J. (1993) *Pressure, power and policy: state autonomy and policy networks in Britain and the United States*. Hemel Hempstead: Harvester-Wheatsheaf.

Smith, M.J. (1995) Pluralism. In D. Marsh and G. Stoker (Eds.) *Theory and Methods in Political Science*. Basingstoke: Macmillan.

Solesbury, W. (1976) The environmental agenda. *Public Administration*, Winter, 379–397.

Sparkes, A.C. (1992) The paradigms debate: an extended review and a celebration of difference. In A.C. Sparkes (Ed.) *Research in Physical Education and Sport: Exploring Alternative Visions*. London: Falmer Press.

Sport England (1997a) *England the Sporting Nation: A Strategy*. London: Author.

Sport England (1997b) *A Sporting Future for the Playing Fields of England: Policy on Planning Applications for Development on Playing Fields*. London: Author.

Sport England (1998a) *Annual Report, 1997/98*. London: Author.

Sport England (1998b) Facilities Planning Model. *Planning Bulletin*, Issue 1 – Playing Fields for Sport. London: Author.

Sport England (1999a) *Best Value through Sport*. London: Author.

Sport England (1999b) *Investing for Our Sporting Future: Sport England Lottery Fund Strategy 1999–2009*. London: Author.

Sport England (1999c) *Planning Policies for Sport: A Land Use Planning Policy Statement on Behalf of Sport*. London: Author.

Sport England (1999d) Planning Obligations for Sport. *Planning Bulletin*, Issue 4. London: Author.

Sport England (1999e) *Land-Use Planning Policy Statement*. London: Author.

Sport England (2000a) Playing Fields for Sport Revisited. *Planning Bulletin*, Issue 8. London: Author.

Sport England (2000b) Facilities Planning Model. *Planning Bulletin*, Issue 8 – Playing Fields for Sport Revisited. London: Author.

Sport England (2001a) *Review of Playing Pitch Strategy*. London: Author.

Sport England (2001b) *Sport Action Zones. Issues, Successes and Lessons for the Future*. London: Author.

Sport England (2002a) Planning for Open Space. *Planning Bulletin*, Issue 12. London: Author.

Sport England (2002b) *The School Sport Co-ordinators Programme: Reflections on the First Year – An Evaluation of the Impact of the First Phase of School Sport Partnerships*. London: Author.

Sport England (2003) Sport in the Greenbelt. *Planning Bulletin*, Issue 13. London: Author.

Sport England (2006) *The Active People Survey*. London: Author.

Sports England (2008) *Sport England Strategy 2008–2011*. Drafts June. London: Author.

Sport England/CCPR (2003) *Towards a Level Playing Field*. London: Authors.

Sport England/NPFA/CCPR (2003) *Towards a level playing field: a guide to the production of a playing pitch strategy*. London: Authors.

Sport England North-West, SENW (2004) *The North-West Plan for Sport and Physical Activity: 2004–2008*. Manchester: Sport England.

Sports Council (1982) *Sport in the Community: The Next Ten Years*. London: Author.

Sports Council (1988) *Sport in the Community: Into the '90s*. London: Author.

Sports Council/NPFA/CCPR (1991) *The Playing Pitch Strategy*. London: Authors.

Sports Council and the Health Education Authority (1992) *Allied Dunbar National Fitness Survey*. London: Authors.

St. Leger, L.H. (1998) The opportunities and effectiveness of the health promoting primary school in improving child health – a review of the claims and evidence. *Health Education Research*, 14(1), 51–69.

Stoker, G. (1991) *The Politics of Local Government* (2nd ed.). London: Macmillan.

Stoker, G. (1995) Introduction. In D. Marsh and G. Stoker (Eds.) *Theory and Methods in Political Science*. Basingstoke: Macmillan.

Stoker, G. (Ed.) (2000) *The New Politics of British Local Governance*. Basingstoke: Macmillan.

Stoker, G. and Mossberger, K. (1994) The post-Fordist local state: the dynamics of its development. In J. Stewart and G. Stoker (Eds.) *Local Government in the 1990s*. London: Macmillan.

Stone, C. (1988) Pre-emptive power: Floyd Hunter's 'Community power structure' reconsidered. *American Journal of Political Science*, 32, 82–104.

Stone, C. (1989) *Regime Politics: Governing Atlanta 1946–1988*. Lawrence: University Press of Kansas.

Stone, C. (1993) Urban regimes and the capacity to govern: a political economy approach. *Journal of Urban Affairs*, 15(1), 1–28.

Stratton, G. et al. (2005) *Physical Activity, Exercise, Sport and Health: Regional Mapping for the North-West*. Liverpool: Liverpool John Moores University.

Strauss, A. and Corbin, J. (1998) *Basics of Qualitative Research: Grounded Theory Procedures and Techniques*. Newbury Park, CA: Sage.

Taafe, P. and Mulhearn, T. (1988) *Liverpool: A City that Dared to Fight*. London: Fortress Press.

Talbot, M. (1998) Physical education: contested positions, competing discourses – the need for renaissance?. *European Physical Education Review*, 4(2), 104–116.

Taylor, A. (1997) 'Arms length but hands on'. Mapping the new governance: the DNH and cultural politics in Britain. *Public Administration*, 75(3), 441–466.

Taylor, G. (1995) Marxism. In D. Marsh and G. Stoker (Eds.) *Theory and Methods in Political Science*. Basingstoke: Macmillan.

Thelen, K. and Steinmo, S. (1992) Historical institutionalism in comparative politics. In S. Steinmo, K. Thelen and F. Longstreth (Eds.) *Structuring Politics: Historical Institutionalism in Comparative Analysis*. Cambridge: Cambridge University Press.

Thomas, N. (2003) Sport and disability. In B. Houlihan (Ed.) *Sport and Society: A Student Introduction*. London: Sage, pp. 105–124.

Thompson, G. (Ed.) et al. (1991) *Markets, Hierarchies and Networks: The Coordination of Social Life*. London: Sage.

Times Higher (2003) School Playing Fields Under Threat, 11th November.

Tomaney, J. and Mawson, J. (2002) *England: The State of the Regions*. London: Polity Press.

Tones, K. and Tilford, S. (2001) *Health Promotion: Effectiveness, Efficiency and Equity* (3rd ed.). Cheltenham: Nelson Thornes.

Truman, D. (1951) *The Governmental Process*. New York: Alfred A. Knopf.

UK Athletics (2007) Road Running Leadership Group created. www.ukathletics. net/media/news/January-2007/article-9. Accessed on June 18th, 2007.

Walker, P.N. (1988) *The Liverpool Competition. A Study of the Development of Cricket on Merseyside*. Birkenhead: Countryvise Ltd.

Walt, G. (1998) *Health Policy: An Introduction to Process and Power*. London: Zed Books.

Wanless, D. (2002) *Securing Our Future Health: Taking a Long-Term View*. Final Report. London: HMSO.

Wanless, D. (2004) *Securing Good Health for the Whole Population*. London: HMSO.

Webster, C. (1996) *The Health Services Since the War*. London: The Stationary Office.

Webster, C. and French, J. (2002) *Promoting Health: Politics and Practice*. London: Sage.

Weir, K. (1992) Ideas and politics of bounded innovation. In S. Steinmo et al. (Eds.), *Structuring Politics: Historical Institutionalism in Comparative Analysis*. Cambridge: Cambridge University Press.

Whannel, G. (1983) *Blowing the Whistle: The Politics of Sport*. London: Pluto Press.

Wildavsky, A. (1979) Changing Forward versus Changing Back. *Yale Law Journal*, 88(1). November

Wilson, D. (2003) Unravelling control freakery: redefining central–local government relations. *The British Journal of Politics and International Relations*, 5, 317.

Wilson, D. and Game, C. (2006) *Local Government in the UK* (4th ed.). Basingstoke: Palgrave Macmillan.

Wold, B. and Henry, L. (1998) Social and environmental factors associated with physical activity in young people. In S. Biddle et al. (Eds.), *Young People and Health Enhancing Physical Activity*. London: HEA.

Wolfenden Committee on Sport (1960) *Sport and the Community*. London: CCPR.

World Health Organization (1986) *The Ottawa Charter*. WHO.

Yin, R.K. (1994) *Case Study Research: Design and Methods* (2nd ed.). London: Sage.

Young, K. (1977) 'Values' in the policy process. *Policy and Politics*, 5, 1–22.

Zafonte, M. and Sabatier, P.A. (1998) Shared beliefs and imposed interdependencies as determinants of ally networks in overlapping subsystems. *Journal of Theoretical Politics*, 10(4), 473–505.

Zahariadis, N. (1995) Comparing lenses in comparative public policy. *Policy Studies Journal*, 23(2), 378–382.

Zahariadis, N. (1999) Ambiguity, time and multiple-streams. In P.A. Sabatier (Ed.) *Theories of the Policy Process*. Boulder, CO: Westview Press.

Zahariadis, N. (2003) *Ambiguity and Choice in Public Policy: Political Decision Making in Modern Democracies*. Washington, DC: Georgetown University Press.

Zahariadis, N. and Allen, C.S. (1995) Ideas, networks and policy streams: privatisation in Britain and Germany. *Policy Studies Review*, 14, 71–98.

Index